THESEUS AND ATHENS

THESEUS
AND
ATHENS

Henry J. Walker

New York   Oxford
OXFORD UNIVERSITY PRESS
1995

Oxford University Press

Oxford   New York
Athens   Auckland   Bangkok   Bombay
Calcutta   Cape Town   Dar es Salaam   Delhi
Florence   Hong Kong   Istanbul   Karachi
Kuala Lumpur   Madras   Madrid   Melbourne
Mexico City   Nairobi   Paris   Singapore
Taipei   Tokyo   Toronto

and associated companies in
Berlin Ibadan

Published by Oxford University Press, Inc.,
200 Madison Avenue, New York, New York 10016

Library of Congress Cataloging-in-Publication Data
Walker, Henry J.
Theseus and Athens / Henry J. Walker.
p. cm.
Includes bibliographical references and index.
ISBN 0-19-508908-1
1. Greek literature—Greece—Athens—History and criticism.
2. Theseus (Greek mythology) in literature.   3. Kings and rulers in
literature.   4. Athens (Greece)—Civilization.   5. Heroes in
literature.   I. Title.
PA3015.R5T48   1994
880.9'351—dc20   93-44486

1 3 5 7 9 8 6 4 2
Printed in the United States of America
on acid-free paper

D. M. Patris

Preface

I would like to tell, or rather warn, the reader what the scope of this work is. It is nothing like an analysis of the myth of Theseus as a whole. It concentrates instead on his image as an ideal ruler of Athens, and as a model for Athenian citizens to follow. I have always been surprised at the powerful grip that the idea of monarchy had on the citizens of Athens and has continued to hold on those of many other democracies since. There are no doubt strong psychological reasons for this rooted in the individual psyche, but I am more interested in the phenomenon as it affected the Athenians as a whole, so I tend to adopt more political explanations for it.

My work falls into two main parts. The first includes chapters 1 and 2, and examines the image of Theseus up until the the fifth century. I try to show why the Greeks were so interested in their former kings, and how Theseus developed in the imagination of the Athenians from a minor local ruler to a great democratic king of the entire country of Athens. The period with which I am dealing in this part is one of comparative obscurity in the history of Athens, and I shall have to rely considerably on the works of previous scholars in the field rather than on the evidence of the Greeks themselves, for they have left us very little indeed.

The second part is the core of my book. It focuses on the image of Theseus as Athenian citizen and king in several major works of classical literature from the fifth century—the poems of Bacchylides and the plays of Sophocles and Euripides. Each of the four chapters in this section examines the major contradictions in the fifth-century image of Theseus, which is what these writers were implicitly doing in their own creative works. Thus, each chapter asks a question about the way in which the Athenians visualized their early history, a past which was surrounded by an aura of mythical splendor. How could the Athenians accept a young warrior from a primitive age as a role model for Athenian adolescents? How could they admire a Bronze Age warlord as a great ruler of their country? How could they imagine such a king to be the founder of Athenian democracy? And how could a hero-king represent the higher ideals of their republic? The imagination of the Athenians, wrapped up in the magical world of Greek myth, seems to have thrived on contradictions such as these.

The brief final chapter looks at what happened to Theseus at the end of the fifth century when the world of the city-states and their mythical heroes started to collapse. It shows how the historians of Athens wished to preserve the traditions of their country for future generations, and how they tried to create an official version of the story of Theseus, who had now become a historical figure rather than a mythical hero.

I would like to thank Frederick Ahl, Kevin Clinton, Gordon Kirkwood, and Phillip Mitsis of Cornell University and Nicole Loraux of the École des Hautes Études en Sciences Sociales for guiding the research that led to this book. And I would like to thank my editor, Angela Blackburn, and my anonymous readers for transforming that research into this book. I would also like to thank my Dean, Martha Crunkleton, my Chair, Lorrie O'Higgins, and my colleagues at Bates College for their friendship and support. Finally, I would like to thank my wife, Nikky Singh, for inspiring me and encouraging me to complete this work.

Lewiston, Maine   H. J. W.
September 1993

Contents

THESEUS AND ATHENS

Everybody who writes a work about Heracles or Theseus seems to make the same mistake. They imagine that because they are writing about one hero, their work will also have a certain unity.

Aristotle, Poetics

1

Myth and Ritual: Hero Worship in Greece and the Origins of the Theseus Myth

Kings and Republics

After the fall of the Mycenaean kingdoms, the Greek world went through the long period of relative poverty and obscurity known as the Dark Ages, out of which the Greek republics emerged in the eighth century. Surprisingly enough, these republics made no attempt to repress their monarchist past. On the contrary, they guarded the memory of their legendary kings as a precious heritage, and most of the literary works produced in these republics celebrated the great achievements of these kings, whom they referred to as heroes. The Greek states actually worshipped these kings and offered sacrifice to their tombs. Even more surprisingly, this hero worship was not a remnant from the age of the kingdoms, preserved throughout the Dark Ages by the conservatism of religious ritual, but rather an innovation that first appears with the rise of the Greek republics. This survival, or indeed revival, of monarchist sentiment, which was actually encouraged by the Greek republics, is very unusual, especially since the tales about these ancient kings made it perfectly obvious that their moral values were quite different from, indeed violently opposed to, those expected of a good citizen in a Greek state.

Nowhere is this paradox more glaring than in the case of Athens, the most democratic and egalitarian of all the Greek republics. The masterpieces of drama and sculpture commissioned by the democracy itself glorify the highly antidemocratic deeds and attitudes of the heroic kings. Most of these kings, however, were not actually Athenian. When it came to celebrating their own heroic kings, the Athenians took a somewhat eccentric course. As the great hero of their country, they chose a relatively minor legendary figure from the Attic countryside, Theseus, king (or perhaps more accurately lord) of the region around Aphidna. He was a typically violent and self-centered hero, perhaps wilder than most, but the Athenians tried to brush up his image and portray him, quite anachronistically, as a democratic leader of their state. It is to the strange development of the image of Theseus as a role model for all Athenians that the present work is devoted. After tracing the development of Theseus as a political figure, I shall examine his portrayal in the works of fifth-century literature in which he plays a significant role, and end with the work of Hellanicus who, around 400 B.C., produced what was supposed to be a historical version of his life story. Before embarking on this task, however, we shall first have to look at the role of hero cults in Greece as a whole and at the origins of the figure of Theseus himself.

Greek Heroes

When Schliemann discovered a magnificent gold death mask in a Bronze Age tomb at Mycenae, he sent an excited telegram to the king of Greece announcing that he had discovered the grave of Agamemnon. He was completely wrong about the dating of the tomb, and the king buried there could not have been contemporary with Agamemnon and his famous sack of Troy, but Schliemann's mistake reveals more about Greek attitudes toward their heroes than the accuracy of a more scholarly archaeologist would have done. His reaction was, in fact, not very different from that of a Greek hero worshipper, and his mistake is precisely the kind of one that an ancient Greek might have made. The essence of hero cult is a tomb of awe-inspiring antiquity, a great name from Greek legend, and the enthusiastic human imagination that unites the two into one conception, the Greek hero.[1]

Even such a formulation is, however, deceptively simple, for we find heroes without tombs, and heroes without names, and heroes who are, in fact, minor gods and spirits who were demoted to this new rank. Nevertheless, insofar as it is possible to speak of rules and exceptions in so confusing a matter, the type of hero worship that combined an ancient tomb with a legendary figure was the normal one, and the other types were assimilated to it.[2] It was rare that this type was fully realized in practice, so we often find that a hero at a genuine Bronze Age tomb will remain nameless, or that a legendary king celebrated by the poets is worshipped at a place where there is, in fact, no Bronze Age structure of any type to be found. This should not surprise us in any way, for the Greeks were relying not on the science of archaeology but on chance finds and on that feeling of awe attached to some particular structure which suggested that some supernatural being was present, one of the Great Dead.

Hero worship developed with the rise of the city-state. In the Mycenaean Age, the age of the legendary heroes themselves, there is no trace of worship at tombs. The Mycenaeans treated the remains of their former kings with a lack of respect that would raise eyebrows in the most secular of ages. The bones of their dead monarchs were treated as so much rubbish and swept into a corner of the tomb to make way for a new corpse.[3] The only trace we can find of a slightly different attitude is when the kings of Mycenae, on the eve of their decline, include the most ancient royal cemetery (Grave Circle B) inside the newly extended walls of their palace. This cemetery was already four centuries old at the time, and by protecting it inside their new fortifications the kings of Mycenae betrayed some sort of respect for the past, though we cannot tell whether they performed any type of worship at these graves. The kings and their palaces would long have disappeared before anyone thought of praying at these Mycenaean tombs to the Great Dead.

A precursor of hero cult appears to have been practiced on the island of Euboea during the Dark Ages.[4] At this time the inhabitants of Euboea began to treat the tombs of their recently deceased rulers with an extraordinary respect that has been described as heroization. The most famous example of such honors paid to royal graves occurs in Eretria. Around 680 B.C., the walls of this city were extended to include the graves of members of its royal family who had died between 720 and 680 B.C. The city was placing itself under the protection of its Great Dead.[5] At Lefkandi on Euboea, we have an even earlier example of such honors being paid to recently deceased monarchs. Around 1000 B.C. a warrior, a woman, and some horses were buried in the floor of a large building, which was later filled in to form a tumulus. What makes this building even more interesting is that the site chosen for it was on top of a Mycenaean chamber tomb.[6] The inhabitants of Lefkandi were, or course, honoring their own lord and lady rather than the Mycenean heroes, but they seem to have been quite confident that they were upholding the traditions of the Mycenaean kingdoms. This confidence is not entirely unexpected since Euboea was one of the first regions of Greece to emerge from the poverty and isolation of the Dark Ages. The Euboean cities of Chalcis and Eretria seem to have led the Greeks to the Levantine trading post of Al Mina[7] and thus to have reestablished those vital links with the outside world that had been lost since the days when the Mycenaeans traded at Ras Shamra. The two city-states eventually came to blows in the first major war fought in Greece, involving several states on both sides, since the Mycenaeans had launched their last

great expedition, the Trojan War itself. The Lelantine War is the only conflict in all those five centuries that was serious enough to be remembered
and handed down to us. The Euboeans were, therefore, the first Greeks who
could claim that their achievements rivaled those of the great Mycenaean
age and that their own kings deserved to be honored even after death.

It was not until the eighth century B.C. that Greece as a whole recov-
ered economically, and the tiny republics, which came into existence at
this time, became obsessed with their Mycenaean past and felt that they
could justifiably claim those mighty kings as their predecessors. By this
time, there had been a complete break in their tradition; they had experienced the long centuries of the Dark Ages, so when the Greeks started to
worship at the Mycenaean graves, they were honoring the tombs of a people
from whom they felt very distant and whom they treated with corresponding respect. This temporal and cultural gulf separating the Great Dead from
their worshippers is an essential aspect of hero worship.[8] The new phenomenon of hero cult, which arises from their respect for these ancient kings,
is found at two different types of location. They made offerings at such
Mycenaean graves as were known to them at this time, but they also worshipped at hero shrines, which they themselves erected to the heroes of
Greek legend.

Grave cults started to crop up throughout Greece during the eighth
century and were especially common in Messenia, the Argolid, and Attica.[9]
Since these Mycenaean graves were discovered by chance, it is not surprising that the Greeks were often unable to figure out which hero might
be the occupant of the grave. As a result, grave cults often have anonymous heroes as their object,[10] but this is not always the case. A wall was
built in this century around a group of Mycenaean graves at Eleusis, and
these graves were identified as the resting place of the Seven against
Thebes.[11] From Homer, we learn that a conspicuous tomb in Arcadia was
identified as that of an obscure local hero called Aepytus (*Iliad* 2: 606).[12]
Even when the hero could not be identified, it was still a source of great
prestige both for the local villagers and for the citizens of the entire state
to establish a link with the legendary Mycenaean Age, to discover the presence of one of the Great Dead in their midst and to win his favor by paying
homage to his grave.

The second type of hero cult took place at hero shrines, and shrines of
this nature are especially relevant to the cult of Theseus. Such worship is
quite different from the first type of hero cult in that it does not take place
at a grave; it is located instead in a region that is associated with the legendary career of the hero in question. A shrine is erected to the hero at this
place, and this new shrine (rather than an old Bronze Age tomb) becomes
the center of the hero cult.[13] The motivating factor behind this type of hero

cult is not the discovery of an impressively ancient grave but rather the legends about a particularly famous hero, which incite his successors (for this is how the Greek states now see themselves) to establish a more physical link with him. Homer and the epic poets must have played a major role in the development of hero shrines, because the heroes to whom they are raised are usually heroes renowned throughout Greece, heroes with a Panhellenic reputation. It was once thought that this type of hero worship was the earlier form and dated back to the tenth century,[14] but now archaeologists seem to acknowledge that it also begins toward the end of the eighth century. Two of the most famous Homeric heroes were among the first to be honored in this way. Sometime before 700 B.C. shrines were erected to Agamemnon near Mycenae and to Menelaus at Therapne.[15] These cults are particularly interesting because they were initiated by Dorians, who were, therefore, already beginning to take over the traditions of the people they had conquered. As we shall see shortly, the Dorians were much more innovative and aggressive in promoting hero cults than were the descendants of the Mycenaean Greeks.

The other two hero shrines erected in the eighth century are found in Attica. Both are a little unusual in that they honor a local Attic hero without any great legendary career. The first is the shrine of Academus, which was built in the eighth century, perhaps after the discovery of a Mycenaean house nearby.[16] If this was what motivated its building, it might be more accurate to agree with de Polignac that this is really a case of a grave cult, since the Mycenaean house may have been mistaken for a tomb.[17] The second case from Attica is more like that of Agamemnon and Menelaus, for it is the cult of the first human king of Athens, Erechtheus. Here we are dealing once again with a hero who was well known throughout Greece. Indeed, our main evidence for the existence of his cult at this time comes from Homer himself (*Iliad* 2: 546–551). Homer tells us that the young Athenians honor Erechtheus every year by sacrificing bulls and rams to him (*Iliad* 2: 550–551).[18]

One might be inclined to brush aside the evidence from Homer as a later interpolation, but it would make perfect sense for the city of Athens to have erected such a hero shrine in the eighth century. The hero cults established throughout Attica at Mycenaean tombs and at the Academy were dedicated to local heroes and were an attempt by the people living in the countryside to assert their autonomy against the encroaching power of the capital city.[19] These cults were a manifestation of a regional (though far from separatist) spirit which, as Thucydides reminds us, was still alive three centuries later at the time of the Peloponnesian War.[20] The establishment of a cult to Erechtheus would have been a good reply on the part of the city to regional sentiment. Erechtheus was a hero with a Panhellenic reputation (in contrast to the obscure and even anonymous heroes of the Attic countryside), and the epic tradition that recorded his name also declared that Athens was a single united state[21] and not a loose confederation of autonomous villages.[22] Thus, the capital city had good reason to promote this hero and the epic tradition associated with him.

Hero shrines were not, as we have seen, located at Mycenaean tombs, so there was nothing to prevent a hero from having several shrines in his honor, sometimes even in different states. The Greeks, however, assimilated the two types of hero worship and often referred to hero shrines as hero graves. This led to the extremely odd result that a hero was often said to have several different burial places. Oedipus had no less than four "graves"—one in Thebes, another in the sanctuary of Demeter at Eteonos, a third at Colonus in Attica, and a fourth in the city of Athens.[23] The assimilation of hero shrine and hero grave also led to a slightly distasteful innovation in the worship of heroes, one that we first hear of in the sixth century and that the Spartans seem to have been responsible for. As far as we can tell, the Spartans were quite content with hero shrines alone, and they did not worship heroes at Mycenaean tombs, but they made up for this lack by raiding such tombs elsewhere. They then built what undoubtedly were exceptionally efficacious hero shrines by burying the stolen corpses in them, and thus they created a hero shrine that truly was a hero grave. By so doing, they deprived the other state of that hero's protection and transferred it to themselves.[24] The Spartans did not steal just any old corpse from any old tomb; with the help of oracles they deliberately tried to find the grave of a particular epic hero, though in practice they were delighted if these investigations led to any corpse that looked vaguely heroic and Mycenaean. The most famous example of such a hunt was the Spartan quest for the bones of Orestes during their war against Tegea, which took place around the middle of the sixth century B.C. The people of Tegea seem to have had no idea that they possessed the remains of Orestes, and they certainly had no idea where these remains might be located. The Tegeates were quite impressed, however, when the Spartans found the body of an ancient warrior and removed it to their own land, declaring that it was indeed the body of Orestes. In fact, the Tegeates were so impressed that they accepted the claim of Sparta to be the protector of the pre-Dorian peoples of the Peloponnese, since it now possessed the great hero of those peoples. As a result, the Tegeates and many other non-Dorian states of the Peloponnese became allies of Sparta.[25] The possession or seizure of a hero's corpse was a serious matter, and the Spartan example was followed by other states. Although such behavior might seem a little grotesque to our eyes, the Greeks felt that it was perfectly natural, and Sophocles had no qualms about devoting a large part of his *Oedipus at Colonus* to a tug-of-war between Athens and Thebes over the remains of Oedipus. The very indignity of such squabbles is in itself a remarkable testimony to the overriding importance of hero cults throughout the age of the city-state, and to the extraordinary lengths to which the Greeks would go to win the favor of a hero.

The main function of hero worship was, then, to legitimize the authority of the city-states and to create a sense of solidarity among their citizens.[26] By respecting the Great Dead, by building shrines and inaugurating festivals in their honor, by assuming the role of their successors, the city-states invested themselves with the glory of the heroic age. To this general rule, the cult of Theseus was no exception. In fact, he was an ideal candidate for a hero shrine because he had a very colorful career and was well known throughout Greece. He was, however, unusual in one important respect: unlike Erechtheus, he did not come from the city of Athens. He was adopted by the city from outside, but by the end of the sixth century he was already honored as the greatest of its heroes, the archetype of all Athenians. Before examining his cult and the development of his image as an Athenian hero, we must first look into the origins of Theseus himself. We know that he was not originally an Athenian, so where did he come from?

The Origins of the Myth of Theseus

The Theory of Hans Herter

This seemingly simple question has been a source of great scholarly controversy. My own answer, to anticipate a little, is that Theseus came from Aphidna in the northeast of Attica, but in saying this I am going against the view of the greatest scholar of the myth of Theseus, Hans Herter. In his classic article on the subject, "Theseus der Jonier," Herter argues that Theseus was a very ancient hero of all the Ionian peoples rather than a specifically Attic hero. In his approach to this problem, Herter followed the principles of the "Historical School."[27] This school of mythological analysis held that the Greek myths were developed by tribes, and the stories followed these tribes in their wanderings. By examining myths carefully we can find traces of the early homelands of these tribes, and we can see how the myths were affected by the movements of the tribes and the various places in which they stayed. When employed without caution, this method can produce some unusual results, such as Bethe's conclusion that the Trojan War had really been fought in Greece![28] In exploring the origins of the myth of Theseus, Herter does not, of course, apply this approach in so radical a fashion, and the results of his research are much more plausible and attractive. So whatever the faults of the school itself may be, Herter's interpretation must be examined on its own merits.

An earlier attempt had been made by Toepffer to explain the origins of Theseus by the methods of the Historical School. Toepffer wished to explain why it is that episodes from the story of Theseus are located in places so divergent as Thessaly, Attica, and Trozen. True to the tenets of the Historical School, he concluded that these different locations reflected stages in the wanderings of a Greek tribe. Theseus and his friend Peirithous are the heroes of a Thessalian tribe, which is remembered in myth as the Lapiths. According to Toepffer, this tribe migrated from Thessaly by sea, landing first on the northeast coast of Attica near Marathon, and finally settling at Trozen. Since this tribe had inhabited all three regions, stories about Theseus are likewise located in all three of them.[29] Herter develops a more sophisticated version of this theory. He believes that the Lapiths represent the ancient Ionians, and that the legends told about the Lapiths recall the occupation of Thessaly by the Ionians before the Dorians invaded Greece.[30] Herter concludes that Theseus is an "Attic-Thessalian hero" common to all the Ionians and honored by them in their myths.[31]

Herter's theory is attractive in that it explains, as does Toepffer's interpretation, why the Attic hero Theseus fights against the Centaurs in Thessaly and why he is born and reared in Trozen. It is also more economical than Toepffer's explanation, since Herter does not have to postulate any unprovable prehistoric migrations. If Theseus is indeed a Pan-Ionian hero, it is perfectly reasonable that other Ionians apart from the Athenians should have invented stories about him. It is indeed true that the location of the battle with the Centaurs in Thessaly and the birth of Theseus in Trozen create difficulties for those who believe that Theseus is an Attic hero, but are they really enough to make a Pan-Ionian out of Theseus? The answer to this question is the point on which Herter's theory stands or falls.

The Thessalian Theseus

The earliest evidence we have that associates Theseus with the Lapiths of Thessaly is from the *Iliad* (1: 265):

> Θησέα τ' Αἰγεΐδην, ἐπιείκελον ἀθανάτοισιν.
>
> And Theseus the son of Aegeus, equal to the immortals.

This line occurs in a speech of Nestor where he recalls the courage of the Lapiths, whom he himself had joined in their fight against the Centaurs when he was younger. In keeping with his theory, Herter claims that

Theseus is not an Athenian in this passage, so we have Homeric evidence for his Ionian Theseus.[32] Unfortunately, most scholars believe that this line is an interpolation, but even if we accept it, the role that Theseus plays in the battle against the Centaurs and his friendship with the Lapith Peirithous do not prove that he himself was a Lapith.

Peirithous first meets Theseus at Aphidna, and their friendship is an old element in the myth. Nilsson wonders what Peirithous, a Thessalian hero, is doing in Attica.[33] It is as important to ask this question as it is to inquire why Theseus should be found among the Lapiths, which is the issue Herter implicitly brought up when he argued that Theseus was originally a Thessalian. Nilsson concludes that Peirithous, the friend of Theseus, is really a minor Attic hero.[34] If Herter can plausibly claim that Theseus and Peirithous and even Aegeus are originally Thessalian, Nilsson is equally convincing when he argues that they are all from Attica. The Greeks frequently confused heroes who bore the same name, so Herter is quite right in suggesting that a Thessalian hero called Theseus might easily have been forgotten when he was later overshadowed by the Athenian Theseus, but Nilsson is also justified in claiming that a minor Attic hero called Peirithous would quickly have been confused with the more famous Peirithous from Thessaly. A weakness in Herter's argument is that such a displacement of Theseus or Aegeus from Thessaly to Attica could only have happened if Athens had been powerful enough to distort the tradition in its own interests. The *Iliad*, however, equates the man who fought the Centaurs (Herter's "Thessalian Theseus") with the man who killed the Minotaur (Herter's "Attic Theseus"), so the legends about the battle against the Centaurs must already have been transferred to Attica. Athens did not, however, enjoy the kind of prestige that would have enabled it to alter a Panhellenic epic until the sixth century at the earliest. We must, therefore, accept that Theseus and Aegeus were Attic heroes from the very beginning. Otherwise, we shall have to conclude that the Homeric lines are sixth-century interpolations, in which case our evidence for a Lapith or Thessalian Theseus disappears.[35] In short, the evidence for Theseus' early association with Thessaly is simply not strong enough to enable us to speak of a Lapith or Thessalian Theseus.

The Trozenian Theseus

The second main argument that Herter advances for the existence of a Pan-Ionian Theseus is the hero's birth at Trozen. He points out that Trozen had once been an Ionian city, and it maintained some Ionian traditions even after the Dorian invasion.[36] As far as Herter is concerned, the story about Theseus' birth is part of Trozen's ancient Ionian heritage. One branch of the Ionians brought the story of Theseus both to the northeast of Attica and to Trozen.[37] The Athenians later took over the myth for themselves alone, and the Trozenian tales, which would have localized all his adventures near Trozen, died out. As Herter sees it, the story of his birth was an exception to this rule. It was so strongly rooted in Trozen that even the Athenians had to acknowledge that city as his birthplace.[38]

Even if we were to accept that the birth of Theseus at Trozen was a very old part of the myth, though in fact there is no evidence for this story before the fifth century B.C., it should not lead us to doubt his Attic origins. Founding heroes often come from "outside," and this feature actually increases their effectiveness in renewing their land and setting up civilized institutions.[39] It is by no means clear, however, that the myth originally stated that Theseus was born in Trozen or concerned itself with the issue of his birth at all. Here we come up against the problem of homonyms once again, for Nilsson points out that Pittheus, the maternal grandfather of Theseus, may in fact have been an Attic hero, who was later confused with his better known Trozenian namesake.[40] Aethra, the daughter of Pittheus, certainly seems to be from Attica at *Iliad* 3:144. Her role in this passage, as Nilsson points out, presupposes the story that Theseus had abducted Helen to Attica.[41] Nilsson is therefore convinced that the presence of Pittheus and Aethra in the myth of Theseus does not prove him to be a Trozenian, and that the connection with Trozen is a later addition to the story of Theseus.[42]

The series of adventures that Theseus undergoes on his journey from Trozen to Athens supports Nilsson's view. Most scholars agree that this cycle did not develop until late in the sixth century, though Herter argues that it was invented to reconcile the original Trozenian home of Theseus with the site of his achievements as an adult.[43] If, however, the birth story were really an old one, it is very surprising that this cycle should not have appeared until the sixth century. Nilsson suggests that these stories were probably invented to support the claim of Athens to the Megarid,[44] and this is surely a better explanation than to attribute the cycle's creation to a very belated embarrassment on the part of the Athenians that their hero was born in Trozen. As in the case of Thessaly, there just is not enough evidence to prove that Trozen is the home of the myth of Theseus.

The Ionian Theseus

The two major arguments that Herter adduces to prove that Theseus was a Pan-Ionian hero are not as strong as they might first appear. There is a further and more serious flaw with his theory, and this is the absence of any cult or myth devoted to Theseus in the Ionian cities of Asia Minor.[45]

Herter realizes that this is a difficulty, but his only explanation for this silence with regard to Theseus is that Theseus became less relevant to those Ionians who colonized Asia, and that he eventually disappeared from their worldview.[46] It is extremely unlikely that this is what happened. The Ionians would not have forgotten their own national hero and yet have preserved such an extraordinarily rich tradition about the Achaean heroes who are remembered so vividly in the works of Homer. The more obvious solution is that Theseus had never been an Ionian hero in the first place.

The only trace that Herter can find of the Theseus legend in the Ionian colonies is an obscure story about the foundation of Smyrna. According to this story, Smyrna was founded by Theseus, though in one version he is not our mythical hero but simply an aristocrat of the Eumelid family who happens to bear this name.[47] Smyrna was not, however, an Ionian colony; it was established by Aeolians and only later taken over by Ionian refugees from Colophon.[48] The story that Theseus founded Smyrna must date from the eighth century at the very earliest, so we are not dealing with an old Ionian tradition that was brought over from the mainland.

The only other connection between Theseus and the Ionians of Asia Minor is the story that Oenopion, the first ruler of Chios, was the son of Ariadne and Theseus. The more usual version of the story declared that Oenopion was the son of Dionysus and Ariadne. The names of Oenopion ("wine-face") and his brother Staphylus ("grape-bunch") make it quite clear which of these versions is the original one. There are only two sources for the other version, which makes Oenopion the son of Theseus, and these are a poem written by the pro-Athenian Ion of Chios,[49] and a vase painting executed by the Lewis Painter.[50] Clearly, this version was created to justify the position of Athens as leader of the Ionians.[51] It tells us more about the success of Athenian propaganda than it does about the Pan-Ionian nature of Theseus.[52]

The Attic Theseus

Our attempts to find a home for Theseus in Thessaly, Trozen, and Ionia have proved disappointing, so we must conclude that he is firmly rooted in Attica alone. In this respect he differs completely from Heracles, whose myths and cults are scattered all over Greece. With Heracles we can say that he is equally at home in Tiryns or Thebes because he is "one of those heroes of whom myths were told everywhere."[53] The elements in the myth of Theseus that would lead us to believe he is also such a hero have been created for posterity by the Athenians. Herter's theory that Theseus was a Pan-Ionian hero is a tribute to the success of the Athenians in raising their local hero to the status of "another Heracles."

It is generally agreed that Theseus comes from the northeast of Attica (Herter himself accepts this, though he would add that this is simply one of his homelands).[54] This region around Aphidna and Marathon is the site of some of the oldest episodes in the legend of Theseus—his abduction of Helen, his meeting with Peirithous, his struggles against the Bull of Marathon.[55] As far as Helen is concerned, her abduction is very definitely associated with Aphidna, but as early as the seventh century, we find that the Dioscuri attack Athens as well. There they find Aethra, whom they bring back to Sparta as a slave, though some versions seem to have insisted that the entire story took place in Aphidna alone.[56] Herter also points out that Aphidnus, the eponymous hero of Aphidna, is the only one of all the local Attic heroes to support Theseus against the Dioscuri.[57] This part of Attica is the real homeland of Theseus, and we should not be misled by his adventures abroad. His connections with Thessaly and the Centaurs are not central to his myth but derive from his friendship with Peirithous. His participation in the battle against the Centaurs does not make him any less of an Attic hero, just as Nestor's involvement does not make him any less of a Pylian. There is, furthermore, no evidence for his connection with the Saronic Gulf until the end of the sixth century, and none for the story of his birth in Trozen until the century after that. Finally, his connection with the Ionian colonies is an innovation dating to the time of the Athenian empire. In short, Theseus is, as Nilsson concluded, "of local Attic origin."[58]

We have seen that the countryside of Attica and the city of Athens itself were no strangers to the new hero cults of the eighth century, and we found that they worshipped both at hero graves and at hero shrines, as did many other Greek states. The Athenians never associated any Mycenaean tomb with Theseus, so he was worshipped at hero shrines alone. As we shall see later when we examine the cult of Theseus, none of his hero shrines were located in the Attic countryside, and this strongly suggests that he was already considered to be an Athenian by the time that hero cults had first developed. The Attic Theseus is ignored in cult, but he does survive in myth, because the Athenians left his story more or less as it had been before, and no great effort was made to change the site of his deeds from rural Attica to the city of Athens. The starting point of the voyage to Crete may, perhaps, have been altered from Marathon in the northeast to Phaleron, the old landing point of Athens,[59] and in some versions he carries Helen off to Athens rather than to Aphidna,[60] but otherwise his feats were situated in various parts of Attica and elsewhere, as they always had been. There were only two major innovations in his myth. First, Theseus was now looked upon as a king of Athens and was forcibly inserted into the list of Athenian kings. It is this change in his citizenship from Diacrian[61] to Athenian that explains the hostility between him and Menestheus, who was not an interloper.[62] The second innovation is that the synoecism of Attica was attributed to Theseus. Homer always speaks of Attica as a united state, so this synoecism must have been a part of Athenian myth by the time the *Iliad* was composed. This means that Homer must also have considered Theseus to be an Athenian hero rather than a local Attic one.[63]

There is a close connection between these two innovations in the myth. Theseus changes from a local hero to a national ruler at precisely the time that the inhabitants of Attica transfer their loyalty from their region to the capital city. He emerges as an Athenian hero when Attica is united into a polis centered on Athens. The new state took over an Attic hero with a Panhellenic reputation, just as it had taken over the land of Attica itself and her institutions. It is difficult to say exactly when Theseus changes from an Attic to an Athenian hero, but the Homeric picture of Athens as a united state and the purely Athenian nature of his cult make it clear that Theseus has become an Athenian by the eighth century. In cult and literature Theseus is, therefore, always an Athenian, though traces of his rural origins can often be detected in the background because the Athenians did not bother to erase them.

The Myth of Theseus

Theseus the Athenian was something of a wild bandit, if we can judge by his appearance in the works of early archaic artists and writers. He was not only a menace to those around him; he also fought against the gods themselves. He kidnapped Helen and held her in Aphidna. This was not just a crime against an ordinary woman, for originally Helen had been a goddess.[64] In Attica, she was worshipped at Thorikos, and perhaps at Rhamnous also.[65] His abduction of Ariadne was a similar offense, because she too was a goddess; and, finally, he helped Peirithous in his attempt to abduct Persephone, but this time he had to be punished for his misdeed by being detained in the Underworld. Helen, Ariadne, and Persephone are all vegetation goddesses, and it is doubtless their disappearance every winter that gave rise to the stories about their abduction.[66] The friendship between Theseus and Peirithous, which had a permanent memorial in the mixing-bowl at Colonus[67] (the one they had used in swearing to be friends), was not just a case of "honor among thieves." If it led them to help each other in their careers as rapists, it also obliged Theseus to fight against the Centaurs. This rather more honorable joint effort with Peirithous was to become very important in the fifth century, when the Centaurs came to be seen as representing the forces of barbarism against civilization. Finally, Theseus was renowned throughout the archaic age as the man who had killed the Minotaur. The archaic Theseus is, therefore, an abductor of women, all of whom are vegetation goddesses, and he is a fighter against monsters, all of whom are half-human and half-animal. As a candidate for the representative of all that Athens stood for, Theseus would seem to be a most unlikely choice, and yet one day he would become the hero who, moralized beyond recognition,[68] was the "prototype of the Athenians."[69]

The fight with the Minotaur has remained the most popular episode in the myth of Theseus, and it may also be the oldest one we know of. The monster is represented on bronze tripods from Olympia that were made in the second half of the eighth century and may even predate Homer. The only problem with these fragmentary decorations is that we cannot tell whether anyone was shown fighting against the Minotaur. In other words, we have a Minotaur but no sign of Theseus. On the other hand, it is interesting that the Minotaur is portrayed as a man with the head of a bull, exactly as he is when he fights with Theseus in later art.[70] The first clear representation of Theseus fighting the Minotaur, with the other young male and female victims looking on, and Ariadne holding the string that will help them get out of the labyrinth, dates from around 670 to 660 B.C.[71] It goes against the norm in having a Minotaur with the body of a bull and the head of a man (something like a Centaur),[72] but almost all other representations follow the precedent of the eighth-century tripods. This suggests that the tripods represent not just any bull-headed monster but rather the very Minotaur that Theseus fought. There does not seem to be any good reason to doubt that this artistic tradition goes back to the eighth century. In any case, the story of Theseus and the Minotaur is well established by about the middle of the seventh century in art, when it even appears on a vase from Sicily.[73] The first literary reference to it occurs in Sappho (born circa 630 B.C.) who mentioned the fourteen victims of the Minotaur in a lost poem (fr. 206 *PLF*).

Apart from the bronze tripods, our earliest source for the myth of Theseus is Homer himself. Homer is the first to tell us about the abductions of Ariadne, Helen, and Persephone, and about the battle against the Centaurs. In all, he mentions episodes from the myth no less than four times (*Iliad* 1: 265, 3: 144; *Odyssey* 11: 321–325, 631), but scholars have argued against the authenticity of all four on the grounds that they might be Athenian interpolations. For my purposes it does not matter greatly whether these passages are genuine or not, because in each case we find that the episode is known to people living shortly after Homer's time. To excise all four passages and then elevate their absence into the a priori principle that the myth of Theseus is completely unknown to epic poetry seems quite unjustified. Even if we deny that Homer referred to these episodes in his original version of the poems, it is fairly clear that they must have been familiar to his contemporaries.

Homer does not tell us about the Minotaur, but the story of Ariadne's abduction is related briefly at *Odyssey* 11: 321–325. Theseus appears in quite a good light there, because he does not desert Ariadne. Instead, Homer says that after Theseus and Ariadne reached Dia (a small island just north of Crete[74]), Artemis killed her. Dionysus only enters the story to "testify" against Ariadne.[75] Ameis and Hentze condemn the last line of *Odyssey* 11: 321–325, because the form of the god's name (Διονύσου) is Attic,[76] and this casts doubt on the whole passage. If Homer did not mention the story himself, however, it was certainly current in his time. We find the tale of Theseus and Ariadne in Hesiod's *Theogony* (circa 730–700 B.C.) at lines 947–949, where he presents the more familiar version of the story, according to which Dionysus marries her. Ariadne is also mentioned in the *Catalog of Women* (early sixth century),[77] among other sexual partners of Theseus.[78]

After Ariadne helped Theseus escape from the labyrinth, she joined him and the other rejoicing victims of the Minotaur in a dance to celebrate the defeat of the monster. Perhaps Homer knew about this because he mentions a dancing floor that Daedalus built for Ariadne at Cnossus (*Iliad* 18: 591–592). This little incident from her story probably appeared on the chest of Cypselus at Olympia (circa 570 B.C.),[79] and is clearly depicted on the François Vase (also circa 570 B.C.), which was painted by the Attic artist Cleitias. He shows Ariadne and her nurse welcoming Theseus and the young Athenians, so he felt that the dance took place at Cnossus and may have been following Homer in this.

A veiled reference to Helen's abduction occurs in the *Iliad* at 3: 144. To punish Theseus, Helen's brothers had taken his mother Aethra as a hostage, and in this passage of the *Iliad* we are told that his mother is still in captivity and acts as a servant to Helen. This line has also been suspected,[80] but we find once again that the episode is well known in the generation after Homer. The kidnapping of Helen is depicted on a wide range of artifacts dating from about 680 to 660 B.C. They range from vases[81] to reliefs in bronze or gold[82] to a bronze cuirass,[83] and they are found throughout the Peloponnese (Argos, Corinth, Olympia) and even as far as Crete. The story is also well known to poets throughout Greece in the century after Homer. The Spartan poet Alcman (circa 650–600 B.C.) gives the story of Helen's abduction by Theseus and Aethra's capture by the Dioscuri.[84] Somewhat later, the Sicilian poet Stesichorus (circa 630–555 B.C.) recounts a curious tale that Theseus had made Helen pregnant, and that their child was Iphigenia, whom Helen gave to her sister Clytemnestra.[85] The rescue of Helen by her brothers and their capture of Aethra as a reprisal appears on the chest of Cypselus at Olympia (circa 570 B.C.)[86] Finally, it also appears in the *Sack of Troy*, and it was probably mentioned in the *Cypria*, two cyclic epics that were probably written sometime in the sixth century.[87] In the *Sack of Troy*, we read that Demophon and Acamas had joined Menestheus' army for the specific purpose of freeing their mother, and that they brought her home after the fall of Troy,[88] while the *Cypria* gave the usual story about Helen being abducted, and the attack by her brothers on Aphidna and Athens.[89] By this time the story of Helen and Theseus has been widely known throughout the Greek world for well over a century.

The third of Theseus' abductions is also mentioned by Homer. He makes a brief reference to Theseus' descent into Hades with Peirithous and their attempt to carry off Persephone at *Odyssey* 11: 631. Odysseus is eager to see men of a former era, and he knows that as punishment for their attempted abduction Theseus and Peirithous have been kept alive in Hades. He wants to see them, but suddenly becomes afraid of Persephone and decides not to bother. He realizes that he himself has committed a similar offense, for he has violated her kingdom by entering it while still alive, and that he too may be punished for this. Ameis and Hentze once again argue that the line should not be there. They take it to be a "patriotic interpolation of Peisistratus," thus agreeing with Hereas of Megara,[90] but the story goes back before the time of Peisistratus. Its first appearance in Greek art is on a shield relief from Olympia (580–570 B.C.),[91] where we see Heracles coming to rescue the heroes, which means that it was already a Panhellenic myth almost a generation before Peisistratus came into power. The story appeared again in the *Minyas*,[92] a minor epic written in the sixth or fifth century,[93] and in the undatable *Descent of Peirithous*.[94] Finally, we have a sizeable epic fragment dealing with this story, though it is not certain whether it comes from the *Descent of Peirithous* or the *Minyas*.[95] In this fragment, Theseus speaks with Meleager and tells him that Peirithous has a better right to Persephone than Hades, being a closer relative to her than the King of the Underworld is. Once again, the story is an old one, and even if our evidence does not go quite as far back as the sources for the episodes about Ariadne and Helen, we certainly can reject the notion that it was a creation of the Peisistratid era.

Homer's epics, in their present form, seem to have raked up every scandalous tale about Theseus, but they also mention his role in the great battle against the Centaurs. At *Iliad* 1: 265 Nestor finishes off his list of the champions on the Lapith side with the words:

Θησέα τ' Αἰγείδην, ἐπιείκελον ἀθανάτοισιν.

And Theseus the son of Aegeus, equal to the immortals.

Scholars have objected to this line because it is absent from many of the manuscripts, because it also appears in the *Shield of Heracles* at line 182, and because Theseus is not mentioned in the other Homeric descriptions of the battle against the Centaurs at *Iliad* 2: 742 and *Odyssey* 21: 295.[96] In these last two passages, Homer does not just fail to mention Theseus; he does not mention any Lapith whatsoever, with the exception of Peirithous himself, and it would be hard to leave him out of a story about his own wedding. As far as the line's reappearance in the *Shield* is concerned, Van der Valk points out that the *Shield* often imitates the *Iliad*, so it should not make us doubt that the Homeric line is genuine. Furthermore, the Homeric lines recognize the special role of Peirithous in the story (as at *Iliad* 2: 742 and *Odyssey* 21: 295ff.) by placing him first in the list of the Lapiths. In the *Shield*, on the other hand, he is lumped in with all the others. For that matter, the names of the Lapiths in the two poems are not the same, and the *Iliad* does not name any of the Centaurs. The *Shield* is clearly a derivative work. Finally, we must consider the line's absence from some manuscripts of the *Iliad*. Van der Valk claims that Aristarchus, who athetized the line, is responsible for its absence from the good manuscripts.[97] Aristarchus' reasons for doing so were its appearance in the *Shield* and his fear that it might have been inserted by the Peisistratids.[98] On the other hand, Dio and Pausanias had this line in their texts of the *Iliad*, since they refer to it, and this is a strong argument in favor of its authenticity, as those who condemn it admit.

If we reject the Homeric reference, the first literary text to mention that Theseus fought against the Centaurs is the Hesiodic *Shield*, which dates from the turn of the sixth century. Mazon has argued that the poem was written just after the Sacred War of 590 B.C.,[99] Huxley has argued that it was written shortly before it.[100] Russo has come up with an interesting piece of evidence supporting these views, since it shows that the passage in the *Shield* must be genuine and that it must date from before 570 B.C. at any rate. The clue to the date and authenticity of the passage is the depiction of the battle of the Lapiths and the Centaurs on the François Vase.[101] This vase is the first work of art that clearly shows Theseus fighting as an ally of the Lapiths. Cleitias, who painted it around 570 B.C., uses some of the names from the *Shield* for his warriors, and the mysterious name Melanchaites (ΜΕΛΑΝ[Χ]ΑΙΤΗΣ) appears above one of his Centaurs. This is not the name of any of the Centaurs but the word does appear in the *Shield* at line 186; it is an epithet describing one of the Centaurs: μελαγχαίτην τε Μίμαντα ("and black-haired Mimas"). Russo claims, quite convincingly, that Cleitias misinterpreted this line and mistook the adjective for the name of another Centaur, Melanchaites.[102] This would show that the *Shield* was written before 570 B.C., and that the passage from the *Shield* about the Centauromachy is genuine.

In its early form, therefore, the myth of Theseus consists of five main episodes: the abductions of Helen, Ariadne, and Persephone, and the fights against the Minotaur and the Centaurs. They seem to be known as early as the eighth century, but even if we reject the evidence of the *Iliad* and the *Odyssey*, it is quite clear that they were famous throughout the Greek world by the end of the seventh century. By the mid-seventh century, the abduction of Helen had appeared on vases from Crete to the Peloponnese, and the killing of the Minotaur was known in the Cyclades, throughout the Peloponnese, and had reached as far as Sicily. This extraordinarily wide distribution of the myth of Theseus no more than fifty years after the composition of the Homeric epics makes it quite clear that the myth of Theseus must have been known to the epic tradition. Otherwise, it would be difficult to explain how Theseus became a Panhellenic hero, which he certainly was by the middle of the seventh century.

The Cult of Theseus

From Athens itself we do not get any illustrations of the myth until the second quarter of the sixth century, when the dance on Crete, the battle with the Centaurs, and the abduction of Helen appear on Attic vase paintings. The city of Athens is, however, the only center of the cult of Theseus. This might seem a little odd at first, since the legend of Theseus comes from the northeastern part of Attica. We might expect that there should be some cult of Theseus in this region, but in fact there is none. Herter is embarrassed by this absence and suggests that there must have been a hero cult of Theseus at Marathon in historical times.[103] This cannot, however, have been the case because the belief that there are no cults of Theseus outside the city of Athens is not based on an argument from silence, or on the inability of archaeologists to come up with any evidence of such a cult to this date. It is based on an explicit statement to this effect by Philochorus.[104] The Athenians themselves were perplexed by the absence of any cult outside the city, and this is why they invented the curious aition that Theseus had generously handed over all his cults places in Attica to Heracles.[105] All our ancient sources clearly indicate that there never was a cult of Theseus at Marathon, or anywhere else in the Attic countryside for that matter.

There is, however, a fairly simple explanation for this discrepancy between the myth of Theseus, which comes from the area around Aphidna, and the cult of Theseus, which is located in Athens alone. The myth of

Theseus goes back to a time when Aphidna and its lord had some sort of independent existence, an autonomy which came to an end when Attica was united as a city-state. The cult of Theseus, on the other hand, is a product of the newly united state of Athens. He was worshipped at hero shrines, and this type of worship does not begin until the age of the city-states. So, as far as hero cult is concerned, Theseus is purely Athenian. This is why all his shrines were within the boundaries of the city and its suburbs. There was, therefore, no transfer of his cult from the northeast of Attica to the capital, but rather a new invention of such a cult in Athens.

The main hero shrine of Theseus was in the center of Athens. Unfortunately, archaeologists have not yet discovered the location of the Theseion, so we cannot tell when it was built. Aristotle, however, informs us that it was already in existence by the middle of the sixth century. In the *Constitution of the Athenians* he tells how Peisistratus disarmed the Athenians after calling them to an assembly in the Theseion.[106] Aristotle's testimony has been doubted, however, since Polyaenus, writing in the second century A.D., says that the trick of Peisistratus took place in the Anakeion,[107] and Pausanias says that the enclosure of Theseus (the word he uses is *sekos*, and this may be important) was not built until Cimon came back from Skyros.[108] Jacoby believes that we should trust Pausanias' statement about the hero shrine[109] and Rhodes holds the same opinion.[110] On the other hand, Aristotle's account receives some support from the story in Plutarch, which says that the Theseion was built by the Athenians during Theseus' lifetime, and from the end of Euripides' *Madness of Heracles*, which also dates it to the mythical era.[111] All of these show that the Athenians believed the Theseion was much older than the fifth century. Jacoby, who seems to contradict himself on this issue, points out that all the *Atthides* agree in assigning a very early foundation to the Theseion, and that we should infer that the hero shrine was built even earlier than the sixth century.[112]

Whatever we may think of the anecdote about Peisistratus disarming the Athenians, it seems unlikely that Aristotle would have located a sixth-century event in a fifth-century building. It is quite possible that several versions of the anecdote went round and that no one really knew where it actually happened, but Aristotle would at least have known whether or not there was a Theseion in Athens in the time of Peisistratus, so we can trust him when he says that it did exist then. This point is brought up by Thompson and Wycherley who quite rightly declare that, as far as the dating of the Theseion is concerned, it is irrelevant whether the people assembled in the Anakeion or the Theseion; the important point is that Aristotle's text shows that there was already in the sixth century B.C. a "simple but extensive temenos." They also explain the apparent divergence between Aristotle and Pausanias on this issue. Pausanias speaks only of a temple (*hieron*) and an enclosure (*sekos*); he does not deny that there was already a holy precinct (*temenos*) or a Theseion in Athens, and these are the rather precise terms used by Euripides, Aristotle, and Plutarch.[113] It would have made perfect sense for Cimon to bring the bones of Theseus to a holy precinct that had been dedicated to the hero some centuries earlier and then build a new shrine for the bones within this older Theseion.[114]

Archaeologists still argue about the site of this Theseion, which was the most important of his hero shrines in Athens and located somewhere in or near the Agora. Recently, however, some new theories have been advanced about its possible site that might support an early dating for the Theseion. In the 1960s, Thompson had searched for the Theseion in the Agora,[115] and later in the area around the Agora.[116] Shortly afterward, Vanderpool pointed out that it definitely could not be in the area we call the Agora, and that Pausanias had been misread. Whenever Pausanias refers to our Agora, he calls it the *Kerameikos*, so when he says that the Theseion lay near the *agora*, the only place we can be sure it does not lie is in what we call the Agora.[117] Vanderpool suggested that the Theseion must have been near the Roman agora.[118] Perhaps this would be further evidence that it was built before the sixth century, which is when the Classical Agora was laid out. The Athenians would have been more likely to erect the Theseion in the Classical Agora, if the Theseion was later.

By the time that Philochorus was writing in the fourth century, Theseus had no less than four sanctuaries, all of them in the city or suburbs of Athens. The main Theseion was the old one in the city center, and the others were in the Peiraeus, in the western suburbs, and at Colonus.[119] He had been fully accepted as an Athenian hero for centuries, but there were still some peculiarities in his cult indicating that he had not been from Athens originally. One of these, a very important one, was revealed by Herter. All the most ancient cults of Athens, including that of Athena herself and of the hero Erechtheus, are located on the Acropolis. The main sanctuary of Theseus, on the other hand, is in a newer district in the northern part of the city. If Theseus had genuinely been an Athenian hero from the very beginning, his hero shrine would have been situated on the Acropolis.[120] The location of the shrine of Theseus thus exposes him as a hero who was not originally an Athenian.

His priestly family, the clan of the Phytalidai, is also slightly unusual. This family came from the deme of Lakiadai, and its members were supposedly descended from the hero Phytalus, whose tomb was in that deme. Lakiadai was a suburb of Athens, situated beside the Sacred Way and on the southern bank of the Cephisus.[121] In other words, it was just inside the city line.[122] Those who went north and crossed the river left urbanity behind them and entered the rustic world of their fellow citizens who dwelt in the Attic countryside. It is precisely this marginal position of the Phytalidai that explains why they became the priests of Theseus.

The Phytalidai played an important role in the cults of both Demeter and Theseus, and for the same reason in each case. The origins of their privileges in these cults were explained by remarkably similar legends. When Demeter first comes to the city of Athens, she stops at the Cephisus and is welcomed by Phytalus. In return for his kindness she rewards him with a fig-branch that will enable him and his descendants to purify anyone who might be polluted. The area around was known as Holy Fig Tree (*Hiera Syke*) to commemorate this function of the Phytalidai.[123] There was an altar to Zeus Meilichios, the god of purification,[124] on the far side of the Cephisus, so that a visitor could be purified before entering Athens.[125]

When Theseus comes to the city after killing various bandits on the road from Trozen to Athens, he also stops at the Cephisus and is welcomed by the Phytalidai. They purify him, and in return for their kindness he rewards them by putting them in charge of his cult.[126] The region of the Holy Fig Tree is therefore a sort of "quarantine station," as Deubner put it,[127] and the Phytalidai function almost like sponsors for the immigrant goddess and hero. They were supposedly the first to welcome the goddess Demeter and the hero Theseus, and they continued to play a role in their cults, as well as in the cult of Zeus Meilichios.[128] The very fact that the Phytalidai were involved in their cults shows that Demeter and Theseus were not originally Athenian, and that they come from places that were once independent of the city.

The feast day of Theseus fell on the eighth of Pyanopsion, and the festivities in his honor were called the Theseia. The Phytalidai were responsible for offering libations and sacrifices to Theseus,[129] but some other noble families of Athens also helped by contributing to the cost of the festival.[130] These families were supposedly descended from the fourteen victims of the Minotaur whom Theseus had saved from the Labyrinth.[131] The festival later became a very elaborate affair with processions, huge sacrifices, and athletic events,[132] but if the Theseia were celebrated at all in the sixth century,[133] they were doubtless relatively minor events and may have amounted to no more than a sacrifice to the hero.

By around 600 B.C. Theseus had for over a century been well known in Greek literature and art as an Athenian king who fought against the Minotaur and the Centaurs, and who abducted Helen, Ariadne, and Persephone. His deeds had been celebrated by Greek writers and artists from all over the Greek world, and by this time his fame was spreading even beyond this world to Etruria, Lydia, and Phrygia.[134] In Athens he had some sort of sacred space dedicated to him, but this area probably did not have a building in his honor. The Theseion was no more than a plot of land set aside for him.

Up to this point, his story had remained fairly static, but especially after the middle of the sixth century, new episodes were added to it. Steischorus is our first source for two new love affairs of Theseus. According to Stesichorus (circa 630–555 B.C.), Demophon was his son by Iope, and Acamas was his son by another woman. Unfortunately the papyrus that gives us this information breaks off at this point, so we have to guess that Phaedra was the mother of Acamas, and that the third child, presumably Hippolytus, was his son by "the Amazon Hippolyta."[135] Theseus' victory over the Bull of Marathon appeared for the first time on vases produced between 550 to 540 B.C.[136] At the end of the century, in the period stretching from 520 B.C. to 490 B.C., a series of Attic vases depicted his rape of the Amazonian queen, Antiope.[137] Finally, in the last decades of the century, Athenian artists started to organize his deeds in a cycle. This cycle includes the episodes of the Marathonian Bull and the Minotaur, but most of it consists of a whole new series of events that take place on his journey as a youth from Trozen to Athens. These new adventures were especially invented in the final decade of the sixth century to round out the cycle. This decade also marks a turning point in the popularity of the myth of Theseus as an artistic theme in Athens. Before 510 B.C. Heracles is the favorite hero of Athenian vase painters, and Theseus only appears on one Attic vase in twenty. After this date Theseus becomes much more popular, and artists paint him on almost one out of every four vases.[138] Why are all these new episodes invented in the second half of the sixth century? What brings about this extraordinary rise in the popularity of Theseus at the end of the century? These are questions I shall try to answer in the next chapter.

Notes

1. Kearns defines a hero as a combination of an intermediate being (i.e., between mortal and divine) who receives cult and a narrative, historical dimension (Kearns 1989, 135). This covers both spirits who are given a biography and demoted to the status of heroes, as well as mortals (real or legendary) who are given a cult and promoted to the status of heroes. We are concerned mainly with the latter type of hero.

2. This generalization does not, of course, do justice to the extraordinary variety of Greek heroes (see Kearns 1989, 1–4 and 129–132), but it is one that the Greeks themselves would have made. Hesiod, at *Works and Days* 161–165, defines heroes as warriors of a race that no longer exists, especially those who fought at Thebes or at Troy. His definition is hopelessly inadequate, but it does show that the word "hero" immediately brought to mind the notion of Thebes, Troy,

and legendary battles, rather than an agricultural or mantic spirit such as Echetlaios, the plough-man, or Trophonius, the sender of prophetic dreams. The value of Hesiod's statement lies precisely in its casual nature.

3. Mylonas 1951, 98.

4. This early "heroization" of contemporary kings occurs only on Euboea, though at a later period founders of new colonies are honored in this way (Whitley 1988, 175).

5. de Polignac 1984, 141–142.

6. Catling 1982, 16–17.

7. Boardman 1964, 63–66.

8. Coldstream distinguishes between genuine hero-cult and the "tendance" of contemporary tombs as follows: "But when later offerings follow after a gap of several centuries—in fact after the whole of the Dark Age—then we are clearly dealing with a hero-cult . . ." (Coldstream 1976, 9). In this article Coldstream concludes that it was in fact this cultural difference, insofar as it affected burial customs, that led the Greeks (quite correctly) to associate Mycenaean tombs with the heroes celebrated by Homer (Coldstream 1976, 13–14). The validity of this conclusion (doubted by Whitley 1988, 174–175) does not affect the importance of his criterion for distinguishing between "tendance" (such as we find on Euboea) and true hero worship.

9. Coldstream has a useful map showing every known case of grave cult (Coldstream 1976, 12, Fig. I). Grave cults are found in Messenia, Arcadia, the Argolid, Corinthia, Attica, Boeotia, Phocis (one doubtful case), and also on the islands of Cephallenia and Delos.

10. This point is brought out by Coldstream and Whitley, but they qualify their statements by pointing out that the hero of the tomb may have been anonymous only to its first discoverers (Coldstream 1976, 14) or that he may be anonymous only to us (Whitley 1988, 174).

11. It is generally accepted that these are the graves mentioned by Pausanias (1: 39, 2) and Plutarch (*Life of Theseus* 29). See Whitley 1988, 176. Kearns, however, reminds us that although people may have started worshipping at these tombs in the eighth century, we cannot tell whether they identified them with the graves of the Seven as early as this (Kearns 1989, 130–131).

12. Price 1973, 140; Kirk 1985, 217. Pausanias (8: 16, 1–3) is our only witness for the existence of this tomb, which has not been discovered by modern archaeologists.

13. Archaeologists rightly emphasize this distinction (Coldstream 1976, 15; Snodgrass 1982, 11; Whitley 1988, 174 note 6).

14. Offerings dating from this period were found on Mt. Hymettus, at Olympia, and in the Polis Cave on Ithaca, and it was thought that they were dedicated to Heracles, Pelops, and Odysseus respectively. It now seems more likely that the offerings were really made to Zeus on Mt. Hymettus and at Olympia, and that the cult in the Polis Cave honored the nymphs. In each case the hero was included in these cults at a later date (Coldstream 1976, 16–17; Snodgrass 1982, 111–112; de Polignac 1984, 130 note 12). Coldstream thinks that the cult of Odysseus might

be very ancient, and that it could be attributed to the survival of a local tradition about this hero: "It would not be surprising if Odysseus had had a share in the cult from the beginning . . ." (Coldstream 1976, 16). But de Polignac is surely right in concluding that "this cave cult has nothing heroic about it" (1984, 130 note 12).

15. Coldstream 1976, 16; Snodgrass 1982, 112; Whitley 1988, 174. De Polignac doubts that even these are old hero cults, and believes that the shrine of Menelaus was really a temple to Helen and that the Agamemnoneion was simply the center of the festival supposedly founded by Clytaemnestra to appease his ghost (1984, 131 note 12).

16. Coldstream 1976, 16; Snodgrass 1982, 111–112. Both of these archaeologists suggest that the cult might even date back to the ninth century.

17. de Polignac 1984, 130.

18. Archaeologists agree that this annual cult took place on the Acropolis, but they are not sure whether the shrine of Erechtheus was erected in the eighth century on the site of the old Mycenaean palace (Coldstream 1976, 16) or in the sixth century at the entrance gate to the Acropolis (Price 1973, 136–137; Bérard 1983, 51).

19. Whitley 1988, 178. It is surely significant that in Attic myth, all the local heroes of Attica, with the notable exception of Aphidnus, are opposed to Theseus, who was responsible for the unification of Attica (Herter 1936, 197–199). Academus, for example, betrayed the hiding place of Helen to the Spartans (Plutarch, *Life of Theseus* 32).

20. Thucydides 2: 16, 1–2.

21. Kirk 1985, 179.

22. Αὐτονόμῳ οἰκήσει ("living under their own laws") is the expression used by Thucydides to describe the political situation in the villages of Attica before the synoecism (Thucydides 2: 16, 1).

23. Kearns 1989, 50. The presence of two hero graves in one state (in Athens and at Colonus) is particularly objectionable, and Kearns argues that we must choose between them. She suspects that the grave at Colonus might be the original one (Kearns 1989, 208–209).

24. Such attempts to win over the heroes of another state were quite common, though they did not always take this form (Kearns 1989, 47–48).

25. Sealey 1976, 83–84.

26. As Kearns remarks, the hero unites the community and personifies its essential characteristics (Kearns 1989, 133).

27. This school of thought was criticized by Nilsson several years before the appearance of Herter's articles (Nilsson 1932, 5–10).

28. Bethe's particular application of the historical approach was analyzed and condemned by Nilsson (Nilsson 1932, 6–7).

29. Toepffer 1897, 155–156 and 157–158.

30. Herter 1936, 236–237.

31. Ibid., 234.

32. Herter 1936, 223, and 1973, 1046.

33. Nilsson 1932, 174–175.

34. Ibid., 174–175. Leaf had reached the same conclusion in his commentary on the *Iliad*: "It is doubtful if there ever was a Peirithoos in any but Attic legend" (1900, note to *Iliad* 2: 742).

35. Kirk believes that the Homeric lines are sixth-century interpolations and that the association of Theseus with the Lapiths was invented at this later date. He suggests that the story may have been created by Peisistratus to honor his Thessalian allies (1974, 155).

36. The state had at least one extra non-Dorian tribe, and its citizens continued to celebrate the Apatouria (Herter 1939, 274).

37. Herter 1936, 204.

38. Herter 1936, 205, and 1939, 275.

39. de Polignac 1984, 138. He emphasizes however that Theseus is an exception to this rule, being a real Athenian who is only recognized as such on reaching adulthood (de Polignac 1984, 138 note 33).

40. The eponymous hero of the deme Pithus in Attica is called Pittheus (Nilsson 1932, 167). Toepffer made the same connection (Toepffer 1897, 156). This confusion would also have the attraction of making Theseus a cousin and suitable rival of Heracles. Iolaus explains the family connection in Euripides' *Children of Heracles* at lines 207–212.

41. Nilsson 1932, 167–168.

42. Calame believes that Trozen did not become the birthplace of Theseus until after the city welcomed the Athenian refugees of 481 B.C. (Calame 1990, 423).

43. Herter 1936, 205; 1973, 1052–1053.

44. Nilsson 1953, 747.

45. Friis Johansen 1945, 51–52.

46. Herter 1936, 225; 1939, 245.

47. Herter argues that this name in itself would show that the Ionians had at least heard of the hero Theseus (Herter 1936, 225), but in fact the Greeks deliberately avoided naming their children after heroes (Nilsson 1932, 192), as Herter himself points out when he discusses Aegeus (Herter 1936, 208).

48. Herodotus 1: 150. His account is supported by the archaeological evidence, in that the pottery changes from Aeolian to Ionian in the eighth century (Boardman 1964, 49–50).

49. Plutarch quotes a line of his in which he refers to Chios as follows: τήν ποτε Θησείδης ἔκτισεν Οἰνοπίων, "which Oenopion son of Theseus once founded" (*Life of Theseus*, 20).

50. Jacoby believes that this work depicts Theseus as the father of these two children (Jacoby 1947a, 6–7).

51. Calame 1990, 427.

52. Just as, according to Plutarch, the bad reputation of Minos is a tribute to the influence of Athenian literature: "It truly seems a hard fate to incur the hatred of a city that possesses the gifts of eloquence and poetry" (*Life of Theseus*, 16).

53. Nilsson 1932, 208.

54. In his brief review of the connections between Greek myth and Mycenean

cities, Schefold says with refreshing simplicity, "From Aphidnae in Attica comes Theseus, the first abductor of Helen" (Schefold 1966, 13). If we had to pick one particular place, Aphidna would indeed be the best choice.

55. Toepffer 1897, 152–153; Nilsson 1932, 170; Herter 1936, 190–191 and 193–195. These scholars assume that the capture of the Bull of Marathon is a very ancient part of the myth of Theseus. We have no evidence for this episode until the sixth century, so I would not like to rely on it, but the other arguments for Theseus' being a native of northeast Attica are quite convincing.

56. Alcman (fr. 21, *PMG*) seems to have mentioned the sack of Athens and the capture of Aethra alone, both of which occurred while Theseus was absent. Hesychius' Lexicon (see Alcman fr. 22, *PMG*) explains Alcman's phrase Ἀσαναίων πόλιν ("city of the Athenians"), which must surely come from this poem, as τὰς Ἀφίδνας ("Aphidna"). This peculiar interpretation is obviously the work of someone who believed that the episode occurred in Aphidna and decided to twist Alcman's text to produce this meaning. In *Cypria* F 12 (*EGF*), we read that the Dioscuri attacked Aphidna, which was vigorously defended by the local hero, Aphidnus. Then they sacked Athens, during the absence of Theseus. Some manuscripts even say that the Dioscuri sacked Aphidna, rather than Athens, which shows that there were some versions of the story abroad in which Athens did not enter into the picture at all. This confusion, which was felt by the ancient Greek scholars who read Alcman and the *Cypria*, is in itself significant, and it suggests that the story which located everything in Aphidna died hard. We can take it that this story was the older one, since nobody would have had any incentive to transpose an Athenian legend to a remote spot like Aphidna, and since even the Athenian version says that the Dioscuri attacked Aphidna first (Herter 1936, 195–196).

57. Toepffer 1897, 153; Herter 1936, 199–200 (See *Cypria* F 12 *EGF*).

58. Nilsson 1932, 167.

59. The major evidence for its starting at Marathon is the separate *theoria* of the Marathonian Tetrapolis to Delos (Herter 1936, 218 and 218 note 1). This *theoria* to Delos tells us more, however, about the early autonomy of the Tetrapolis and the importance of Delos to the Marathonians (and indeed to all the Ionians) than it does about any early connection between Theseus and Marathon. It seems more likely that the Cretan voyage never started in Marathon, and that Theseus first becomes an Athenian, and only then is equated with the slayer of the Minotaur.

60. Herodotus tells us that Theseus detained her in Aphidna (Herodotus 9: 73, 2), but Alcman has her being rescued from Athens (fr. 21, *PMG* = Pausanias 1: 41, 4) and so did the Chest of Cypselus (Pausanias 5: 19, 2).

61. Herter uses this phrase to describe Theseus' origins in the northeast, without narrowing them down to a specific city such as Aphidna or Marathon. Diacrian literally means "someone from beyond the hills." "Hillbilly" would be an accurate translation, but somehow it has failed to win general acceptance.

62. Kullmann 1960, 74–75.

63. Ibid., 76–77.

64. Helen is well-known as a goddess in Sparta (Herodotus mentions her temple at 6: 61, 3), but she was also honored as a goddess in Attica (Nilsson 1932,

74 and 170, and Herter 1936, 200). Skutsch sees Helen as being (in part) a Spartan vegetation goddess called Welena (Ϝελένα). This goddess disappeared to the south every winter, just as vegetation itself disappeared in the cold months of the year. Her sojourn in the south gave rise to the story that Helen had been in Egypt throughout the Trojan War, while her disappearance gave rise to the story that she had been abducted by Theseus, which in turn provided a model for Homer's story that she ran away from Sparta with Paris (Skutsch 1987, 190).

65. Kearns 1989, 158.

66. Nilsson points out that Helen and Ariadne, since they are originally vegetation goddesses and are raped, are similar to Persephone in both these respects. Both of them are also hanged: according to one version of her story, Ariadne hangs herself after she is deserted by Theseus, and images of Helen were hung on a plane tree (Nilsson 1941, 292–293).

67. Sophocles, *Oedipus at Colonus*, 1593–1594. Pausanias (at 1: 18, 5) says that the memorial was near the Acropolis.

68. "In the voluminous Theseus narratives the few genuinely early elements are almost completely overgrown by the inventions of the poets and even of the Attidographers. The 'democratic' king, who (first in these writings?) achieved synoecism, is so different from the ancient hero of the Tetrapolis that it is hardly possible to speak of legend in this connexion: the late epos contains too much of conscious invention" (Jacoby 1949, 393 note 20).

69. Herter 1939, 313. Herter goes too far, however, when he says that the Athenians "called their country the Thesean land, and loved to call themselves Theseïdai." It is true that the Athenians sometimes did this, but it is far more usual to find *Erekhtheïdai* or *Kekropidai*.

70. Brommer 1982, 38.

71. Cycladic relief amphora from Tinos in the Basel museum (Schefold 1966, 40 and plate 25a; Brommer 1982, 38–39 and plate 25).

72. Artists of this period seem to have liked monsters with four feet, since another relief amphora shows Medusa with the body of a horse (Schefold 1966, 34 and plate 15b; Brommer 1982, 39; Boardman 1967, 93 illustration 53).

73. Brommer 1982, 39.

74. Stanford 1959, 393 commentary on 11: 321–325.

75. Presumably he tells Artemis that Ariadne has lost her virginity. West suggests that Dionysus was already married to Ariadne and that she left him for Theseus (West 1966, 418 commentary on 949).

76. Ameis and Hentze 1879, 102.

77. 580–550 B.C. (March 1987, 158) or 560–520 B.C. (West 1985, 136).

78. Fr. 298 (West-Merkelbach) tells how Theseus left Ariadne for Aigle. Fr. 147 says that Hesiod also mentioned Theseus' affair with Hippe, and suggests that he told of many others too.

79. The chest showed Theseus with a lyre and Ariadne holding a crown (Pausanias 5: 19, 1). Friis Johansen, Schefold, and Brommer argue from these details that the artist must have had the victory dance in mind (Friis Johansen 1945, 29; Schefold 1966, 75; Frank Brommer 1982, 85).

80. This passage is accepted as a genuine reference to Theseus' abduction of Helen by Herter and Brommer (Herter 1936, 263; Brommer 1982, 93). Kirk acknowledges that Aethra is indeed the mother of Theseus, but he follows Aristarchus in condemning the line as an Athenian interpolation for that very reason. He also points out that maidservants are not named after the other two Homeric occurrences of the formulaic line οὐκ οἴη, ἅμα τῇ γε καὶ ἀμφίπολοι δύ' ἕποντο, "she was not alone, for two maidservants followed with her" (Kirk 1985, 282 commentary on 3: 144).

81. The earliest are a late Geometric vase from Argos in the Princeton museum (Brommer 1982, 94) and a Protocorinthian lekythos (Schefold) or aryballos (Brommer) in the Louvre, which dates from 680 B.C. (Schefold 1966, 41–42 and figure 9; Brommer 1982, 94–95).

82. We find Helen's abduction on shield-reliefs from Olympia (Brommer 1982, 94) and on gold reliefs from Crete (Brommer 1982, 96).

83. The bronze cuirass (670–660 B.C.) comes from Olympia (Schefold 1966, 42 and plate 26).

84. Alcman fr. 21 and 22. (*PMG*).

85. Stesichorus fr. 14 (*PMG*).

86. This part of the chest is described by Pausanias at 5: 19, 2 (Herter 1936, 193; Schefold 1966, 72 and figure 26; Brommer 1982, 96).

87. Davies suspects that all of the cyclic epics date from the second half of the sixth century at the earliest (Davies 1989, 4), and he argues that the *Cypria* dates from around 500 B.C. (Davies 1989, 3). Bernabé seems to accept that the *Sack of Troy* was a Homeric composition, since he dates it to the end of the eighth century (Bernabé 1987, 89), and he suggests the seventh century as the date of the *Cypria* (Bernabé 1987, 43).

88. Proclus' summary of the *Iliupersis* (*EGF*, p. 62); *Iliupersis* F 4 (*EGF*).

89. *Cypria* F 12 (*EGF*). The only problem with this fragment is that we cannot tell for certain that it came from the *Cypria* rather than from some other epic.

90. Ameis and Hentze 1879, 114.

91. Schefold 1966, 68–69 and figure 24; Brommer 1982, 101 and figure 15.

92. *EGF* F 1.

93. Huxley suspects it was composed by Lesches and dates it to the early sixth century (Huxley 1969, 120); Bernabé dates it to the early fifth century (Bernabé 1987, 137).

94. In his catalog of the works of Hesiod, Pausanias mentions one that told how Theseus and Peirithous went together into the Underworld (Pausanias 9: 31, 4–5).

95. The fragment has been published as coming from the Hesiodic poem (fr. 280 West-Merkelbach). The same story also appeared in the *Minyas* (F 1 *EGF*), so the fragment might come from this poem rather than from a Hesiodic work. See *EGF*, p. 145 where Davies suggests that the *Minyas* and the *Descent of Peirithous* might be alternative names for the same work.

96. Kirk believes that the line is a sixth-century Athenian interpolation (Kirk 1985, 235 commentary on 2: 742–744). From the silence of the other Homeric

accounts of the battle, and from the reappearance of *Iliad* 1: 265 in the *Shield*, Brommer argues that the passages about the battle against the Centaurs are either unreliable or say nothing about Theseus. He actually doubts the authenticity of the passage in the *Shield* as well (Brommer 1982, 104). Russo in his commentary on the *Shield of Heracles*, while accepting that the line from the *Shield* is genuine, agrees that the Homeric line must have been copied from there (Russo 1965, commentary on line 182). It is curious that Plutarch does not mention this passage when he records the statement of Hereas that Peisistratus had interpolated line 631 into *Odyssey* 11 (Plutarch, *Life of Theseus*, 20, 1). This would only be an "argument from silence" for the authenticity of *Iliad* 1: 265, but if the involvement of Theseus in the battle against the Centaurs had been a recent invention, surely Hereas would have had a very good case in claiming that Peisistratus had interpolated this line rather than the one in the *Odyssey*, and surely Plutarch would have presented this claim instead of the rather dull ones he cites.

97. Van der Valk 1964, 521 note 153.

98. Ibid., 521.

99. Mazon dates it to 590–560 B.C. (Mazon 1992, 124–125).

100. Huxley dates it to around 600 B.C. (Huxley 1969, 110–111).

101. Schefold 1966, 62 and plates 50 and 51; Simon 1976, 74 and plates 52 and 54; Brommer 1982, 105.

102. Russo 1965, 32.

103. Herter 1936, 191. Herter also suggests that the Phytalidai, the priestly family of Theseus, must have originally come from Marathon (Herter 1939, 290). They seem, however, to be from Lakiadai, a suburb of Athens.

104. Jacoby, *FGrH*, 328 (Philochorus) fr. 18.

105. Euripides, *Madness of Heracles* 1328–1333.

106. Aristotle, *Constitution of the Athenians* 15, 4.

107. Polyaenus 1: 21, 2.

108. Pausanias 1: 17, 6. Diodorus says the same thing at 4: 62, 4.

109. "That is the tradition as to the entire sacred precinct . . . which could not have been forgotten and which cannot be doubted" (Jacoby, *FGrH*, commentary on 327 (Demon) fr. 6, p. 208).

110. Rhodes 1981, 211 commentary on 15 iv.

111. Plutarch, *Life of Theseus*, 23: 5; Euripides, *Madness of Heracles*, 1328–1333.

112. "The Atthides seem uniformly to have assigned the foundation of this sanctuary to the time of Theseus himself. . . . Even if Aristotle's evidence ('Aθπ. 15, 4) for its existence at the time of the Peisistratids drops out it may be inferred from the general agreement that it was older than the sixth century B.C." (Jacoby, *FGrH*, commentary on 328 [Philochorus] fr. 18, p. 309). In a footnote, he makes the following statement, which seems to correct what he had said in his commentary on 327 (Demon) fr. 6, p. 208: "F18 yields the fact that the city τέμενος of Theseus was not established as late as 475 B.C., for if it had been Ph. could, and must, have known. The discussion about the age of the city Theseion (see on Demon 327F6) ought to take this piece of circumstantial evidence much more into

account than it has done hitherto" (Jacoby, *FGrH*, note 10, p. 225 to commentary on 328 [Philochorus] fr. 18).

113. Barron, though he does not believe that there was a Theseion before 476/5 B.C., provides a useful analysis of these terms: *temenos* refers to the parcel of land set aside for the cult; *sekos* refers to the tomb; and *hieron* refers to the temple (Barron 1972, 21).

114. Thompson and Wycherley 1972, 124. Boardman is dubious about the existence of a sixth-century Theseion, partly because its rebuilding in 476/5 B.C. would have violated the oath of Plataea. This objection is only valid, however, if the sixth-century Theseion was a "substantial building," and Boardman acknowledges that the oath probably would not have been violated by the construction of a new enclosure on an old site (Boardman 1982, 16–17).

115. At that time, Thompson thought it might be the building usually identified as the Heliaia (Thompson 1966, 42–43 and 46–48).

116. Thompson and Wycherley 1972, 125.

117. Vanderpool 1974, 308–309.

118. Ibid., 309–310.

119. Jacoby, *FGrH*, commentary on 328 (Philochorus) fr. 18, p. 309.

120. Herter 1936, 184 and 188–189.

121. Toepffer 1889, 250.

122. The Cephisus formed the city line of Athens at this point (Deubner 1932, 48; Parker 1983, 139 note 143).

123. Toepffer 1889, 250.

124. Zeus is the real god of purification, not Apollo (Parker 1983, 139). In this role, Zeus usually bears the title Katharsios, or Meilichios (Parker 1983, 139 note 143).

125. Deubner 1932, 48.

126. Plutarch, *Life of Theseus* 23. 5; Deubner 1932, 224; *RE*, vol. 20.1 columns 1,176–1,177.

127. Deubner 1932, 48.

128. *RE*, vol. 20.1 columns 1,176–1,177. Kearns suggests that the Phytalidai owed their connection with Theseus to their convenient location on the road from the Isthmus to Athens; they may have used the geography of his myth to justify their control of his cult (Kearns 1989, 121).

129. Jacoby suggests that the old cult of the Phytalidai was distinct from the cult at the city shrines to Theseus and may have been performed at Lakiadai alone (*FGrH*, commentary on 328 [Philochorus] fr. 18, p. 309). Deubner on the other hand believes that the Phytalidai were always in charge of the shrines of Theseus in the city (Deubner 1932, 224).

130. The Phytalidai did not belong to this group, and Jacoby argues that their connection with these families must therefore be artificial and late. He believes that the role of the Phytalidai and these other families in the cult must have been invented in 475 B.C. (*FGrH*, commentary on 327 (Demon) fr. 6, p. 208). It seems unlikely to me that the contribution by these families to the festival would have acquired such a strong place in the tradition if it had only started in 475 B.C., since

it had disappeared by the fourth century when the state paid for the cult. As far as the Phytalidai were concerned, there were better reasons for entrusting the cult to them than that they happened to come from the same deme as Cimon, as Jacoby suggests (*ibid.*)

131. Plutarch, *Life of Theseus* 23. 5; Deubner 1932, 224; Ampolo and Manfredini 1988, 234–235 commentary on chapter 23, line 26.

132. This trend continued and the festival reached its acme in the second century B.C. (Deubner 1932, 225–226).

133. Calame believes that festival dates from Cimon's discovery of the bones of Theseus in 476/5 B.C. (Calame 1990, 405 and 444).

134. His fight against the Minotaur appears on Etruscan vases from the first half of the sixth century (Brommer 1982, 45) and on terra-cottas at Gordion and Sardis from the second half of the century (Brommer 1982, 55).

135. Stesichorus fr. 16, lines 21–26 (*PMG*). It was Lobel who reconstructed the missing words as "the Amazon Hippolyta." What the papyrus actually has is: ἐκ δὲ τῆς Ἀμ[αζόνος Ἱππο]λύτη[ς], "and from the Am[azon Hippo]lyta . . ."

136. Brommer 1982, 28.

137. Ibid., 112.

138. Theseus appears on only 5 percent of Attic vases before 510 B.C., but after this date, the figure jumps up to 23 percent (Boardman 1975, 2).

2

Benevolent Dictators
and the Paradox
of a Democratic King

Theseus and the Peisistratids

The end of the sixth century does indeed mark a turning point in the legend, and several prominent classical scholars have provided one reason why
this change might have come about. The answer given by Herter, Nilsson,
Kirk, and Connor is that the sixth-century Athenian dictators, Peisistratus
and his sons, decided to promote Theseus as the great hero of Athens. These
scholars have gathered quite a number of arguments for their view, but I
am not convinced that this view is correct. In fact, Theseus does not become really popular until after the Peisistratids are expelled. We shall later
explain why it is not altogether incongruous that the citizens of a democracy might promote a legendary king as their hero. Before that, however,
we shall examine the received opinion and see why it is not fully backed
up by the available evidence. The arguments for the standard view can be
divided into three main groups corresponding to the ways in which the
Peisistratids supposedly promoted the myth of Theseus: according to this
view, the Peisistratids patronized literary works about Theseus, they used
the stories about him to justify their foreign policies, and they claimed
Theseus as the true founder of several new institutions that they themselves
had introduced at Athens.

Poets Laureate to the Peisistratids

The Peisistratids did patronize literature, but we cannot say that they ever
required their poets to write about the myth of Theseus. The only extant

ancient writer who makes any sort of association between Peisistratus and Theseus is Hereas of Megara.[1] According to him, Peisistratus interpolated line 631 into Book 11 of the *Odyssey*:

Θησέα Πειριθόον τε, θεῶν ἐρικύδεα τέκνα.

Theseus and Peirithous, the glorious children of gods.

At this point in the epic, Odysseus hopes to see some ancient heroes, and mentions these two as examples. Herter discusses this line from the *Odyssey* and points out that there is nothing in the manuscripts to indicate that the line is interpolated. He quite rightly distrusts the evidence of a writer "whose anti-Athenian bias is notorious."[2] It might seem a little suspicious that out of all the ancient heroes (πρότεροι ἀνέρες, "men of yore") whom he hoped to see, Odysseus should happen to choose Theseus and Peirithous and them alone. They constitute, however, just like Odysseus himself, a very special case; Odysseus, Heracles, and Theseus and Peirithous are the only men who went down to Hades alive. Odysseus has just seen the ghost of Heracles, so it is natural that he should think next about his other two predecessors on this journey to the Underworld.

Hereas also says that Peisistratus deleted the following line from Hesiod's *Aigimios* (fr. 298 Merkelbach-West):

Δεινὸς γάρ μιν ἔτειρεν ἔρως Πανοπηίδος Αἴγλης.

For a dreadful love for Panopeus' daughter Aegle tortured him.

This line explains why Theseus deserted Ariadne, and the excuse does not do much credit to the hero. Connor points this out as one of the "indications of Pisistratid interest in the legends of Theseus."[3] Hereas' story is, however, a very odd one and not entirely trustworthy. It is plausible that Peisistratus might have tampered with the Homeric texts used for the Panathenaic Games, and that such revisions might have had a considerable effect on the manuscript tradition, but it is very unclear how Peisistratus, or any other Athenian for that matter, could have influenced the text of this Hesiodic work. In any case, these two remarks by Hereas are the only direct ancient evidence we have for believing that Peisistratus took an interest in literary representations of the Theseus myth, though if we were to believe Hereas he seems to have been more interested in forgery and interpolation than in the promotion of new works.

Peisistratus' son Hipparchus was something of a dilettante and invited Anacreon of Teos, Lasus of Hermione, Simonides of Ceos, and other writers to the court of the tyrants at Athens. Perhaps we should seek some evidence for a new literary interest in Theseus among their works. We shall have to give up on Anacreon; he would have been quite happy to write any number of poems praising available Athenian boys or flute-girls, but heroic deeds were not quite his line. Lasus wrote dithyrambs, but nothing survives that would indicate a poem about Theseus. There are, however, a few fragments of Simonides that refer to the Cretan voyage. One describes the sail that the crew were to hoist if Theseus was still alive on their return from Crete (fr. 45 a *PMG*). This sail given by Aegeus was not white, as in the normal version, but scarlet:

> Φοινικέον ἱστίον ὑγρῶι
> πεφυρμένον ἄνθει πρίνου
> ἐριθαλέος.

> A sail dyed scarlet with the soft
> luster of the luxuriant
> kermes-berry.

Another, presumably from the same poem, mentions that the ship's helmsman was "Phereclus, son of Amarsyas" (fr. 45 b *PMG*). Finally, there is an almost comic statement from the poor herald, who rushes to bring the good news to Aegeus, but discovers that he has already committed suicide. The messenger addresses the dead king in the following words (fr. 46 *PMG*):

> βιότου κέ σε μᾶλλον ὄνασα πρώιτερος ἐλθών.

> I would have been of more use to your life had I arrived earlier.

Finally, Simonides must have written about the abduction of Antiope, because we are told by Apollodorus that he called her Hippolyta, not Antiope.[4] Connor quotes the first of these passages (fr. 45 a *PMG*), and he considers it clear evidence that the patronage of the Peisistratids had given birth to a new branch of literature devoted to the hero.[5] "Simonides", he claims, "was one of the first Greek poets we know to treat Theseus."[6] This statement is true as far as it goes, but Simonides was, in fact, only one among many early Greek poets who refer to Theseus.[7] Simonides had many predecessors in writing about Theseus, and we cannot conclude from his work that the Peisistratids patronized a new literature glorifying the deeds of Theseus. Simonides enjoyed a very long poetic career, and did not die until 468 B.C., when he was almost ninety years old. We cannot assume that he wrote these poems in the time of the Peisistratids, since it is more likely that they belong, like most of his work, to some later stage of his long life. Unless Simonides was a most ungrateful wretch, I think it unlikely that he worked for

Hipparchus at all. He was chosen by the democracy to write most of the official epigrams inscribed on its monuments, and among these epigrams were his lines celebrating the assassination of Hipparchus![8]

Finally, Connor claims that the Peisistratids may have commissioned an epic about Theseus, the *Theseïd*.[9] Herter takes the same view because he also looks upon Theseus as the political forerunner of the Peisistratids in that he was a strong ruler of a centralized state. The Peisistratids would, therefore, have had a natural interest in promoting an epic devoted to this heroic monarch.[10] Unfortunately for this view, there is absolutely no evidence that such an epic was written in the sixth century. There were at least two poems of this name in existence in ancient Greece, but we know only five things about them. First, a man called Diphilos, who wrote iambic verse, was the author of a *Theseïd*.[11] He was probably the same Diphilos who mocked an otherwise unknown philosopher by the name of Boidas, in which case he lived before 423 B.C.[12] We know so little about Diphilos' *Theseïd* that we cannot even state whether it was a serious epic or another of his funny poems.[13] Second, we know that an epic *Theseïd* existed by the fourth century, since Aristotle mentioned it disparagingly in his *Poetics* (at 1,151a20).[14] Third, an Athenian called Nicostratus or Pythostratus wrote an epic *Theseïd*, but he wrote in the fourth century at the earliest.[15] It is possible that his work might be the one mentioned by Aristotle, since he clearly is not talking about a comic poem. Fourth, we have a remark by Plutarch that the author of a *Theseïd* wrote about the insurrection of the Amazons.[16] The theme of the latter poem is so bizarre that Boardman concluded it must have been much later than the fifth century.[17] Fifth, we know that an author of a *Theseïd* wrote that the golden-horned deer of Keryneia was female.[18] These five pieces of information are all we know about any *Theseïd*, and it is quite clear that none of them lead us toward the Peisistratid era. Huxley, therefore, is doubtful about the existence of a sixth-century *Theseïd*,[19] and Wilamowitz poured scorn on the very idea.[20]

Herter has a further argument for his belief that a *Theseïd* had been composed in the sixth century, and this is "the agreement between the monumental and literary tradition about a definite form of the sagas."[21] The "definite form of the sagas" that he refers to is the Cycle, which consists of five adventures of Theseus that took place along the Saronic Gulf (Sinis, Phaia's sow, Skiron, Kerkyon, and Procrustes), the capturing of the Marathonian Bull, and the killing of the Minotaur. The myth of Theseus was indeed unusual in that its episodes were organized into this Cycle, which appears for the first time on works of art around 510 B.C.[22] Herter believes that a *Theseïd* must have inspired it, and in order to make this *Theseïd* a Peisistratid epic, he has to assume that it must have taken quite a while for the epic to influence these artists.[23] If, however, the appearance of the Cycle is to be attributed to the influence of an epic, it should surely have been a recent and exciting stimulus, a work composed sometime around the expulsion of the Peisistratids rather than several decades earlier during their regime. We must turn, however, to Herter's original assumption, for the existence of the Cycle by no means proves that someone had written a *Theseïd* by this period. Artists were, after all, no less inventive than writers, and we do not have to assume a literary source for their works. They had a rich, oral tradition on which they could draw, and we sometimes find surprising differences between artistic and literary representations of myth.[24] Neils has shown that the creation of the Cycle by vase painters can be explained in terms of art history alone.[25] We do not have to posit a literary model for the Cycle; on the contrary, the variety of its depictions argues against the existence of a sixth-century *Theseïd*.[26] Whether we turn to Greek writers and scholiasts or to Greek artists, there is no evidence for this hypothetical poem.

The only definite connection we can establish between the Peisistratids and any literary work devoted to Theseus is that Simonides wrote a poem or two about him, and that Simonides was a contemporary of the Peisistratids (but he was also a contemporary of Aeschylus and even of Socrates). If the Peisistratids did commission some poets to write works dealing with Theseus, no record of their doing so has survived.

"The Prototype of the Successful Monarch"[27]

A politician was not restricted to sponsoring works of literature if he wanted to use myths to bolster his position. He could establish a more direct link between himself and the figures of myth either by imitating such heroes, or by altering the myth to provide a heroic precedent for his own behavior. One of the most extraordinary cases of such an assimilation to the men of the heroic age was the theatrical return of Peisistratus to Athens in 556 B.C., which marked the beginning of his second tyranny. He dressed a tall woman up as Athena, and sent heralds to proclaim that the goddess was escorting him back to her city. However we may interpret this episode,[28] we need have no doubts that Peisistratus was quite glad to use myth for political ends. Herter, Nilsson, Connor, and Kirk believe that the Peisistratids used the Theseus myth in this way.

They claim that the Peisistratids used preexisting myths, changed some of them, and even invented new ones to supply mythical precedents for their actions.[29] Connor admits that some of the parallels he draws between episodes in the Theseus story and historical events in the time of the Peisistratids might be regarded as coincidences,[30] but this objection can in fact be applied to all of them. There is simply no ancient evidence that the

Peisistratids looked upon Theseus as their mythical predecessor. The theory that they did so is a recent one developed by modern scholars. The first Athenian we know to have used the myth of Theseus in this way is Cimon, but in his case, several ancient sources tells us about this.[31] If the Peisistratids had made such extensive use of the myth of Theseus as this theory requires, surely some ancient author would have mentioned it, just as Herodotus records that Peisistratus used Athena for such political purposes. Unfortunately, no such statement has survived.

In short, modern scholars may draw many parallels between various details of the myth of Theseus and events in the careers of the Peisistratids, but there is no evidence that the Athenians or the Peisistratids themselves ever did so. In the particular cases brought up by these scholars, it can nearly always be shown that the parts of the myth they believe to have been promoted or invented by the Peisistratids either did not appear during the era of the Peisistratids, or were not completely suitable as parallels for their achievements.

Peisistratus made his final and successful bid for power in 546 B.C., and some scholars have spotted what they believe to be significant parallels between the heroic deeds of Theseus and the tyrant's coup d'état. Peisistratus landed at Marathon; then, with the help of his Thessalian allies he defeated the Eupatrids at Pallene; finally he marched on Athens where he disarmed the citizens during an assembly meeting. This last event has not been discussed by these scholars, and we shall examine it later in this chapter, but first we shall see how they have inferred parallels between the myth of Theseus and Peisistratus' return to power.

Peisistratus defeated the Eupatrids at Pallene and this was also the site of Theseus' victory over the Pallantids. Connor refers to the victory of Theseus as an "ancient exemplar" for that of Peisistratus, and Herter more cautiously suggests that the historical battle of Pallene may have colored the image of the mythical one.[32] Unfortunately, the earliest representation of this battle occurs on the east pediment of the Hephaisteion, which was built around 450 B.C., and it is not even certain that it really portrays the battle against the Pallantids.[33] Our first literary source, Euripides' *Hippolytus*,[34] is even later. We have, therefore, no reason to associate this particular episode with the Peisistratids.

In any case, Nilsson points out that it would have been quite embarrassing for Peisistratus to draw any parallel between the mythical and historical battles, because he had gained a victory over the Athenians, not for them.[35] Figueira agrees with this, and argues that Theseus would, on the contrary, have appealed more to the Eupatrids.[36] Living near the capital city, the Eupatrids would probably have thought that the Pallantids resembled their own enemies, Peisistratus' supporters from "beyond the hills." Figueira's theory is as valid as that of Connor, but in fact there is no evidence that anyone in the sixth century drew any parallel between the victory of Theseus over the Pallantids and the victory of Peisistratus at Pallene.

Theseus' subjection of the Marathonian Bull has been related by Connor to the landing of Peisistratus at Marathon in 546 B.C.[37] This view might seem to receive some support from vase painting in that the first representation of this event occurs on a contemporary piece of pottery, the Paris Amphora of 550–540 B.C.[38] Theseus, however, had been associated with Marathon long before then.[39] In any case, to identify Peisistratus with Theseus and his Athenian opponents with the bull seems a little grotesque, and it is even less plausible than the similar equation made in the case of Theseus and the Pallantids.

Kirk points out that Peisistratus had been supported by Thessalian cavalry, and he proposes that it was Peisistratus who invented the story of the friendship between Theseus and the Lapiths of Thessaly.[40] Unfortunately for this theory, the François Vase, which is the first Athenian vase to show Theseus helping the Lapiths, dates from before the Peisistratid age (570 B.C.). Our first definite literary source for this friendship,[41] the Hesiodic *Aspis*, was composed even before this. Once again, the equation of Theseus and Peisistratus has very little foundation.

All in all, we have absolutely no reason to believe that Theseus was promoted as a hero during the regime of Peisistratus. There is, however, one final and rather more convincing parallel that has been drawn between our hero and Hippias, Peisistratus' other son and successor. Connor has compared Theseus' victories over the bandits on the Saronic Gulf with the operations of Hippias against pirates, and he suggests that in this case, we may be dealing with a fabrication of myths by the Peisistratids.[42] Peisistratus himself had actually seized Nisaea earlier in his career,[43] and his son might with reason have been especially proud of the achievements of two generations of Peisistratids in this region. The idea that some political motivation stood behind the invention of these episodes is quite plausible. These stories appear together as a group around 510 B.C.,[44] and we find the same five episodes in every case: Sinis, Phaia, Sciron, Cercyon, and Procrustes. We have already seen that their appearance was felt to prove the existence of a sixth-century *Theseïd*, sponsored by the Peisistratids or their opponents. Although we have no reason to believe in this purely hypothetical epic, and should doubtless accept Neils's explanation that the Cycle was inspired by an oral legend,[45] it is still quite possible that this oral legend was politically motivated. Even the cautious Brommer believes that "a political decision must have stood behind this [cycle]."[46] Sciron and Cercyon are, after all, local heroes of Megara and Eleusis who have been turned into the villains of the Athenian myth, where they are defeated by the virtuous Theseus.[47] The Cycle must have been created during a period when the Athenians were involved in the Megarid, and it must have been inspired by this involvement.

As we just saw, Nilsson and Connor take it that these adventures were based on the activities of Peisistratus and his sons in the Megarid.[48] If we consider the Cycle as a whole (in other words, the depiction of all five Saronic adventures on one work of art, to which are added the Marathonian Bull and the Minotaur), this theory will not work, since the entire Cycle must have been a product of the new democracy. There is, however, one vase that depicts two of these adventures, and it was produced before 510 B.C. This is a cylix thrown by Skythes around 515 B.C., which an unknown painter illustrated with Theseus and the sow on one side, and Theseus attacking an unidentified youth (who might be Skiron) on the other.[49] Here we have two new episodes that have been added to the myth of Theseus, date from the reign of Hippias, and have probably been inspired by his foreign policy. These two episodes painted in the time of Hippias and the later development of the full Cycle by vase painters under the democracy are a visual representation of the perennial Athenian dream of ruling the Isthmus.[50] It is a dream that lasts from the time of Solon down to the Peloponnesian War,[51] and if under Hippias one artist tentatively expresses it through two adventures of Theseus, it must await the age of Cleisthenes before it reaches its fullest embodiment.

Aetiology for Peisistratid Reforms

Theseus did not, however, just engage in battles with wild animals, bandits, and Centaurs. He was also the king of Athens, though his image as a great reformer belongs rather to the Classical period than to the sixth century. Nevertheless, there are several institutions that he is said to have set up whose real origins lie in the age of the Peisistratids, and some modern scholars have argued that these aetiological stories also date from the Peisistratid era. One of these is the Panathenaia. Herter and Connor point out that Theseus was supposed to have renewed the Panathenaic Festival of Erichthonius and they claim that Peisistratus really did expand this festival, so this event would have been included among the deeds of Theseus in order to glorify his historical successor.[52] The Panathenaia were indeed changed during the archonship of Hippocleides in 566 B.C. The Greater Panathenaia were introduced in this year, and they were a special form of the Panathenaia, celebrated every four years, which included athletic competitions in addition to the normal annual ceremonies.[53] This is, however, long before the time of Peisistratus, who did not even attempt to gain power until 560 B.C., and was not firmly established as a tyrant until over a decade after that. Peisistratus' only innovation was to add Homeric recitations to the new Greater Panathenaia. The anecdote about Theseus, however, has nothing to do with the Greater Panathenaia, because it refers to the old (pre–566 B.C.) annual Panathenaia. The story was clearly invented to reconcile two contradictory accounts about the origins of the annual Panathenaia, one which attributed them to Theseus, and another which claimed they had already been established by Erechtheus. None of these aetiological myths have anything to do with the Peisistratids.

Certain details about the Cretan voyage have also been connected with the Peisistratids, on the grounds that the Delian Crane Dance is portrayed for the first time on the François Vase (570 B.C.),[54] and that, in later times, a sacred triaconter used to set off from Brauron, Peisistratus' hometown. It was supposed to be the very ship that Theseus had used on his Cretan expedition.[55] Some scholars have argued that Peisistratus initiated the sending of the ship from Brauron to Delos, and that he promoted the story that Theseus and the other young Athenians performed a victory dance on Delos. Both the custom and the myth supposedly arose from the interest that Peisistratus had in the sacred island. It is very unlikely, however, that Peisistratus developed either of them, and his interest in Delos was not so remarkable that we should attribute any Delian elements in the myth of Theseus to the inventiveness of the tyrant. The François Vase has nothing to do with Delos whatsoever, since Cleitias is depicting a victory dance on Crete, not a Crane Dance on Delos.[56] There is no evidence for the unusual story that Theseus and his friends celebrated their victory with a Crane Dance on Delos before the time of Plutarch.[57] The sending of the sacred ship cannot be attributed to Peisistratus either, because it is an ancient custom revealing the earlier autonomy of the Marathonian Tetrapolis, rather than an innovation of the tyrants. The Tetrapolis sent a separate religious delegation not only to Delos but also to Delphi.[58] Finally, the Athenians had been involved with Delos long before the age of Peisistratus. As early as Solon's time, we find a law referring to priests called *Deliastai*,[59] but the island had been the religious center of the Ionians for centuries before that, so the association between Athens and Delos must have been even more ancient.[60] Peisistratus did, it is true, purify Delos in 543 B.C.,[61] but he did this because he was interested in the Cyclades in general,[62] and because he wanted to counterbalance the influence of the Alcmaeonids at Delphi, the other great center of Apollo's worship.[63] Peisistratus seems to have looked upon Delos more as an Apollonian center than as a place that had close links with the Theseus legend. So with the Athenians involved in rites at Delos at least half a century before his time and the victory dance not being situated on Delos until long after his day, Peisistratus falls out of the picture altogether.

Finally, there is some evidence from coinage that might establish a link between Peisistratus and Theseus. Connor points out that coins during the Peisitratid era bore an ox head and that Theseus had supposedly issued similar coins.[64] The ox head was, however, only one device among many (there are fourteen altogether) found on the so-called *Wappenmünzen*.[65] It is true that these early coins were minted in the mid-sixth century[66] and therefore originate in the reign of the Peisistratus, but this is a fairly recent discovery. Although *we* may know that the *Wappenmünzen* began under Peisistratus, there is absolutely no way that the person who attributed their introduction to Theseus could have known this.[67] The inventor of this story was simply making a wild guess;[68] he was not trying to honor Peisistratus or reflect his achievement.

We have seen various aetiological myths which tell us that Theseus founded or renewed the Panathenaic Festival, instituted the custom of sending the sacred ship to Delos, and invented coinage. There is no evidence that any of them were current in the sixth century or that they have any connection with the Peisistratids.

There is one final episode in the myth that makes its first appearance toward the end of the Peisistratid era, though it can hardly be connected with any of their achievements.[69] Representations of the rape of Antiope first appeared in Greek art around 520 B.C., and the theme remained surprisingly popular up until 490 B.C.[70] It even appeared on the pediment of the Temple of Apollo Daphnephoros at Eretria, which makes this the first sculpture we have that portrays Theseus.[71] Its style has been compared with that of the sculpture on the Alcmaeonid pediment at Delphi, and as a result the Eretrian temple has been dated to 515–500 B.C. Thus the Eretrians may have started building it toward the end of the Peisistratid regime.[72] Since the Knights of Eretria supported Peisistratus and offered their city as a base to him in 546 B.C., it is possible that this political alliance may have had something to do with the theme of the pediment, if it does indeed date from the time of the tyrants. Tyrrell and Neils, on the other hand, suggest that it might have commemorated the victory of the Athenian democracy over Chalcis in 506 B.C., since the Eretrians would hardly have been displeased at the annihilation of their ancient rivals.[73] In any case, the pediment honored the mythical Attic hero, though, mercifully, no one has tried to see in it a reference to any of the marriages of Peisistratus.

A more fundamental parallel can, however, be drawn between Peisistratus and Theseus. It lies not in any particular achievement of the one or the other, but rather in the political role they played in Athens. Herter refers to Theseus as "the ideal of monarchy," "the prototype of the successful monarch," "the mythical archegete of the monarchy."[74] According to Herter, it is because Theseus was a great monarch that the Peisistratids patronized the writing of a *Theseïd* and established a national cult to honor the hero (for Herter believes that they did both these things).[75] Like most mythical heroes, Theseus was a king, but it is a different matter to try to make him into "the prototype of the successful monarch," or "the archegete of monarchy." If Peisistratus wanted to look for a model of princely behavior in the heroic age, surely he could not have found a better one than his namesake, Peisistratus the son of Nestor. In fact, as Herodotus tells us, the tyrant was actually named after the mythical Peisistratus, and believed himself to be his descendant.[76] Connor supports a modified version of Herter's theory, for he argues that what Theseus and Peisistratus had in common was that both were pan-Athenian leaders. He reminds his readers that Peisistratus had helped conquer Salamis earlier in his career, had reconciled the widely dispersed Athenians to his rule, had established district judges, and used to tour the country on inspection trips.[77] The parallel is too vague to be effective, however, since the same type of comparison could be made with many Athenian leaders and would apply equally well to Solon or Cleisthenes.[78] Every Athenian leader we know of was pan-Athenian like Theseus, but once again there is no evidence whatsoever that any sixth-century political figures ever drew this comparison.

All these similarities between the achievements of Theseus and various events of the Peisistratid era might have provided the tyrants with some reasons for choosing Theseus as a heroic role model; there is no evidence that they actually did so. The significance of the Peisistratids in the development of the myth of Theseus has been greatly exaggerated. Theseus does begin to emerge as a figure on Athenian vase painting in the sixth century, but this is a very gradual development, and it cannot be attributed to the Peisistratids. Shapiro, in his work on art under the tyrants, takes a very sensible approach to this issue. He avoids the temptation to attribute too great a role to them, and instead he describes the emergence of Theseus as a phenomenon that belongs to the sixth century as a whole, as a development in which the ages of Solon and Cleisthenes are just as important as the age of the Peisistratids.[79] The really significant growth in the popularity of Theseus does not occur until after 510 B.C. That is the watershed in the story of Theseus, not 546 B.C.

If we look at the representations of Theseus in Athenian art and literature from the early sixth century to about 510 B.C., we shall get a fairer view of things and be able to put the role of the Peisistratids into a proper perspective. From about 570 B.C. (before Peisistratus came into power) we have

the first depictions of the Minotaur and the great François Vase. One
Minotaur painting is very remarkable, in that we see not only the Minotaur,
Ariadne, Theseus, and the other victims, but also the goddess Athena.[80] It
is very seldom that she is shown coming to the aid of Theseus.[81] On the
François Vase Cleitias painted, among other mythological scenes, the landing on Crete, with the dance of the fourteen victims, and also the battle of
the Lapiths and Centaurs.

From the time of Peisistratus himself we have the Bull of Marathon
appearing for the first time on a vase dating from 550–540 B.C.;[82] the fight
between Theseus and the Minotaur becomes popular with the Group E
painters around 540 to 530 B.C.;[83] and Exekias in the same decade produced
vases with portraits of Theseus and of his sons, Acamas and Demophon.[84]
From the reign of the younger Peisistratids, we find the first painting of
any of Theseus' adventures on the Saronic Gulf (the sow and perhaps
Skiron, on a cup dating from 515 B.C.),[85] and also the first depictions of the
rape of Antiope (from 520 B.C. on). Finally, we may have one literary source,
since Simonides wrote some poems about Theseus at some stage in his long
life, which extended from the sixth century into the following one.

Throughout the sixth century, Athenian artists clearly demonstrate an
interest in their local hero, and the Peisistratid era is, of course, a part of
this sixth-century trend, but it is not an exceptional stage in this development. Under the Peisistratids, the most popular hero on Attic vase paintings is Heracles. It is not until after the expulsion of Hippias that Theseus
will change from being an Athenian hero to the favorite hero of the Athenians.

It seems almost like a case of poetic justice that several scholars should
have turned the theory of Herter, Nilsson, Kirk, and Connor on its head
and declared that Cleisthenes promoted the myth of Theseus and looked
upon the hero as his mythical forerunner. Jacoby, Schefold, and Sourvinou-
Inwood, using the same methods as the proponents of the Peisistratid theory,
have reached precisely the opposite conclusion.[86] Just like their opponents,
all three of them believe that there was a sixth-century *Theseïd*, but they
believe it was commissioned by those Athenians who were opposed to the
tyrants, and that Theseus represents their leader, Cleisthenes.[87] They have
also tried to establish various parallels between the fate of the democratic
opposition in Athens and the career of the mythical hero. Their conclusions
are important in that they clearly show that, in applying this sort of approach
to Greek myth, equally competent scholars can come to completely different results. The fault does not lie with one group or the other but with the
method itself. Vidal-Naquet rightly condemns both those who try to see
Theseus as representing Peisistratus and those who think he is Cleisthenes.[88]
Any attempt to attribute the dissemination of this myth to any one politi-

cal personality seems futile. As Kron has pointed out, *all* Athenian politicians used Theseus as a model;[89] he stood for the whole of the Athenian state.[90]

Hero Worship and Tyranny

One important point must, nevertheless, be conceded to Herter. His main reason for associating Theseus with the Peisistratids was that Theseus was a heroic king and could therefore have been promoted as a model only by another autocrat. This is something that Herter states again and again,[91] and he feels that it is a complete distortion of the hero's nature when he is turned into a democratic hero in the fifth century.[92] Herter is absolutely right in believing that a heroic king should never have been a model for a democracy; but the Athenians were considerably less rational than Herter would have liked them to be. Pausanias had given voice to a similar disappointment at the outrageous anachronism of the Athenians for precisely the same reason,[93] and Herter clearly admires the way in which Pausanias has restored Theseus "to his rights as an absolute ruler."[94] The discrepancy between the kings of the heroic age and the people who admired them is particularly obvious in the case of democratic Athens, but the problem applies to the Greeks in general. Why should any Greek state, apart from one governed by a monarch or a tyrant (both of which were considered exceptional in the Greek world), have looked up to these heroic kings?

The issue we are bringing up here is once again the function of heroic myth and cult in the city-states of Greece. The Greek city-states developed in the eighth century, but this was also the age when the Greeks started to worship heroes and when Greek epic reached its highest point in the works of Homer. These three phenomena are related. The Homeric poems and hero cult bear witness to a heightened interest in the heroic age of the Mycenaean kingdoms. Now that some form of state had been reestablished in Greece, the people of the eighth century naturally looked back to their age of greatness, indeed the last age when there had been centralized governments in Greece. Epic and cult were two different ways of making a connection with that great age, but the connection could not be too close. The great difference between the two ages is that the states of the Mycenaean age were monarchies, whereas those of the eighth century were aristocratic republics. These new republics wished to cloak themselves in the aura of the heroic monarchies, without introducing any monarchist element in their constitutions, for the essence of the aristocratic system was the equality of the "peers" within the small circle that controlled the state. The one thing that could not be endured in the republics was that "desire to triumph over an adversary, to affirm one's superiority over others,"[95] which was the hall-mark of the heroes. And yet, the very popularity of the Homeric epics among the Greeks of this era reveals how fascinating they found those heroes whom they could not have tolerated for one moment as their peers. Their dilemma was to retain the glory and authority of the heroic age while rejecting its behavior and its values, and to this dilemma the cult of the heroes in the new city-states provided the perfect solution.

A living king, who might claim to be descended from the last Mycenaean rulers and thus guarantee continuity with that great era, would have been intolerable. A dead hero, on the other hand, proved to be very convenient.[96] The function of these hero shrines, established by the new aristocratic governments, was to legitimize their authority, to stand as a symbol of the "ethnic and dynastic continuity" linking the republics with the old Mycenaean kingdoms that had preceded them.[97] The mantle of the hero-king falls upon the aristocrats as a group;[98] they have divided his authority among them and cast votes for his power.

Ironically, illogically, and yet quite definitely, the heroes are not "proto-types of monarchy." They are, on the contrary, patrons of aristocracy, and it is as such that they are honored in the new city-states. A tyrant, on the other hand, has nothing to do with heroes.[99] The hero and tyrant are not mythical prototype and working model, but rivals. A tyrant has no desire to defuse the spirit of monarchy by burying it alive in a hero shrine; he wishes to bring it back to life and embody it in his own person. He resur-rects once again in all its dreadful details the specter of sacred majesty, which the city hoped it had buried forever. He appropriates for himself all the power of the old kings,[100] which the aristocrats had so carefully done away with by dividing it up among the elected magistrates of the city.[101] Peisistratus provides an excellent illustration of the fundamental difference between aristocratic hero cults and the revival of autocracy. In Athens, the Acropolis had been the center of royal power but was now reserved for the gods alone; it was the religious center of the city. The Agora, down in the lower city, was the center of republican government. Peisistratus staged a coup d'état no less than three times in Athens, and on each occasion he headed straight for the Acropolis. There were practical reasons for this, since the Acropolis was an easy place to defend, and it would be hard to dislodge him once he was installed there. But there was more to the appeal of the Acropolis than this. His first take-over was a crude affair in which he relied on armed supporters, but his second bid for power was the famous charade in which he was escorted to Athens by the goddess Athena her-self. Whether he fancied himself as Heracles or not is irrelevant;[102] the important point is that he is directly replacing such a hero and claiming the patronage of the goddess. He does not have to rely on hero cults since he is a heroic monarch himself.[103]

Peisistratus' final restoration to absolute power culminated in his disarming of the Athenians. Aristotle's account of this event, even if we do not believe it to be historically accurate, does provide us with a good insight into the rivalry between hero cult and tyranny, since the anecdote is based on the opposition between the hero shrine of Theseus and the position of Peisistratus on the Acropolis.[104] In this story, the citizens of Athens, or those at any rate who are rich enough to afford armor, attend a military review at the Theseion.[105] This is an archetypal Greek assembly, in which the armed *laos* (citizen body) gathers together in a traditional meeting place, which is often protected by a hero tomb, such as the typically Greek assembly of the Trojans around the tomb of Ilus (*Iliad* 10: 414–415).[106] Peisistratus, for his part, plays the role of the archetypal tyrant to perfection. He does not speak to the Athenians as an equal in their assembly. He asks them to approach the Acropolis and listen to his speech as he addresses them from above. He talks down to them from a position of absolute authority, from the seat of their gods and their former kings. A stronger contrast could not be made between the republican hero, who patronizes the assembly of peers, and the tyrant, who has no peers but the gods and heroes themselves. The anecdote goes on to tell how the agents of Peisistratus gathered up everybody's weapons (apparently the citizens had not brought their weaons with them to the foot of the Acropolis) and piled them up in the Theseion. Peisistratus then told them to go home (for they had now lost the right to bear arms and with it the right to participate in government) and leave the state to himself. As Bérard has put it, "the function of the hero shrine is turned against the people."[107] Peisistratus has broken all the rules of an assembly held under the protection of the city's hero, and he has abused the trust that the people placed in its sanctity.

The logical connection between Hero and Tyrant is belied by history; they are, in fact, opposed as rival heirs to the old kingdoms. The one grants his blessing to the new dispensation, the other seeks to restore the old system on his own behalf. It is not at all surprising that a sacred space should have been assigned to Theseus by the government of the aristocratic republic rather than by Peisistratus. Nor should we be surprised when we discover that Theseus enjoyed exceptional popularity after the Peisistratids had been expelled. Boardman has shown that Theseus scenes were, in fact, quite rare on Attic pottery during the era of the Peisistratids. Depictions of Heracles, on the other hand, were very common and were far more popular in Attica during this period than they were anywhere else in Greece:[108] 44 percent of Attic vases at this time have Heracles scenes, whereas the average figure for selected artifacts from the rest of Greece is about 26 percent.[109] During the same period Theseus is found on only 5 percent of the vases from Attica. In the first quarter of the fifth century, Theseus rises in popularity and almost comes to equal Heracles: he is represented in 23 percent of pottery paintings, while Heracles goes down to 19 percent.[110] From this evidence, Boardman proposed that Peisistratus identified himself with Heracles,[111] but perhaps he was not too serious about this suggestion.[112] The important point is that the rise in the frequency of Attic vases depicting Theseus coincides with the restoration of the republic, with the creation of the Theseus Cycle, and with the building of the Athenian Treasury at Delphi, which glorifies Theseus on its metopes.[113]

Theseus and Cleisthenes' Democracy

The years around 510 B.C. clearly mark a turning point in the development of the myth of Theseus, but some proponents of the Peisistratid theory argue that the new popularity of Theseus is a delayed result of the policy of the Peisistratids.[114] This does not explain why Theseus remains popular after 510 B.C., nor why the promotion of Theseus by the Peisistratids should have been so ineffective until this date. Their only aim in promoting the myth would have been to glorify themselves, but such a policy is pointless unless it is immediately effective.[115] If the Peisistratids planned to promote Theseus as their mythical predecessor (though we have no evidence for this plan), they failed to do so in time, and it was, in fact, the restored government of Athens that put their plan into effect and reaped its benefits.

Both Connor and Herter acknowledge that the popularity of the Theseus myth after 510 B.C. is awkward for their theory, but they point to the absence of Theseus from Cleisthenes' eponymous heroes and suggest that this indicates some dissatisfaction with a hero promoted by the Peisistratids.[116] Connor refutes his own point himself: "The fact that one tribe was named after his son Acamas shows that his exclusion from the list was not due to any feeling against Theseus."[117] Herter and Kron have supplied the real reason for this omission. Theseus, they point out, was the hero of the entire people and the entire state; he could not, therefore, become the hero of just one tribe.[118]

We have already seen that the innovative cup of Skythes, which shows Theseus fighting the sow on one side and perhaps Skiron on the other, may have been inspired by Athenian hostility to Megara in the time of Hippias. This dispute between Athens and Megara, which was largely over Salamis, was finally settled through outside arbitration when the Spartans handed the island over to the Athenians. Plutarch, our source for this Spartan decision, thought it occurred in the time of Solon,[119] but one of the five Spartan arbitrators happens to be called Cleomenes. Bury and Meiggs therefore date the Spartan arbitration to around 509 B.C.[120] This dating is attractive because the Spartans, having set up a new government in Athens, would naturally want to settle the country's external affairs as well.[121] It would also explain why Cleisthenes might have established a cleruchy on the island (if indeed he did do this), because such an action would be senseless if Athens had been in secure possession of the island since the time of Solon. These events seriously threatened Megara and strengthened the position of Athens on the Saronic Gulf. They are, in addition, almost exactly contemporary with the first appearance of the vases depicting Theseus fighting the series of bandits on the Saronic Gulf, and probably also with the construction of the Athenian treasury at Delphi, which has the adventures of Theseus and Heracles sculpted on its metopes.[122] The complete series of adventures along the Saronic Gulf begins at the Isthmus with Sinis, continues along the coast through Megara and Eleusis, and comes to an end on the Cephisus with Procrustes. It celebrates an imaginary Athenian mastery over the entire region. The early appearance of the fight against the sow and Skiron was inspired by Athenian involvement in the Megarid; the emergence of the entire Cycle was inspired by the final victory of Athens over Megara, which resulted from her secure possession of Salamis. It was, of course, largely a Spartan achievement, but the Athenians naturally chose to attribute it to Theseus rather than to Heracles.

An extremely important feature of the new Cycle created by Athenian artists around 510 B.C. is that it rivals the Labors of Heracles. This is a point recognized by all scholars,[123] and Plutarch even makes it a part of the myth of Theseus when he tells us that the Athenian hero was fired to tackle these bandits by his admiration for Heracles.[124] When Theseus becomes very popular after 510 B.C., he is not only a hero common to all Athenians, but also the Athenian alternative to Heracles. This would make perfect sense in the period following Cleisthenes' victory. Heracles was, after all, taken to be a Dorian hero, and we would hardly expect the Athenians to honor him after 510 B.C. The Spartans had, of course, helped them to expel the Peisistratids, but the Athenians preferred to forget that, and later they even affected to believe that the dictatorship had been ended by their own heroes,[125] Harmodius and Aristogeiton, who assassinated Hipparchus in 514 B.C. This was partly just a matter of national pride, but their lack of appreciation for the help they had got from the Spartans was not entirely unjustified. The Spartans had, after all, undone whatever favor they might have won with the Athenians by sending their army back to Athens to impose the government of Isagoras upon them. The years after 510 B.C. also mark a turning point for Athens herself. She could not challenge

Sparta's position as the leading state of mainland Greece, but she began to assume her position as leader of the Ionians, and when they rebelled against Persia, she granted them the aid that the Spartans refused.

The Athenians had, therefore, good reasons for asserting the prowess of a hero of their own, and for setting him up as a rival to the universally admired hero of the Dorians. Plutarch records a saying of the Athenians, which, though it may date from a later period, reveals why a fixed cycle of deeds was established for Theseus. They claimed, Plutarch tells us, that Theseus was a "second Heracles" (ἄλλος Ἡρακλῆς).[126] The hope that this claim would one day be accepted by all the Greeks is what inspired the creation of the Cycle.

A significant symbol of the new official popularity of Theseus is the Athenian Treasury at Delphi, erected in the early days of the new democracy (somewhere between 510 B.C. and the early 480's B.C.)[127] It was decorated with metopes that depict his adventures, and these metopes make it quite clear that the Athenians in this very period after 510 B.C. were already deliberately comparing Theseus with Heracles. The nine metopes on the long southern side show the adventures of Theseus, and this is the prestigious side of the Treasury, the one that the Delphic pilgrims would have seen as they went up to the Temple of Apollo. The corresponding metopes on the less conspicuous northern side show the labors of Heracles. On the shorter sides of the Treasury, the six eastern metopes facing the road portray a battle against the Amazons, while the six western metopes at the back of the building show Heracles and the cattle of Geryon.[128] The most easterly metopes at the corners of the long sides stress this comparison, because the last one on the southern side shows Theseus with an Amazon, while the corner metope on the northern side shows Heracles with an Amazon, and both lead into the eastern metopes which represent a full-scale war between Greeks and Amazons.[129]

The middle metope on the southern side is also remarkable, in that it portrays Theseus alone with Athena. This is very unusual since Athena was felt to be the special protector of Heracles.[130] In fact, the relationship between Athena and Heracles is almost one of intimacy.[131] Boardman has argued that the reason Athena is so seldom shown beside Theseus is that she was felt to be the special protector of Heracles, and it took the Athenians a long time to get used to the idea that she could be represented as helping Theseus instead.[132] Whatever the reason, this metope is unique. As Brommer remarks, Athena is never represented alone with Theseus, so the purpose of this relief is clearly to raise Theseus to the status of Heracles.[133] The sculpture becomes even more striking when we consider that Athena is conspicuously absent from the scenes with Heracles. As Boardman puts it, this metope is "a very deliberate compliment to the hero, and at Herakles' expense."[134] It is unique both in crediting Theseus with the same high favor that Heracles had enjoyed and in showing that Theseus is by now the greatest hero of Athens, just as Athena is the patron-goddess of the city. The function of this metope is thus identical with that of the Treasury as a whole.

A final monument to Theseus, created in the first decades of the democracy, occurs in the work of the first Athenian prose writer, the mythographer Pherecydes.[135] His work on Athenian myth, the *Attica*, naturally covers the career of Theseus.[136] Pherecydes mentioned Alope, who was the daughter of the Eleusinian king, Kerkyon.[137] This suggests that he must have been familiar with the Cycle, something we could probably assume even without this passage, given the popularity of the Cycle at this period. The story of the Minotaur naturally took pride of place in Pherecydes' work, and he made Theseus something of a trickster, since he escaped the wrath of Minos by sabotaging the Cretan ships.[138] When he turned to the war against the Amazons, Pherecydes stressed that this was a private expedition which Theseus and his charioteer Phorbas undertook without the help of Heracles. Pherecydes is referring, of course, to the campaign in Themiscyra, which ended with the abduction of Antiope, and this alone suggests that he wrote his work before 490 B.C.[139] Theseus is still something of a wild man, as he was in earlier archaic literature, and his treatment of Ariadne, Antiope, and many other women are still a large part of his story.[140] There are, however, some interesting new traits that suggest Pherecydes regards him as something of a civilizing hero, perhaps even a civilized hero. The episodes involved with the Saronic Gulf are always regarded as an achievement aimed at benefiting humanity, and the somewhat refurbished Theseus who performs them betrays surprising new elements of intelligence[141] and piety.[142] His first appearance in prose seems to have had a sobering effect on his character, but this is a trend that belongs to the new image of Theseus that emerges under the democracy.

The Cycle, the Treasury at Delphi, and the *Attica* of Pherecydes mark a new stage in the development of Theseus as an Athenian hero,[143] just as the expulsion of the Peisistratids marked the beginning of a new heroic age for Athens. In the new era that started now, this adventurous state would develop a radical form of democracy, this new power would assert itself in every way against the established power of Sparta.[144] The Spartans themselves augmented the effect of this contrast with Athens by making an equal but opposite change in their own policy. Up until the creation of the new Athenian system, tyranny was the antithesis of everything that Sparta believed in, but after the establishment of Athenian democracy the Spartans altered their views in a sudden U-turn that shocked their own allies.[145] From now on, the Spartans became the champions of oligarchy, and they started to look upon the new government of Athens as their greatest enemy.[146] This is why the Athenians turned now more than ever to the figure of Theseus.

They were embarking on a new political adventure and needed the sanction of tradition, a sense of continuity with the past. They were ready to act independently of Sparta and needed to be reassured of their ancient glory. Theseus had never been anything more than one of many Athenian heroes, but after 510 B.C. he became the greatest hero of Athens, and just as Athens would one day be able to challenge Sparta, so Theseus developed into a worthy rival of the great Panhellenic Dorian hero, Heracles himself.

The revolution of Cleisthenes resulted in the birth of a new Athens, a radically "secular" state insofar as such a thing was possible at this time.[147] What his reforms involved above all else was a consciously political manipulation of the state religion.[148] The story that he bribed the Delphic prophetess, whether true or not, certainly seems to have captured his attitude with some accuracy.[149] He played around with the traditional religion of Attica in a manner that might have made downright atheism seem kinder. His great innovation was the creation of the ten eponymous heroes, who were referred to as *Archegetes*. This was the term used to describe the founding hero of a new colony, and Cleisthenes did indeed act as if he were creating a new city and establishing a completely new religious tradition rather than reforming a very ancient one.[150] A good example is his treatment of the old hero Erechtheus who was demoted from his royal status on the Acropolis to that of an ordinary tribal hero along with the other ten in the Agora.[151] For Homer, Erechtheus had been the patron of the city; for Cleisthenes, he was just one hero among others.[152] In spite of his cavalier attitude toward ancient beliefs, and even though his reforms were entirely political in inspiration, Cleisthenes still had to give his new city the sanction of the gods and heroes if he did not wish to scandalize his new political allies, the Athenian people.[153]

For the ordinary Athenians, the heroes were very much alive. The Athenians clung to their belief with especial tenacity in times of crisis, and all sorts of incredible stories arose about the first great international test that the new democracy had to face, the Battle of Marathon. Many of the soldiers claimed that they had seen Theseus, clad in full armor, leading them into battle against the Persians.[154] Since this was a battle in which the Athenians and the Plataeans had to face the Persians alone, it is not surprising that the Athenians should have believed they were helped by the intervention of a purely Athenian hero. The official painting of the battle in the Stoa Poikile showed this miraculous apparition.[155] After the battle, the local people of Marathon commemorated it by sending a sculpture of the Bull of Marathon, which Theseus had overcome, to the Acropolis.[156]

The war with Persia also had a peculiar effect on one little episode in the myth of Theseus. The abduction of Antiope, since it involved an expedition by an Athenian hero into barbarian territory, was gradually associated in Athenian thought with their own raids against Persia during the Ionian revolt. The first clear example of this association dates from 500 to 490 B.C., and it occurs on a vase painted by Myson. On one side he shows Theseus and Peirithous running away with Antiope, and on the other he shows Croesus, victim of the Persians and friend of the Greeks, on his funeral pyre.[157] The significance of this comparison becomes clear when we recall that the major military action by Athens during the Ionian revolt of 499 B.C. was the burning of Sardis, once the capital of Croesus, but by this time the center of Persian rule over Ionia. This connection between Amazons and Persians was so clear by 490 B.C. that a campaign fought against the Amazons in their own land was seen as inappropriate after the Battle of Marathon. Consequently, the abduction of Antiope disappears from Attic vases after 490 B.C., but it will later be replaced by a new episode in the myth of Theseus, the Amazonian invasion of Attica, where Theseus and his people will have to defend their country against an incursion by these barbarians, just as the fifth-century Athenians had to defend Attica against the Persians.[158]

Ten years later, when the Athenians had to evacuate their city, they removed their women and children to Trozen.[159] At this time they proudly "recalled" that it had been the home of Theseus, though it is quite likely that they invented the episode of his birth in Trozen at this time. The story of Theseus and the sword left by his father under a rock at Trozen does not appear in Attic art until after the Persian invasion.[160] As Calame points out, in Bacchylides 18 the adventures of Theseus start at the Isthmus, not in the Peloponnese,[161] so Bacchylides does not seem to have thought of him as a Trozenian. The Decree of Themistocles is the first text that assumes a connection between the hero and Trozen. This decree commemorates the evacuation of Athens, and it says that the Athenians were placing their families at Trozen under the protection of "the Archegete of the land." Unfortunately, the decree does not say which land, Athens or Trozen, and there is a lacuna where the name Theseus or Pittheus would have appeared; but in either case, the important point is the connection with the story of Theseus' childhood in Trozen.[162] The myth of Theseus thus played a considerable role in both the Persian Wars.

Cimon and Theseus

Theseus was clearly a popular hero by this time, but the human leader at Marathon, Miltiades, did not fare as well as the mythical one. His son Cimon, on the other hand, was very successful in winning the favor of the Athenian people and in exploiting popular religion to his own advantage.

In this respect he could be compared with Cleisthenes, but Cimon utilized his popularity to promote his own conservative program rather than yielding to the democratic movement, as the Alcmaeonid reformer had done. His greatest coup in this publicity campaign was the return of the remains of Theseus to Athens.

In 476/5 B.C. the Athenians received an oracle commanding them to recover the body of Theseus and honor him as a hero.[163] Some time after this,[164] Cimon, who was campaigning against Dolopian pirates on the island of Skyros, found some bones there,[165] claimed they were the remains of Theseus, and brought them back to Athens. "The rejoicing Athenians," Plutarch tells us, "welcomed the body with magnificent processions and sacrifices, as if he himself were coming back into the city."[166] Cimon was not establishing the cult of a neglected hero whom he had chosen for personal reasons. If he had any choice in the matter, he would doubtless have gone for a more Panhellenic hero such as Menestheus rather than the purely Athenian Theseus. Cimon was, instead, capitalizing on the reputation of a hero who was already the most popular one in Athens. Plutarch says as much: "As a result of this," he remarks, "the people were especially endeared to Cimon."[167] The son of Miltiades had repaid a debt that his father owed to the Athenian hero.[168]

Podlecki argues that Cimon's theatrical coup may have been in response to the rising popularity of Themistocles. There was, he points out, a natural rivalry between the man responsible for the victory at Salamis won by the democratic oarsmen of the triremes, and the man whose father had won the Battle of Marathon, an old-style campaign fought by the wealthy hoplites. Cimon had at last matched the wily politician who had solved the oracle about the Wooden Walls by finding the answer to another oracle and an even older question about the location of Theseus' body.[169] The sort of political capital that Cimon hoped to gain from the expedition to Skyros and his rivalry with Themistocles, which lay behind this campaign, are completely within the normal rules of politics in an ancient city-state.

Podlecki has tried to discover what Themistocles' answer might have been to this sudden increase in Cimon's popularity. From certain elements in the aetiology of the Oschophoria, he argues that Themistocles may have reorganized this festival and changed the myth of Theseus in ways that would improve his own image.[170] Unfortunately, these connections between Themistocles and the myth of Theseus are as difficult to establish as the ones that scholars have tried to make between the same myth and Cleisthenes or the Peisistratids, an enterprise rightly condemned by Podlecki himself.[171] Moving to the world of the stage, we are, perhaps, on more solid ground. Aeschylus' *Persians* had glorified Salamis, and in 476 B.C. Themistocles may have reminded the Athenians of his victory by commissioning another tragedy on the subject.[172] Cimon may have got a chance to answer him in 468 B.C., when he and the other generals for the year were allowed to judge the dramatic contest. Sourvinou-Inwood suggests that they pronounced Sophocles victor with his play *Aegeus*, and that this drama may have played a significant role in making Theseus "the mythological projection of the triumphant people of Cimonian Athens."[173] Cimon's bringing back of the remains of Theseus would be just another part of this propaganda war with Themistocles, and he would not be setting himself up as some sort of second Theseus, but simply trying to make himself more popular, to win a few more votes. It is probably not just a coincidence that the precedent for his theatrical coup is to be found in his favorite city, Sparta.[174]

After Cimon had returned with the bones of Theseus, a new hero shrine was erected in the center of the city to house the remains. It was either a totally new sanctuary complete with hero shrine, or else a new hero shrine built in a preexisting sanctuary to Theseus.[175] I have taken the latter view, though in all probability the old Theseion would have been no more than a space set aside for his cult and would not have included any building. Cimon would have built his impressive new shrine in this old sacred space. The return of the bones and the building of this new shrine gave new life to the cult of Theseus. Perhaps it was at this time that the state appointed its own priests to look after the cult of Theseus, and these priests would have replaced the Phytalidai in Cimon's Theseion.[176] It is not clear whether the other three Theseia (in the Peiraeus, in the western suburbs, and at Colonus) were in the hands of the Phytalidai or of state priests, or whether they even existed at this time.

When the remains of Theseus were brought to Athens they were welcomed with processions and sacrifices.[177] The sacrifices to the hero on his feast day, the eighth of Pyanopsion, had originally been financed by noble families supposedly descended from the fourteen victims saved from the labyrinth by Theseus. By the fourth century, the families of the fourteen victims had dropped out of the picture and the Theseia were financed by a special tax.[178] The state may have taken control of the Theseia after the return of the hero's bones. This annual festival was celebrated with processions, libations, and sacrifices.[179] It must also have included some competitions, and these probably date from the time that Cimon came home with the remains of Theseus, since Euripides is supposed to have won an athletic victory at the Theseia when he was a boy.[180] By the third century, the Theseia included a parade by the ephebes, a torch race, and all kinds of athletic events, but it probably was not quite so elaborate in the early fifth century.[181]

Nothing is known about the form of the new Theseion, but Barron conjectures that it was a square space surrounded by a stoa on three or four sides.[182] It was decorated with paintings, but these works did not attempt in any way to glorify Cimon himself. The dramatic return of Cimon from Skyros with his unusual cargo was thus quite different from Peisistratus' performance in which the tyrant was led into the city by a woman dressed up as the goddess Athena.[183] The paintings in Cimon's Theseion illustrated three episodes from the myth of Theseus: the invasion of Attica by the Amazons, the battle with the Centaurs, and his visit to Poseidon's palace under the sea.[184] The last of these paintings was by Micon, and it is generally assumed that he painted the others.[185] In fifth-century art, the Amazons and the Centaurs often stand for the barbarians, so the two paintings that showed these battles doubtless recalled Athenian successes in the Persian Wars;[186] the third painting may have honored the thalassocracy of Athens in that it associates the king of Athens with the Queen of the Sea, and Theseus had paid this underwater visit during a dispute with Minos, the first of the Greeks to rule the waves.[187] The Theseion honors the Athenians, therefore, rather than Cimon, though he did gain popularity by honoring them and their hero in this way.

We might wonder why Cimon did not draw a direct parallel between himself and the hero, but such self-glorification was very much frowned upon in the democratic city. Centuries later, Plutarch was still shocked at the thought that Cimon and his fellow generals had been authorized to erect three herms after their Eion campaign of 476/5 B.C.[188] None of the offending epigrams on these herms actually mention any of the generals by name,[189] so they may seem quite innocuous to us, but Plutarch thought differently. He criticizes the Eion epigrams as being excessive, since Themistocles and Miltiades never received such an honor. He goes on to say that when Miltiades merely asked for an olive crown, he was told that if he wanted to be honored alone, then he would have to go and defeat the barbarians on his own! This anecdote may not be literally true, but it does show how much the Athenians were opposed to such special honors being paid to private citizens. In fact, Plutarch was not being hypersensitive, because the Eion epigrams were unique in honoring a specific, if unnamed, group of individuals. Normally, public epitaphs and funeral orations mention "the Athenians" in general, rather than any specific Athenians.[190] The Theseion, honoring Athens alone, was therefore a more proper monument.

At about the same period a war memorial with a statue of Theseus was erected at Delphi. Its nature was very different from the anonymous modesty of the Theseion, for it glorified Cimon's father in a most outrageous fashion. This monument was the Marathon Base set up by the Athenians at the entrance to the Sanctuary of Apollo. As Pausanias describes it, the monument consisted of three groups of sculpture. First there was a group depicting Miltiades with Apollo and Athena; then came seven of Cleisthenes' eponymous heroes; and finally there was a group that included Theseus,[191] Codrus, and a third figure who was probably Philaios, the mythical ancestor of Miltiades and Cimon.[192] The monument was probably set up in the middle of the fifth century, though its dating is a controversial matter.[193] The group showing Miltiades with Apollo and Athena must have been quite shocking. It was, as Kron points out,[194] the first time that a man had ever been honored as equal to the gods. The Athenians avoided honoring individuals in this way, and in Athens itself the last public statue of a human had been the one erected in honor of the tyrannicides, but they were a very special case and had been heroized too. No human would be honored with a statue in Athens again until the citizens raised one to Conon.[195] A monument such as the Marathon Base at Delphi could never have been tolerated in Athens itself, but leaving aside its extraordinary character, it bears witness once again to the popularity of Theseus. Delphi was the most famous showplace of Greece, and by glorifying Theseus on both their Treasury and the Marathon Base, the Athenians were showing off Theseus as their greatest hero.

Another monument that also celebrates Theseus dates from after the ascendancy of Cimon, but it is associated with his family. This is the Stoa Poikile, erected around 455 B.C. by a relative of Cimon's called Peisianax.[196] Theseus appeared in two of the four paintings that led to the stoa's being called "the brightly painted portico." The four paintings showed two historical battles, the Battle of Marathon and the Battle of Oinoe, and also two mythical scenes, the Greeks after the capture of Troy and the invasion of Attica by the Amazons. Theseus was shown fighting in the war against the Amazons and he also appeared in the painting of Marathon, as a hero emerging from the soil of Attica.[197] The battles against the Trojans and the Amazons were probably seen as mythical prototypes of the more recent wars against the Persians,[198] but the stoa, like the Theseion, is a discreet monument. It does not establish any close connection between Theseus and Cimon or Miltiades, as Connor argues,[199] though Cimon and his followers certainly played some part in the erection of the Marathon Base and the Stoa Poikile. In each of these monuments, a parallel was drawn between the battles of Marathon and Oinoe, which is rather curious, given the involvement of Cimon. In the Stoa Poikile, these were the two historical battles represented. At Delphi, the Marathon Base was matched by a nearby Argive war memorial, a horse commemorating that same Battle of Oinoe in which the Argives and the Athenians had defeated the Spartans.[200] The connection between the war against the Persians and the war against Sparta is one that conservative Athenians like Cimon would have been very reluctant to make.[201] The presence of Codrus on the Marathon Base might be a further declaration by Cimon that he had abandoned his pro-Spartan policies and that he was completely loyal to the democracy of Athens, since Codrus had defended Athens against the Peloponnesians.[202] The Spartans themselves must have noticed this insult; they certainly were aware of the excessive honors paid to Miltiades by his being presented on the base with gods and heroes. If the Marathon Base is the first such monument we know of, the Spartans eventually came up with a fitting answer to this arrogant piece of Athenian propaganda. After the humiliating defeat of the Athenian navy at Aegospotami, they raised a statue at Delphi which showed the victorious Lysander being crowned by the god Poseidon.[203]

Three great fifth-century monuments that honor Theseus are thus associated with Cimon, but in no case does he try to manipulate the myth to his own advantage. His actions rather bear witness to the already established popularity of Theseus as the hero of the democracy, and they are indeed a major concession to it. This was a concession he made at a considerable cost to his own principles, for there is no doubt whatsoever about Cimon's real political views. He was described by a contemporary, Stesimbrotus of Thasos, as being more Peloponnesian in his character than Athenian. Stesimbrotus also records that Cimon never bothered with "music or any of the liberal arts" and was "completely lacking in Athenian cleverness."[204] Cimon himself made no attempt to conceal his love of Sparta. In 463 B.C., when his political opponents accused him of receiving bribes from Alexander of Macedon, Cimon proudly replied that he was not that sort of person, he imitated Spartans instead![205] He was also in the habit of criticizing Athenian behavior by saying, "but the Spartans are not like that!"[206] It was this extraordinary and, as it turned out, not very well requited love of his for Sparta that eventually led to his ostracism in 461 B.C.

As might be expected from such an admirer of Sparta, Cimon had no great love for democracy, and he was furious with the reforms that Ephialtes carried out in his absence in 462 B.C. Plutarch tells us that he objected to such "absolute democracy" and called for a return to the old aristocratic system of government.[207] Cimon was no Critias, however, and seems to have accepted that he would have to put up with living in a democracy and make the best of it. He opened up his estate to the public and provided meals for the poor, which some people saw as "flattery of the mob and demagoguery."[208] Plutarch defends him from what he believes to be a disgraceful charge by pointing out that he was in fact "aristocratic and influenced by Sparta,"[209] which hardly reassures one as to the purity of Cimon's motives. The publicity he gained by honoring Theseus was part of the same magnanimity, which was not devoid of political motivation.

What noblemen such as Cimon found especially difficult to endure in Athens was the imperialism of the democracy, its oppression of other Greeks, an oppression that paralleled their own reduced status within the state itself. The aristocrats had always been an internationally minded group, and many of their clans had branches in several Greek states.[210] They intermarried,[211] they had friends in foreign lands,[212] they met together at the great Panhellenic games. The ideals of their world have survived through the poetry of Pindar, and what is particularly interesting is Pindar's attitude to the ancient heroes. What we have seen so far is the cult of heroes as an "expression of group solidarity,"[213] a means of legitimizing a new form of state and society. In Pindar we find quite a different tradition. For him the heroes are not so much founders of states as founders of noble lines.[214] Hero cult is thus merely a particular case of ancestor cult, and it is "the chain of blood across generations" that is all important.[215] Bowra summarizes Pindar's views about the heroes of myth and the aristocrats of his own day: "From unions between god and mortal arose the generation of heroes, and from this race are descended the patrons and subjects of his poems."[216] Pindar himself was a member of this elite group, but he plays an essential role for his peers by leading them, or rather reintroducing them, to the exalted world of the heroic age to which, as an inspired poet, he alone has a special access. We find in his thought a very old notion of the heroes that would, perhaps, have been understood by the Attic noblemen of the eighth century who proudly asserted their own heroic past against the claims of the capital city.[217] The success of the city-state in taking over the heroes has given an archaic and curious air to Pindar's views, for the heroes of the city-state seem so obviously public and politicized that we find it difficult to think of them merely as founders of private pedigrees.[218] It is through hindsight alone that this seems to be the case, for we should really wonder instead how the republics ever managed to appropriate the heroes for themselves.

Athenian Myth and Ionian Science

The democracy of Cleisthenes was, as we have seen, as close to a secular state as one could go in ancient Greece, but this secularism was strictly limited. The official history of Athens was still firmly rooted in myth, and the establishment of its democracy was justified through its sanction by the Delphic oracle and the eponymous heroes. The version of their history with which the Athenians remained satisfied up until the end of the fifth century was simply the traditional tales handed down by word of mouth from generation to generation. This tradition was given a more definite but carefully doctored form by the funeral orations, which honored those who had died in battle for Athens.[219] The traditional history encapsulated in the orations clearly and deliberately broke away from the aristocratic or

Pindaric view of the past, where the individual hero or nobleman is all important, and where the poet and his exalted language play an essential role in assuring that the glory of the great will not fade away. The official speeches of Athens rely just as much on the mythical past for their material, but they are made in everyday prose by ordinary elected politicians, and are meant for popular consumption rather than for that sophisticated elite which, apparently, was quite capable of grasping the intricacies of a Pindaric ode.[220] Their most important break from the aristocratic and even the popular notion of the past was, however, their suppression of individualism. In official Athenian speeches neither living commanders nor dead heroes were singled out for praise. They never even alluded to the mythical Theseus but rather to the glorious deeds achieved by the Athenians in his time; theirs was a "myth without heroes."[221]

With this myth they remained content, and a similar attitude can be noticed when we look at their admiration for democracy. Once again they do not analyse it, they do not develop theories in its defense; they are simply content to maintain it as their traditional system. This emotive response to their history and constitution may, perhaps, have been one of the strengths of the Athenian system,[222] but it is, in any case, the only response that we know of. From the side of the Athenian people, we have only the romantic and mythical vision found in the panegyrics, which are full of banal but apparently effective generalities.[223]

The supporters of democracy thus took it for granted, and the tools of Ionian science were used instead by the critics of the system in their efforts to undermine it. The invention of history was one of the spectacular developments of Ionian science, and the first man to write a history of Athens, Hellanicus, came from the island of Lesbos, which was just off the coast of Ionia. He was presumably motivated by a disinterested desire for knowledge, but the Athenians who followed his lead were quite different people. Most of them were conservatives opposed to Athenian democracy, and they wrote their histories of Attica in a conscious effort to undermine the generally accepted view of their countrymen.[224] Likewise, the new science of political theory was turned against the state that granted it the freedom in which it could flourish. We find only antidemocratic theory, which is answered by democratic practice and nothing more. As Plutarch said of Pericles, the only writings the Athenian democrats have left us are their decrees.[225]

If there is any trace of a democratic theory, it is to be found in the works of Protagoras and Herodotus alone. These writers were, of course, foreigners and could not, therefore, be entangled in any sensitive political debates on the subject in Athens. Indeed, it was probably their very remoteness from any such arguments that enabled them to sketch the outlines of a democratic theory. Protagoras' argument that all normal people have an innate capacity to make good political decisions is a defense of the Athenian system against an obvious attack, one that is made by the Theban herald against the Athenian king in Euripides' *Suppliant Women* (lines 420–422). Herodotus argues that the success of Athens is a direct result of the freedom granted its citizens to pursue their own goals without interference, a freedom they have enjoyed since the introduction of Cleisthenes' constitution. The Athenians were doubtless flattered by these thinkers, and Protagoras was entrusted with the task of drawing up laws for their colony at Thurii, while Herodotus became a citizen of that colony and gave readings from his *Histories* in Athens.

The Athenian democrats, on the other hand, deliberately avoided such polemics and would not even incorporate them in their innocuous praises of Athens. They wished rather to win universal admiration for the city than to risk alienating any sector of its population by developing an image of it that would be too partisan, too radical, too specifically democratic. Their speeches presented Athens as being a democracy indeed, but a remarkably discreet one, for they neither justified the system, nor mentioned its distinguishing characteristics, nor even acknowledged when it had been introduced. Even to admit that it had been established by Cleisthenes would have revealed its radical break with the past. To boast of such a break would in itself have been quite alarming in a society where respect for the past was so important, but it might also have alienated the influential aristocrats, and their disaffection would have been an even more dangerous consequence of such a declaration.

These noblemen had good reason to wish that the constitution should not develop too greatly in the direction of democracy, and since their good will and cooperation was vital to the survival of Athens, it was essential they should not be too painfully aware that their wishes had been unfulfilled.[226] Theories justifying the features peculiar to Athenian democracy (such as the lottery system and payment for public office) were, therefore, not only unnecessary but positively dangerous.[227] Wishing to assimilate rather than defeat this important social group, the official orators presented Athenian democracy not as an interestingly innovative system, which might be justified on its own merits, but rather as a very ancient one, or more precisely as a trivial modification, no more than a change of name, on the original aristocratic constitution of Athens. This anachronistic and mythical account was the only politically correct one in Athens, and if the Athenians admired the theories of Herodotus and Protagoras, or the deliberately vague rhetoric of the funeral orations, they had even greater respect for a master in the use of mythical symbols such as Cimon, who reassuringly asserted the unbroken continuity between their own times and the age of the legendary heroes.

Theseus in Periclean Athens

Cimon had made good use of the myth of Theseus from the Battle of Marathon up till the time of his exile in 461 B.C. It has been suggested that the myth of Theseus might have experienced a period of unpopularity under the democratic leaders who came to the fore in the late 460s.[228] We find, however, as with most other aspects of political life, that the democrats preferred to maintain old institutions and convert them to their own use rather than demolish them. When Pericles became the recognized leader of Athens,[229] he continued with Cimon's strategy of promoting the myth of Theseus. Goossens claims that Pericles' special position of control over Athens actually invited more comparisons with mythological personages than was usual.[230] A possible connection with Pericles may occur in Cratinus' *Runaway Women*,[231] where the character Theseus may represent a close friend of Pericles', the seer Lampon.[232] Meinecke suggests that the whole comedy may be a skit on the very Periclean venture of founding the positivist state of Thurii, and that the *Runaway Women* are the effeminate and cowardly Sybarites, who beg Pericles to found their city anew.[233] Normally, however, the literary works celebrating the deeds of Theseus are not so transparent, and a simple equation between the hero and the fifth-century statesman cannot be made.

In works commissioned by the Athenian state, Theseus continues to be as popular as ever. Around 460 B.C. a bronze statue of Theseus lifting the rock to retrieve his father's sword was erected on the Acropolis.[234] In the 450s B.C. a bronze group of Theseus and the Minotaur joined it on the Acropolis.[235] The Royal Stoa was refurbished after the Persian sack, and the roof decoration seen by Pausanias was probably made in the 450s B.C. The artist, who obviously had a sense of humor, decided to play on the acroterion's precarious position on the roof and depicted Theseus throwing Sciron over a cliff.[236] Theseus also had his place in the most spectacular building of the age, the new Parthenon of Iktinos. The invasion of Attica by the Amazons, a fairly recent addition to the story of Theseus, appeared on the shield belonging to the statue of Athena (dedicated in 438/7 B.C.)[237] Plutarch tells us that one of the Greeks was given the features of Pericles.[238] Connor and Goossens believe that the Greek warrior resembling Pericles could only have been Theseus and that Pericles was thus given the most prominent position in the mythical battle.[239] From the middle of the century, we also have the frieze on the temple of Poseidon at Sunium. Along with other mythological scenes, the frieze showed Theseus capturing the Bull of Marathon and fighting against Skiron. It probably showed other episodes from the Cycle, but these are the only two that have survived.[240] Theseus clearly remains a major figure in the official art of Athens.

Perhaps the most famous monument portraying Theseus is the one that for long was thought to be the Theseion, but is now taken to be the Hephaisteion. It was built around 450 B.C., just after the death of Cimon and the conclusion of the Cypriot campaign had put an end to hostile operations against the Persians.[241] It has ten metopes on the east front, and four metopes on both the northern and southern sides of the temple, at the eastern extremity of each side. Furthermore, there is a large frieze going all the way across the temple (from one side to the other of the peristyle, and not just across the *pronaos*) on the east side, and a smaller one on the west side which only goes across the *opisthodomos*. Both of the friezes and the extra metopes on the temple sides depict episodes from the myth of Theseus. The ten metopes on the eastern façade show the labors of Heracles, the eight on the sides show eight deeds of Theseus. The east frieze at the front of the temple probably shows Theseus fighting against the Pallantids;[242] the west frieze shows him battling with the Amazons.[243] On each of the friezes, Theseus is portrayed in the posture of one of the tyrannicides; he appears as Aristogeiton on the east frieze, and as Harmodius on the west one.[244] The temple seems to be celebrating the victories of Athenian democracy against its enemies within and without.

Theseus remains consistently popular in Athenian vase paintings throughout the entire fifth century, and no decline can be detected when Cimon is ousted by the democrats. Taylor has argued that just after Cimon's ostracism, the representation of Theseus in vases depicting the Cycle was changed. After 460 B.C., his pose was deliberately modeled on that of the tyrannicides in the monument by Kritios and Nesiotes.[245] Athenian artists did not hesitate to regard Theseus as a democratic hero, and if they probably had a very different view of the hero and of their country, their attitude to both was no less enthusiastic than that of Cimon. Throughout the century—before, during, and after the ascendancy of Cimon—Athenian artists continued to add episodes to the myth of Theseus. The detail that he visited the bottom of the sea on his way to Crete is found on vases as early as 490 B.C.[246] On vases dating from the early Classical period, we find a new beginning to his heroic deeds.[247] The story now starts when Theseus lifts up a rock to retrieve the sword and sandals left by Aegeus for him. In 458 B.C. Aeschylus mentions the story that Attica was invaded by Amazons and that Theseus successfully organized the defense of his country.[248] This is the first time we hear of this invasion, but it appears on vase paintings soon after.[249] Again, from the heart of the democratic era, we have a new adventure starting off his series of triumphs along the Saronic Gulf. His first great deed on the road to Athens is now his victory over Periphetes, an episode we find only after 450 B.C.[250] Finally, around 430 B.C. Theseus is made a partner in Heracles' quest for the girdle of Hippolyta.[251] These innovations show that Athenian artists were actively engaged in developing the myth of Theseus, but the extraordinary number of vases with paintings of Theseus speaks even louder for his continuing popularity throughout the fifth century. The analysis by Schefold and Jung of vase paintings about the Theseus myth concentrates largely on the fifth century, and the wide range of works discussed by them is a tribute to his status as an Athenian hero throughout this century.[252] In addition to these vase paintings, we also hear of a famous portrait of Theseus, which, of course, has not survived. This was the painting by Parrhasius, which led the rival artist Euphranor to exclaim that Theseus looked as if he had fed on roses. Plutarch, however, felt that it had a refinement and elegance that suited the character of Theseus and of the Athenians as a people.[253] The Theseus of Parrhasius obviously had a lot in common with the graceful Athenians of Euripides' patriotic ode,[254] and he represented the culture of Athens just as Euphranor's Theseus recalled the city-state's strength and power.[255]

Although we have considered the plastic and graphic arts very briefly, it is still quite clear that as far as artistic representations of Theseus are concerned, the second half of the fifth century is no less important than the first. The great age for Theseus is the entire period that stretches from 510 to 410 B.C.[256] For our purposes, however, more important than these sculptures and paintings are the works of literature that survive from the fifth century. For the first time, we are dealing with entire works dedicated to episodes from the myth of Theseus. They explore the implications of the myth in a very fundamental way that reveals how the Athenians looked upon Theseus and how they viewed themselves. It is to these works that we shall now turn.

Notes

1. Hereas is quoted by Plutarch in his *Life of Theseus* at 20, 1–2. The evidence of Hereas is discussed by Connor 1970, 145, and by Herter 1939, 264.

2. Herter 1939, 264. Stanford makes a similar point: "But Megarians were prone to anti-Athenian feelings, so one would prefer less suspicious authority" (Stanford 1959, note to *Odyssey* 11: 631). In his work on interpolation in Homer, Bolling reaches this conclusion from the manuscript evidence: "There is no direct evidence for the existence of texts without this line" (Bolling 1925, 242–243). Bolling, however, is not absolutely sure that Hereas is wrong.

3. Connor 1970, 145.

4. Apollodorus, *Epitome* 1: 16. I owe this reference to Boardman 1982, 11.

5. Podlecki, on the other hand, thinks that this poem comes much later in Simonides' career, and was sponsored by Themistocles, perhaps for the festival of the Oschophoria. Podlecki argues that this festival had been established by Themistocles in the 470s (Podlecki 1975, 18).

6. Connor 1970, 145.

7. As we have seen, the myth is mentioned in both the Homeric epics, in five Hesiodic works, and in the works of three lyric poets, Alcman, Sappho, and Stesichorus, who date from before the time of Peisistratus.

8. Simonides 1 *EG*.

9. Connor 1970, 145.

10. "In any case, we should not hesitate to push back the poem deep into the sixth century, and so we shall rather associate it with the time of the tyranny . . ." (Herter 1939, 284; he maintains this view in Herter 1973, 1,046–1,047).

11. We know this from the Scholium to Pindar, *Olympian* 10, 83. See *IEG*, vol. 2, 61–62.

12. The Scholiast to Aristophanes, *Birds* 96 gives us this information, when he tries to convince us that Aristophanes meant no harm when he mocked Socrates, just as Diphilos was no enemy of Boidas, though his mockery did in fact ruin the philosopher.

13. West argues that the iambic lines quoted by the Scholiast to Pindar, *Olympian* 10, 83 come from the *Theseïd* of Diphilos, rather than from some other poem of his. Since iambic verse was a satirical medium, West concludes that this *Theseïd* was a funny poem (*IEG*, vol. 2, 61).

14. Aristotle, *Poetics*, 1451a20 = T 1 *EGF*.

15. We can set this limit because Diogenes Laertes (at 2: 59) tells us that the poet's brother, Xenophon, wrote a biography of Epaminondas and Pelopidas. The manuscripts of Diogenes Laertes disagree about the poet's name. See *Theseis* T 1 *EGF*.

16. Plutarch, *Life of Theseus* 28 = *Theseis* F 1 *EGF*.

17. In this romantic work, Antiope invades Attica because Theseus has deserted her for Phaedra; but Heracles comes to the rescue and kills her. Plutarch himself thought it too fanciful. Boardman discusses it briefly in his article on Amazons (Boardman 1982, 11)

18. Scholium to Pindar, *Olympian Ode* 3. 50 B = F 1 *EGF*. This poet is probably Diphilus, since the Scholium to *Olympian Ode* 10. 83 uses the same words to refer to him: ὁ τὴν Θησηίδα γράψας, "the man who wrote the Theseïd."

19. Huxley 1969, 116–118.

20. "It was certainly not through a Theseis that has disappeared without a trace that Theseus became an Athenian *allos Herakles*." (von Wilamowitz-Möllendorff 1937, vol. 5, pt. 2, 58–59).

21. Herter 1939, 283–284.

22. Brommer 1982, 73; Neils 1987, 36 and 143. The Cycle first appears in literature in Bacchylides' *Theseus* (Poem 18), which was written well into the fifth century.

23. Herter 1973, 1,046. On this point, Herter is followed by Barrett (Barrett 1964, 3). Barrett, however, is a little uncomfortable with this chronological gap, and he postulates the existence of some other works between the *Theseïd* and the vases depicting the Cycle (Barrett 1964, 3, note 1). Barrett's hypothesis implicitly acknowledges that a mid-sixth-century *Theseïd* would have been too early to influence these vases, and this acknowledgment is a strong argument against the validity of Herter's view.

24. Dugas and Flacelière and Snodgrass emphasize the independence and the popular, "vernacular" nature of the tradition of vase painting (Dugas and Flacelière 1958, 58; Snodgrass 1980, 72 and 191–194).

25. Neils 1987, 32–37 and 143.

26. Neils 1987, 144.

27. I have borrowed this expression from Herter (Herter 1939, 284).

28. Herodotus, 1: 60, 3–5. Connor suggests that Peisistratus was merely Athena's "brave but subordinate charioteer" (Connor 1987, 46). Herodotus, however, reports the proclamation made by the heralds of Peisistratus at this time, and it states that Athena was bringing him home from exile. This suggests that Athena was the charioteer, not Peisistratus. She plays the same role for Diomedes at *Iliad* 5: 840–841.

29. Nilsson 1953, 748; Connor 1970, 145 and 150; Kirk 1974, 152. In fact, the new popularity of Theseus in vase painting occurs around 510 B.C., precisely when the Peisistratids have been expelled.

30. "Some he [an imaginary visitor in Pisistratid Athens] might dismiss as pure coincidence" (Connor 1970, 146).

31. *FGrH* 328 (Philochorus) fr.18; Pausanias 1: 17, 6; Plutarch, *Life of Theseus*, 36, 3; *Life of Cimon*, 8, 5–6.

32. Connor 1970, 147; Herter 1936, 187.

33. Thompson and Wycherley 1972, 147. Some scholars suspect it may be another mythical battle such as the one between Erechtheus and Eumolpus (Brommer 1982, 138–139; Schefold and Jung 1988, 246).

34. Brommer 1982, 137–139.

35. Nilsson 1951, 53.

36. Figueira 1984, 464–465. If we accept that the east frieze of the Hephaisteion shows Theseus fighting the Pallantids, this might provide further support for Figueira's view, since Theseus is portrayed in the pose of the tyrannicide Aristogeiton (Taylor 1981, 153).

37. Connor 1970, 146–147. For a completely different interpretation of this same episode, see Sourvinou-Inwood 1979, 50–53.

38. Brommer 1982, 28.

39. Herter 1936, 190–191, 196, and 200; Nilsson 1932, 170.

40. Kirk 1974, 155.

41. As we saw in Chapter 1, some scholars doubt the authenticity of *Iliad* 1: 265.

42. Connor 1970, 149–150.

43. Herodotus 1: 59, 4, and Aristotle, *Constitution of the Athenians*, 14, 1.

44. Brommer 1982, 73; Neils 1987, 36–37.
45. Neils 1987, 144.
46. Brommer 1982, 68.
47. Herter 1939, 268–270 and 281.
48. Connor 1970, 149–150; Nilsson 1951, 56, and 1953, 747.
49. Neils 1987, 34–35; Schefold 1992, 176.

50. The original Cycle begins with Sinis at the Isthmus, which was suppos-edly marked by Theseus as the border between "Ionia" and the Peloponnese (Plutarch, *Life of Theseus*, 25). See Calame 1990, 224.

51. Calame 1990, 422.
52. Herter 1936, 185, and note 5 on 185; Connor 1970, 146.
53. Davison 1958, 26; Andrewes 1974, 106 and 114.

54. Simon is the most recent scholar to argue fully for the view that the dance shown on the vase must be the Delian Crane Dance rather than a dance on Crete. She says that there is no tradition of a dance by Theseus and the young Athenians on Crete (Simon 1976, 72), but this is not quite accurate (Scholiast to *Iliad* 18: 590; discussed by Friis Johansen 1945, 47–48). She also remarks that the vase has other connections with Delos. One of the Athenian girls is called Asteria, which was a poetic name for Delos, and Artemis is depicted as Mistress of Animals on a handle of the vase, which was the form under which she was worshipped on Delos. These are interesting connections, but not completely convincing (Simon 1976, 73).

55. Plutarch, *Life of Theseus*, 23. The Athenians replaced each part of the ship, bit by bit, as it wore out, so it was in a sense still the same ship! This was the sacred ship whose voyage delayed Socrates' execution (Plato, *Phaedo*, 58a–b).

56. Friis Johansen devoted an entire monograph to demonstrating this (Friis Johansen 1945, *passim*). His strongest arguments are the presence of Ariadne and her nurse; the fact that they are facing Theseus and the young Athenians, and clearly welcoming them to Crete; and the existence of an iconographic tradition that as-sociates the killing of the Minotaur with a dance (Friis Johansen 1945, 4, 9, and 43–46). A host of scholars agree with his view, which has become almost the stan-dard one in the last decade (Dugas 1943, 11–12; Nilsson 1951, 59, and 1953, 746; Dugas and Flacelière 1958, 59–60; Brommer 1982, 84; Shapiro 1989, 146–147; Calame 1990, 119–120). It is only fair to note, however, that some impressive scholars support the view that Cleitias is depicting a Crane Dance on Delos: Schefold 1966, 62; Simon 1976, 72–73; and most recently Neils 1987, 26–27. The main difficulty for the first view is that the ship seems to have just landed on Crete, so a victory dance by the young Athenians and the elation of the ship's crew would be somewhat premature. Shapiro escapes this objection by arguing that the Athenians are not performing a dance (Shapiro 1989, 147).

57. Plutarch says that the steps of the "Crane Dance" of Delos copied the intricate layout of the labyrinth, and that it was therefore inspired by the victory dance of Theseus, which must have been performed on Delos (Plutarch, *Life of Theseus* 21). As Friis Johansen points out, the very name of the dance shows that the Delians did not associate it with the labyrinth or with Theseus (Friis Johansen 1945, 12; see also *RE* vol. 4, col. 2475). The story connecting them, if Plutarch

has recorded it correctly, clearly arises from a relatively late attempt to provide Athenian origins for Delian customs. It reflects the position of Delos as the center of the Athenian empire and must date from the fifth century at the earliest. It is possible, however, that Plutarch (or his source), confused the Delian Crane Dance with a Cretan dance called the Labyrinth (Lucian, *On Dancing*, 49).

58. Sealey 1976, 93. See *FGrH* 328 (Philochorus) F 75.

59. Athenaeus 6: 234 e–f.

60. *RE* , vol. 4, col. 2475; *RE* , vol. 5: 2, cols. 58–59; Herter 1939, 260–261.

61. MacKendrick 1981, 179.

62. Lygdamis of Naxos had helped him to return to power in 546 B.C., and the Naxians had controlled Delos from at least the seventh century.

63. Schefold argues that Peisistratus built a Panhellenic temple on Delos. The Alcmaeonids, in rebuilding the Temple of Apollo at Delphi with Parian marble, would, therefore, have been rivaling this Temple of Peisistratus and the later rebuilding of the temple of Athena Polias in marble by his sons, Hippias and Hipparchus, around 525 B.C. (Schefold 1946, 62–63). MacKendrick also believes that Peisistratus promoted Apollo of Delos out of rivalry with the Alcmaeonids who enjoyed the favor of Delphi and its cult of Apollo (MacKendrick 1981, 179).

64. Connor 1970, 147, and note to illustration 153, 146; Plutarch, *Life of Theseus*, 25.

65. Rhodes 1981, 169, note to *Constitution of the Athenians* 10, ii; Kroll and Waggoner 1984, 327–328.

66. Kroll and Waggoner 1984, 332. MacKendrick follows the older view of Seltman, who believed that the *Wappenmünzen* were issued by aristocratic families, each having its own device. These issues were discontinued by Peisistratus and replaced by the famous Owl series (Seltman 1976, 48–50, 80–81, and 86; MacKendrick 1981, 211–212). It seems more likely that the devices on the *Wappenmünzen* served to distinguish among the annual administrations under which the coins were issued (Kroll and Waggoner 1984, 331).

67. Even Aristotle believed that Athens had a coinage system before Solon's time, since he states that Solon devalued the drachma (*Constitution of the Athenians* 10). See Kroll and Waggoner 1984, 326 and 333. One might argue that the story about Theseus and the ox-coins was invented in the time of Peisistratus, but there is no evidence for this story during the sixth century, and it would not, of course, have been necessary to invent it at a time when the real person who introduced coinage would have been so well known.

68. Others attributed the introduction of coinage to Erichthonios or Lykos (Kroll and Waggoner 1984, 333).

69. Perhaps this is why it has not been brought up by the scholars who wish to say that it was the Peisistratids who brought about the new importance of Theseus.

70. Brommer 1982, 112; Neils 1987, 32–33; Schefold and Jung 1988, 232; Shapiro 1989, 148–149. Boardman believes that they start slightly later, around 510 B.C. (Boardman 1982, 8).

71. Boardman 1978b, 156 and illustrations 205.1–2; Schefold 1992, 173–174.

72. von Bothmer 1957, 126–127.

73. Tyrrell 1984, 8; Neils 1987, 45, note 209.

74. Herter 1939, 309, 284, and 290.

75. Herter 1939, 284 and 290.

76. Herodotus 5: 65. See Nilsson 1953, 748.

77. Connor 1970, 146.

78. Jacoby does precisely this: "Theseus, the achiever of synoecism, is not Peisistratus, but Cleisthenes" (Jacoby 1949, 195, note 23).

79. Shapiro 1989, 144–146.

80. This is the cup thrown by the potters Archikles and Glaukytes (Neils 1987, 24). Shapiro, however, dates this cup to 540 B.C. (Shapiro 1989, 144).

81. Brommer 1982, 130.

82. Brommer 1982, 28.

83. Neils 1987, 25.

84. Neils 1987, 28; Shapiro 1989, 147–148; Schefold 1992, 176. Boardman sees Exekias as a democratic opponent of Peisistratus, who used Theseus as a symbol of his political opposition (Boardman 1978a, 15, 24).

85. Neils 1987, 34–35.

86. Bérard has also come out on the side of Schefold, but he does not argue for this view, which is tangential to his own interests (Bérard 1983, 49). Kearns, while rightly denouncing one-to-one equations, feels that the synoecism is too significant to be lightly brushed aside, and she suggests that the strong opposition to Cleisthenes' democratic "synoecism" of Attica may have obliged him to search for a mythical supporter in Theseus (Kearns 1989, 117–119).

87. Jacoby 1947a, 6, note 6; Jacoby 1949, 195, note 23; Schefold 1946, 67; Sourvinou-Inwood 1979, 27. Schefold, in the work he recently coauthored with Jung, has suggested that the *Theseïd* might even date to the time of Solon (Schefold and Jung 1988, 231), but he still believes in the important role of Cleisthenes in the promotion of Theseus as an Athenian hero, for he dates the establishment of the Theseion to 500 B.C. (Schefold and Jung 1988, 231 and 296). He does not provide any evidence for these new views.

88. Vidal-Naquet 1981, 402.

89. "In no way does Theseus play a role just in the political propaganda of certain Athenian clans, such as the Philaïds, but since Peisistratus he stands as a mythical role-model for all Athenian politicians" (Kron 1976, 224). See Kearns 1989, 119 and Calame 1990, 416–417.

90. "Theseus . . . stood for the entire Athenian state and cannot just be assigned to a portion of it" (Kron 1976, 224).

91. Herter 1939, 284, 290, and 309.

92. Herter speaks of the "sacrifice" that Theseus, "the ideal of monarchy," had to make in becoming a democratic hero (Herter 1939, 309).

93. Pausanias 1: 3, 3.

94. Herter 1939, 310.

95. Vernant 1962, 59. The heroic ideal is expressed by Glacus (*Iliad* 6: 208).

96. "The all-powerful king can no longer be conceived of as a living person; but in exchange, his title can be borne by a dead man" (Bérard 1982, 98).

97. Bérard 1982, 97 and 102.

98. de Polignac 1984, 149.

99. Bérard actually declares that there is a systematic opposition between them (Bérard 1983, 45).

100. Aristotle tells us that "the salvation of a tyranny is to make it more like the rule of a king" (Aristotle, *Politics*, Book 5, 1314a34–35). He may have been thinking specifically about Peisistratus, as Andrewes suggests (Andrewes 1974, 108–109).

101. The Peisistratids did indeed allow well-behaved noblemen to hold the eponymous archonship, but this they obtained as a favor and not as an office that they had a right to apply for. If, like Cleisthenes, who had been archon in 525/4 B.C., they stopped behaving well, they would find themselves obliged to leave the country.

102. Boardman argues that Peisistratus' return to power was supposed to recall Heracles' entry to Olympus (Boardman 1972 and 1975).

103. Tyrants "awkwardly try to set up a direct continuity by occupying the fortified seat of the ancient kings, thus short-circuiting the heroic function" (Bérard 1983, 52).

104. Aristotle, *Constitution of the Athenians*, 15, 4.

105. Or the Anakeion, if we are to follow the version that Polyaenus gives of the story (Polyaenus 1: 21, 2). For our present purposes it does not matter much to whom the hero shrine belongs.

106. Price analyzes this passage and gives instances of other agorai with hero tombs (Price 1973, 137–140).

107. Bérard 1983, 48.

108. Paradoxically, the great Dorian hero was 60 percent more popular in Athens under the Peisistratids than he was in the Peloponnese! (Boardman 1989, 158).

109. The figures for the rest of Greece are as follows: Peloponnesian shield-bands, 25.5 percent; Corinthian pottery, 27 percent; Spartan pottery, 27.5 percent; "Chalcidian" pottery, 23 percent (Boardman 1975, 1).

110. Boardman 1975, 2. See also Boardman 1989, 158.

111. Boardman 1972, 59.

112. Boardman ended an oral presentation of this thesis with the words, "If you believe that, you'll believe anything"! (Moore 1986, 38, note 7).

113. This would be dramatically apparent if it was built in the years 510–500 B.C., but it will still be true even if we date it to within a few years after 490 B.C.

114. Herter 1939, 284 and 1973, 1046; Barrett 1964, 3 and note 1 to that page.

115. Moore has already made this point in a different context: "Political symbolism in art tends to lose its edge and meaning rather quickly and one should be particularly cautious about seeing political allusions well after the relevant event" (Moore 1986, 38, note 25).

116. Herter 1939, 290; Connor 1970, 150.

117. Connor 1970, 150. Kearns remarks on the connections that associate Theseus with several of the eponymous heroes (Kearns 1989, 87).

118. Herter 1939, 290; Kron 1976, 224.

119. Plutarch, *Life of Solon*, 10.

120. Bury and Meiggs 1975, 127 and 526, note 2.

121. Sealey agrees with this dating and concludes that this Spartan decision was part of the settlement of 510 B.C. (Sealey 1976, 147).

122. As we shall see presently, the dating of this Treasury is uncertain. It was built either during the decade 510–500 B.C., or else just after the Battle of Marathon in 490 B.C.

123. Nilsson 1932, 164, and 1951, 53–55; Herter 1939, 281 and 303; Schefold 1946, 66–67; Kirk 1974, 109; Boardman 1975, 2; Neils 1987, 144–146.

124. Plutarch, *Life of Theseus*, 6–7.

125. They were heroes both in the modern sense of the word and in the ancient, because the Athenians offered sacrifices to them (Kearns 1989, 55 and 150).

126. Plutarch, *Life of Theseus*, 29, 3.

127. Pausanias (10: 11, 5) says that it was financed from the spoils of Marathon, so that it would have been built just after 490 B.C., and the French archaeologists who excavated the site accepted his testimony. Others, arguing from the style of the sculpture, believe that the building is earlier and that the trophy monument on which Pausanias read this inscription, though physically near the Treasury, could easily have been erected at a later date (Brommer 1982, 68, note 8). Neils points out that the sculpture is carved in a wide range of styles, which cover the entire period between 510 and 490 B.C., though she agrees that Pausanias' inscription does not refer to the Treasury (Neils 1987, 46–47). Schefold and Jung come up with a compromise by suggesting that the treasury was built at the earlier date but was turned into a Marathon monument in 490 B.C. (Schefold and Jung 1988, 274).

128. Boardman 1978b, 159–160 and illustrations 213 and 213.1–9; Brommer 1982, 68–69; Neils 1987, 47–51; Schefold 1992, 179–181. It should be noted that there is some dispute about the exact arrangement of these metopes, but the arrangement suggested by the original excavator (Coste-Messelière) is followed by Boardman, Brommer, Neils, and Schefold, and that is the one I have given here. See Hoffelner 1988 for a recent discussion and a different arrangement.

129. These metopes may have represented a battle waged against the Amazons by Theseus and Heracles, as Boardman suggests (Boardman 1982, 12–13). Schefold suggests that the corner metopes on the northern and southern sides are to be taken together with the metopes on the eastern side, and that all eight form a continuous battle scene representing this joint campaign of Theseus and Heracles (Schefold 1992, 118). There are, however, several difficulties with this view. First, the western metopes show Heracles fighting alone against Geryon, so it seems likely that the eastern metopes should show some achievement of Theseus rather than a joint expedition with Heracles (see Brommer 1982, 117). Second, there is no evidence for a joint expedition by Theseus and Heracles before 440 B.C. when they appear fighting together against the Amazons on the throne of Zeus in his

temple at Olympia (Pausanias 7: 11, 4). Third, Pherecydes, who wrote between 508/7 and 490 B.C., states that Theseus went on a "private expedition" to the land of the Amazons, after the campaign of Heracles (*FGrH* 3 Pherekydes von Athen fr. 150), so the argument against a joint expedition is not based on silence alone. Finally, if we agree with Boardman that the battle against the Amazons on the Treasury was inspired by Athenian involvement in the Ionian revolt (Boardman 1982, 13), we must remember that Sparta, the leading state of the Dorians, gave no assistance to the Ionian rebels. This would make it all the more appropriate to represent Theseus fighting alone without the assistance of the Dorian hero, Heracles, just as Athens and Eretria had to face the wrath of the Persians alone without the assistance of Sparta, both during the rebellion of 499 B.C. and during the Persian reprisals of 490 B.C.

130. On Attic vase paintings, Athena acts as Heracles' sponsor when he enters Olympus, they fight together against the Giants, and she helps him with his Labors (Boardman 1984, 243).

131. Boardman has examined a remarkable series of vases where she is practically alone with Heracles as he reclines on a couch or plays the lyre (Boardman 1984, 244–245).

132. Boardman 1975, 2–3. This also explains why Heracles could remain popular even after the fall of the tyrants who may have promoted his myth (Heracles' friendship with Athena once again gets him out of a tight corner), and why Theseus never quite supplanted his position as a close friend of the goddess (Boardman 1984, 246).

133. Brommer 1982, 69.

134. Boardman 1982, 5.

135. The phrase, "the first Athenian prose-writer," is Jacoby's, who dated Pherecydes' work to the period between 508/7 and 476/5 B.C. (Jacoby 1947b, 33). His conclusions on the date of Pherecydes have been supported by the further investigations of Huxley (Huxley 1973).

136. The fragments concerning Theseus are *FGrH* 3 (Pherekydes von Athen) fr. 147 to 153.

137. She was also the mother (by Poseidon) of the illegitimate Hippothoon, who was one of Cleisthenes' tribal heroes.

138. *FGrH* 3 (Pherekydes von Athen) fr. 150.

139. As we shall see presently, the abduction of Antiope disappears from Athenian art after this date.

140. *FGrH* 3 (Pherekydes von Athen) fr. 148, 152, and 153.

141. *FGrH* 3 (Pherekydes von Athen) fr. 150.

142. *FGrH* 3 (Pherekydes von Athen) fr. 149.

143. Yet another monument to the hero might be the marble statue of an unidentifed young man on the Acropolis, which dates from about 510 B.C. Neils follows Schrader in taking it to be Theseus fighting against Procrustes (Neils 1987, 45–46), but Brommer has shown that this is unlikely (Brommer 1982, 25).

144. Loraux rightly warns us that we must not transfer the violent hostility of the Pentencontaetia back to the period around 500 B.C., as Herodotus does

(Loraux 1986, 75). The two states do, nevertheless, start to go their separate ways at this time.

145. Herodotus 5: 92.

146. Lévêque and Vidal-Naquet 1964, 48–49.

147. Ibid., 23.

148. "It is a city where religion is profoundly politicized" (Lévêque and Vidal-Naquet 1964, 146).

149. Herodotus 5: 63, 1.

150. Lévêque and Vidal-Naquet 1964, 71.

151. Bérard 1983, 51–52.

152. Kearns 1989, 133. Meanwhile, however, Theseus is beginning to take over the role of Erechtheus as patron of Athens, though we do not have to attribute this development to Cleisthenes.

153. Herodotus 5: 66. 2.

154. Plutarch, *Life of Theseus*, 35.

155. Pausanias 1: 15. Plutarch also records this story (*Life of Theseus*, 35). Sourvinou-Inwood suggests that Theseus' dispute with his stepmother and the related fight with the Marathonian Bull may have been reinterpreted to suit the new events. The stepmother, she argues, was now identified with Medea (Sourvinou-Inwood 1979, 53), and Medea herself was thought of as the founder of the Persian nation, the Medes (Sourvinou-Inwood 1979, 49–50). Theseus' battle with the bull and the expulsion of Medea at sword point became the mythic prototypes of the Battle of Marathon (Sourvinou-Inwood 1979, 50–53). She attributes a major role in bringing about this change in the meaning of the myth to Sophocles' *Aegeus*, which probably came out in the 460s (Sourvinou-Inwood 1979, 56).

156. Pausanias 1: 27, 10. See Brommer 1982, 33–34; Shapiro 1988, 381–382. Shapiro believes it may have replaced an earlier statue erected around 500 B.C. (1988, 378–381).

157. Simon 1976, 106–107 and plates 132 and 133; Boardman 1982, 15–16; Schefold and Jung 1988, 272, 296.

158. Shapiro 1989, 149. Schefold and Jung suggest that the abduction of Antiope was replaced by the Amazonian invasion in 490 B.C. (Schefold and Jung 1988, 232). This new theme appears for the first time in Aeschylus' *Eumenides* (at 685–690) and later still on vase painting (Brommer 1982, 119–120), so it might reflect the sack of Athens by the Persians in 480 B.C. or even a combination of both Persian wars (Boardman 1982, 13–15).

159. Herodotus 8: 41, 1.

160. Brommer 1982, 1. The only other episode clearly located on the Peloponnesian side of the Isthmus, his defeat of Periphetes, does not appear until after 450 B.C. (Brommer 1982, 5).

161. Calame 1990, 423. See Brommer 1982, 2, note 3.

162. For the Themistocles Decree, see inscription 23, lines 8–9, and notes on these lines, in Meiggs and Lewis 1969, 48–49. Some scholars suspect that the decree is not genuine, but if it is a later forgery it is quite a good one. For our purposes, the important issue is that the connection between Theseus and Trozen

assumed by the decree is an accurate reflection of the thoughts of the Athenians around the time of the evacuation. Its accuracy is borne out by the appearance in the decades following 480 B.C. of the story about Theseus finding his father's sword.

163. Plutarch, *Life of Theseus*, 36.

164. Frazer believes that Cimon's expedition to Skyros took place during the archonship of Demotion in 470/469 B.C. (Frazer 1898, commentary on 1: 17). His reason for making this claim is that Diodoros says so (at 11: 60); but if we were to follow Diodoros all that closely, we would believe that the archonship of Demotion was a very eventful one indeed, because Diodoros lists all of Cimon's activities from his taking over of Byzantion in 476 B.C. to his campaign around Karia in 468 B.C. as happening during this archonship. Since Diodoros gives these events in the generally accepted historical order, it seems unlikely that he has made a major blunder here; he has probably just decided to group these events together since Cimon was behind them all, and chosen the archonship of Demotion as a suitable date around which they could be grouped. Podlecki suggests that the oracle may have been given in 476/5 B.C., but that the campaign may have taken place later (Podlecki 1971, 141).

165. Connor suggests that Cimon may have discovered a Bronze Age tholos tomb (Connor 1970, 158).

166. Plutarch, *Life of Theseus*, 36.

167. Plutarch, *Life of Cimon*, 8.

168. Herter 1939, 291.

169. Podlecki 1971, 143.

170. The festival is associated with Salamis, site of Themistocles' great victory (Podlecki 1975, 18–19). The king who killed Theseus, Lycomedes, bears the same name as the man who sent Themistocles into exile (Podlecki 1975, 21–22; cf. Connor 1972, 161–162).

171. Podlecki 1975, 10–13. He does, however, believe in "the development of Theseus from a culture-hero to a political one" during this period at the end of the sixth century.

172. Podlecki suggests that this tragedy was the *Phoenician Women* of Phrynichus (Podlecki 1975, 8).

173. Sourvinou-Inwood 1979, 57.

174. As we saw in chapter 1, the Spartans went to a considerable amount of trouble during the Messenian wars to recover the bones of Orestes. As with Cimon, they had only a mysterious oracle to go on, and in the end, again like Cimon, they only found the body of Orestes by chance. The story is told at Herodotus 1: 67–68.

175. As we saw in chapter 1, neither the ancient Greeks nor modern scholars can agree among themselves on this issue. Among those who believe that Cimon's hero shrine was the first Theseion in Athens we have: Pausanias 1: 17, 6; Diodorus 4: 62, 4; Jacoby, *FGrH*, commentary on 327 (Demon) fr. 6, 208; Barron 1972, 21; Connor 1970, 159; Rhodes 1981, 211 commentary on 15, iv; Bérard 1983, 47. Among those who believe that there was already a Theseion and that Cimon built his new tomb in this older sanctuary, we have: Euripides, *Madness of*

Heracles, 1328–1333; Aristotle, *Constitution of the Athenians* 15, 4; Plutarch, *Life of Theseus*, 23: 5; Jacoby, *FGrH*, commentary on 328 (Philochorus) fr. 18, 309; Thompson and Wycherley 1972, 124.

176. Deubner 1932, 224; Herter 1939, 293; Calame 1990, 154. Jacoby believes that all four sanctuaries honoring Theseus were in the hands of state priests from the very beginning (Jacoby, *FGrH*, commentary on 328 (Philochorus) fr. 18, 309).

177. Plutarch, *Life of Theseus*, 36.

178. Our first evidence for this tax is from 342 B.C. See Ampolo and Manfredini 1988, 235 commentary on chapter 23, line 26.

179. Deubner 1932, 224.

180. Gellius, 15: 20, 3.

181. Deubner 1932, 225–226.

182. Barron 1972, 22.

183. Herodotus 1: 60, 3–5.

184. Pausanias 1: 17, 2–3.

185. By examining the style of vase paintings which he believes are based on the works in the Theseion, Barron concludes that the other paintings were by Polygnotus, and that there was also a fourth work by Polygnotus (depicting Theseus rising from the Underworld) on a fourth wall not mentioned by Pausanias (Barron 1972, 43–44).

186. Herter 1939, 295–296.

187. Thucydides 1: 4.

188. Plutarch, *Life of Cimon*, 7–8.

189. Jacoby shows that the three epigrams form a single poem, and that their order in Aeschines (*Against Ctesiphon*, 183–185) and Plutarch should be rearranged (Jacoby 1945, 198–200). Page follows his rearrangement (Simonides XL, *EG*).

190. Jacoby 1945, 201–202.

191. Vidal-Naquet suggests that Ajax, hero of the Aiantis tribe and associated with Salamis and the naval victory of the Themistocles, was deliberately excluded and replaced by Theseus, associated with Marathon and the hoplite victory of the Miltiades. The erection of the Marathon Base would be yet another stage in the dispute between the conservative, hoplite tradition of Marathon represented by Cimon and the democratic, naval tradition of Salamis represented by Themistocles (Vidal-Naquet 1981, 404). Kearns mentions a theory of Griffiths that Theseus, Codrus, and the mysterious third hero might originally have been among the ten eponymns of Cleisthenes and have been replaced later by Ajax, Hippothoon, and Oineus (Kearns 1989, 81 note 8).

192. Philaios is an emendation of the manuscript reading, Phileus.

193. Pausanias says that it was paid for with booty from the Battle of Marathon, which would mean that it was erected in the 480s. He also says, however, that the work was executed by Pheidias, which would date it to the middle of the fifth century (Pausanias 10: 10). Kron argues that we should accept the later dating because a memorial had already been erected at Delphi after the battle in front

of the Treasury of the Athenians, because Miltiades was in disgrace during the 480s and would not have appeared on a public monument, and because the Polemarch Callimachus rather than a mere Strategos of one of the tribal contingents would more properly have been honored in the 480s (Kron 1976, 216–218). Miltiades was not popularly recognized as the hero of Marathon until much later, so the monument must date from a time when his son was influential enough to have changed the popular verdict on Miltiades. Cimon certainly had such authority during the 470s and 460s, but if we accept that the memorial was the work of Pheidias, then it can only date from the 450s when Cimon returned from exile (Kron 1976, 218). This date is also accepted by Connor (Connor 1972, 163).

194. "We have no earlier example for such an exceptional honoring of a man, who is united with gods and heroes in one group" (Kron 1976, 226).

195. Speaking of the honors paid to Conon after he had destroyed the naval hegemony of the Spartans by defeating them in the Battle of Cnidos in 394 B.C., Demosthenes says the following: "Therefore not only did the people of that time grant him freedom from taxation, but also he was the first man of whom they set up a bronze statue, as they had done for Harmodius and Aristogeiton; for they thought that he too had put an end to no inconsiderable tyranny, by destroying the rule of the Spartans" (Demosthenes 20, *Against Leptines*, 70).

196. Originally it was named the Stoa Peisianakteios (Plutarch, *Life of Cimon*, 4). It is not certain whether he simply proposed the construction or actually funded it (Thompson and Wycherley 1972, 24 and 90; Boardman 1982, 17). Loraux believes he may have funded it, which would be typical of the old-fashioned values of his family. "The aristocratic commemoration of acts of private generosity disappeared in the mid-fifth century" (Loraux 1986, 372 note 281).

197. Pausanias 1: 15.

198. Herter 1939, 296.

199. Connor 1970, 162–163. The Marathon painting naturally showed Miltiades, but the ancient sources (Pausanias 1: 15 and Aelian, *Characteristics of Animals*, 7: 38) mention him as just one soldier among many others and do not suggest that he was given any special prominence, as Connor claims (Connor 1970, 162). Polygnotus, who painted the fall of Troy, used Cimon's sister Elpinice as a model for Laodice, the Trojan woman who had an affair with Theseus' son Acamas. This was not to flatter Cimon, as Connor believes (Connor 1970, 162), since Plutarch, our source for this story, goes on to tell us that it originated from a rumor that Elpinice was Polygnotus' mistress (Plutarch, *Life of Cimon*, 4). I doubt we should take any of this gossip seriously.

200. This interesting point is brought up by Kron (Kron 1976, 218–219).

201. Plutarch recounts that Pericles once boasted that his victory over Samos was a greater achievement than the sack of Troy, but Cimon's sister, Elpinice, replied that he should be fighting against the Persians or the Phoenicians, like her brother, and not against his own allies (Plutarch, *Life of Pericles*, 28, 7).

202. Once again, I owe this insight to Kron (Kron 1976, 226).

203. "The Spartan dedicatory offering for Aigospotamoi was designed in a similar way and evidently in competition with the Marathon monument . . ." (Kron 1976, 226).

204. Quoted by Plutarch in the *Life of Cimon*, 4.

205. Ibid., 14.

206. Ibid., 16.

207. Ibid., 16. The references to the πάτρια νόμιμα and to the "aristocracy of Cleisthenes" are probably anachronistic, since they reflect fictions of political thought developed at the end of the fifth century and throughout the fourth century, but the general attitude sounds plausible enough.

208. Plutarch, *Life of Cimon*, 10.

209. Ibid., 10.

210. Gernet 1982b, 227.

211. Vernant 1974, 71–73.

212. One of the distinguishing characteristics of the happy man, according to the aristocratic Solon (13. 2)—in addition to heirs, horses, and a hunting pack!

213. Burkert 1985, 204.

214. This ambiguity lies within the Greek language itself, for an ἀρχηγέτης can be either of these.

215. "The hero cult, in fact, is not an ancestor cult at all; its concern is with effective presence, not with the chain of blood across generations . . ." (Burkert 1985, 204).

216. Bowra 1964, 66.

217. Whitley 1988, 178.

218. Finley 1986, 48.

219. Loraux 1986, 3–4 and 133–134.

220. Ibid., 50–54.

221. Ibid., 65. Perhaps Xenophon is not as far from the spirit of the funeral oration as Loraux thinks (Loraux 1986, 373 note 294) when he speaks of those events as "wars of the Theseus period" (*Memorabilia* 3: 5, 10), because this is not quite the same as calling them wars fought by or under Theseus.

222. Finley 1973, 27–30.

223. Jones 1986, 42–43.

224. Jacoby 1949, 78–79; Loraux 1986, 3–4.

225. Plutarch, *Life of Pericles*, 8; see Loraux's discussion of theoretical and instrumental writing in Athens (Loraux 1986, 178–179).

226. Loraux 1986, 217–218.

227. Its opponents were, of course, quick to point out these features and condemn them. See the Old Oligarch 1, 2 and Isocrates 7 (*Areopagiticus*) 23–24.

228. Loraux 1986, 66.

229. "In theory it was democracy, but in practice it was the rule of one man" (Thucydides, 2: 65, 9).

230. "The exceptional position of Pericles exposed him more than anyone else to the game of mythological disguises for which the vogue starts in the 5th century" (Goossens 1962, 436).

231. Δραπετίδες.

232. "THESEUS the synoecist . . . perhaps came in as LAMPON" (Edmonds 1957, vol.1, 38). In fr. 49 he boasts that he killed Kerkyon.

233. Meinecke 1839, vol. 2, 43.

234. Pausanias 1: 27, 8. See Brommer 1982, 2; Schefold and Jung 1988, 235.

235. Pausanias 1: 24, 1. See Brommer 1982, 49–53; Schefold and Jung 1988, 254. Schefold and Jung give a possible reconstruction on page 256 (illustration 307).

236. Pausanias 1: 3,1. See Brommer 1982, 17–18.

237. Pausanias 1: 17, 2. See Brommer 1982, 122; Boardman 1982, 18–19; Schefold and Jung 1988, 282–283.

238. Plutarch, *Life of Pericles*, 31. Pheidias also gave his own features to another of the Greek warriors on the shield.

239. Connor 1970, 169–170; Goossens 1962, 436. Connor includes an illustration of the Strangford Shield, a copy of Athena's shield, which shows Pericles-Theseus in the center of the bottom of the shield (Connor 1970, ill. 174, 171).

240. Brommer 1982, 70; Neils 1987, 140–141. Scholars have suggested all kinds of dates for this frieze, ranging from 470 B.C. to 420 B.C. Given that the frieze is part of the temple's restoration after it had been destroyed by the Persians, it seems unlikely that we should go much later than the middle of the century.

241. Thompson and Wycherley 1972, 143.

242. The east frieze may represent Theseus fighting the Pallantids or the gods fighting the giants, but there are difficulties with both these identifications (See Brommer 1982, 138–139).

243. For an analysis of these metopes see Brommer 1982, 69–70 and Neils 1987, 126–128.

244. Connor 1970, 153–155.

245. Taylor 1981, 120–121 and 126.

246. Brommer 1982, 83.

247. Brommer 1982, 2.

248. Aeschylus, *Eumenides* 685–690.

249. Its first definite appearance in vase paintings dates from after 450 B.C. (Boardman 1982, 20; Brommer 1982, 120). The invasion was also represented on the shield of Athena in the Parthenon, and this statue was dedicated in 438/7 B.C. (Pausanias 1: 17, 2; see Brommer 1982, 122).

250. Brommer 1982, 5.

251. Euripides, *Sons of Heracles*, 215–217. Pausanias tells us that the Amazonian war represented on the throne of Zeus at Olympia (dating from after 438 B.C.) included Theseus as one of Heracles' allies (Pausanias 5: 11, 4; see Brommer 1982, 116). Apart from this, there is no clear evidence that this story was depicted on any work of art, though Boardman does, as we have seen, suggest that it might have appeared on the eastern metope of the Athenian Treasury at Delphi (Boardman 1982, 12–15).

252. Schefold and Jung 1989, 231–295.

253. γλαφυρῶς ὁ Παρράσιου γέγραπται καὶ πεποίκιλται καί τι προσέοικε ("The painting of Parrhasius is elegant, refined, and quite a good likeness." Plutarch, *Were the Athenians More Famous in War or in Wisdom? Moral Writings*, 346 A).

254. *Medea*, 824–845. The words βαίνοντες ἀβρῶς ("walking gracefully," 830) in particular recall the γλαφυρῶς ("refined") of Plutarch (see previous note).

255. Euphranor's painting probably dates from the fourth century, and we shall mention it in the last chapter. Euphranor boasted that his Theseus looked as if he had eaten plenty of beef, and the painting caused one patriotic observer to exclaim: "Oh land of great-hearted Erechtheus, whom Zeus' daughter Athena once raised." These anecdotes are recorded by Plutarch (*Were the Athenians More Famous in War or in Wisdom? Moral Writings*, 346 B); the patriot's exclamation comes from Homer (*Iliad* 2: 546–547).

256. Brommer 1982, 148.

3

The Trozenian Outsider

The earliest literary works devoted to episodes in the myth of Theseus that have survived in their entirety are two dithyrambs by Bacchylides, Poems 17 and 18. Simonides, the poet's uncle, had written one or two poems about the hero of which only a few words survive, but Bacchylides' dithyrambs have come down to us complete. Both of these poems present Theseus as an outsider, a hero who deviates from the Athenian norm, a very incongruous role-model for a democratic citizen. Perhaps because they were written by one who was not of Athens himself (since Bacchylides, like his uncle, Simonides, came from Ceos), they reveal important contradictions in the nature of the hero and in the conception that the Athenians had of themselves. One of the primary concerns of the Athenians was to assert the purity of their race, the absolute identity of the citizens with their country and its soil, their complete freedom from any admixture of other elements, of foreign matter. According to Attic myth, every Athenian was literally autochthonous, every Athenian was descended from the very soil of Attica itself. In these poems of Bacchylides, Theseus, who should be the prototype of the autochthonous citizens of Athens, is in fact an embarrassing counter-example to all these proud assertions by the Athenians, and he is clearly cut off from the land that gave birth to them all.

This questioning of the hero's autochthony is an extremely important issue. All the Greek city-states were, as we have seen, haunted by the memory of their hero-kings.[1] In democratic Athens, however, this obsession with the heroic age had a special significance. It was not simply an age of distant, noble predecessors; the Athenians wanted to believe it was an age that still lived on in their country. They wanted to believe that the Athenian people and their democracy were timeless.[2] These beliefs in the timeless presence and purity of the Athenians as a race in Attica and in the eternal nature of their democracy were closely connected. Other Greek states had legends in which their first king or the founders of their aristocratic families were descended from the earth itself. In Attic myth, on the other hand, every citizen without exception was of noble birth, every citizen upheld the spirit of the heroic age, every citizen was descended from the earth.[3] This noble birth, heroic spirit, and autochthonous origin of the Athenians were viewed as a justification of their timeless democracy. As far as Athenians were concerned, their democracy did not put an end to the aristocratic, heroic world of Greek legend; it simply continued and expanded this world. Since every Athenian was, in effect, a heroic aristocrat of mythical origins, it followed that every citizen should take part in the political process. This association of ideas between noble birth from the soil and democratic equality among citizens comes out very clearly in the *Funeral Oration* of Lysias and the *Menexenus* of Plato.[4] To question the autochthonous origin of the people was to undermine the foundation of their democracy.

Bacchylides 17: The Man from the Sea

Sons and Mothers

For each family the myth of autochthony guarantees the legitimacy of inheritance in the male line, just as for the entire city it preserves the belief in the purity of the citizen body. Born from the soil itself, and arising from his father's hearth, there can be no doubt about the son's origins. By the very fact of asserting this, however, the myth reveals how greatly the Greeks were alarmed by the thought that a child's paternity can never be known. Telemachus puts it quite bluntly to Athena in the *Odyssey*:

> Μήτηρ μέν τέ μέ φησι τοῦ ἔμμεναι, αὐτὰρ ἐγώ γε
> οὐκ οἶδ'· οὐ γάρ πώ τις ἑὸν γόνον αὐτὸς ἀνέγνω.[5]

> My mother says that I am his, but I myself
> do not know: for no man knows his own origins.

Biologically unable to reproduce himself and obliged to rely on a woman for this (a dependence he often complains about[6]), the Greek father can never be sure about the identity of his son, he can never really know that his son is a true reproduction of himself. In Hesiod's imaginary description of an unbelievably just city, which enjoys all the blessings that heaven could pour on any people, one of its most important features is that sons resemble their fathers;[7] but this certainty is not the lot of the average Greek father. As for Theseus, the Athenians could not even tell whether his father was Poseidon or Aegeus. This particular ambiguity is not just one of double paternity, though this alone would be enough to undo the false security created by the myth of autochthony; it even denies that Theseus originated on the earth at all. Poseidon is, therefore, more than an alternative father; he introduces into the story of Theseus an account of human birth that denies autochthony completely.

It is as the son of Poseidon that Theseus appears in Poem 17 of Bacchylides, and his paternal home is on the bottom of the sea. In the case of Theseus, Poseidon truly lives up to his epithet of *Patrogeneios* ("ancestral"). A character in Plutarch's *Table Talk*, aptly named Nestor, traces the source of the ancient Greek worship of Poseidon Patrogeneios to their belief that man developed from "the moist element."[8] This belief is found even in Homer,[9] and it was later taken up by the Pythagoreans[10] and by Anaximander.[11] It stands, of course, in stark contrast to the more normal belief that attributed the origins of mankind and the fostering of the young to the earth. In Athens, this belief in autochthony was sanctioned by the state through the cult of Ge Kourotrophos and Demeter Chloe on the south slope of the Acropolis,[12] through the reference to Ge Kourotrophos in the Ephebic Oath,[13] and through the never-ending concern with autochthony in the official funeral orations pronounced over those soldiers who had died for Athens.[14] In adopting the more unusual account about the origins of mankind, and in applying it quite deliberately to the greatest hero of Athens, Bacchylides deliberately undermines the flattering myth of autochthony. Mankind is not born from the Earth, that "secure seat of all the immortals,"[15] but rather from the *pontos*, the unknown sea, which is so close in its nature to the primordial Chaos,[16] the Chaos that came to an end with the genesis of the Earth.

At the beginning of Bacchylides' poem (15–16), Theseus is, indeed, called "the offspring of Pandion," but this is the only tribute paid to the normal version of his birth; his descent from the Attic soil is denied everywhere else in the poem. Bacchylides has brought up the issue of autochthony only to deny it. Theseus is not born from the hearth, the fixed center from which the Greeks oriented space,[17] nor indeed from the earth at all; he is born from the *pontos*, the sea viewed as a space that cannot be oriented. His roots lie in the Cretan Sea, not in the Attic earth.[18] The Cretan Sea is, of course, a well-known one, a charted sea, a *pelagos* that the Greeks are used to sailing on, but this familiarity only extends to the surface of the sea; it does not apply to the underwater home of Theseus, the depths of the sea. Bacchylides quite accurately describes these depths as a *pontos* (line 94) and a "grove of the *pontos*" (πόντιον ἄλσος, 84–85), contrasting it with the familiar surface which he calls a *pelagos* (line 4).[19] He stresses that in this realm of the *pontos* one's location cannot be defined. The last and extremely unreliable reference point for Theseus, the ship of Minos, quickly disappears (lines 90–91) and leaves him completely lost. Instead of waiting for Theseus to return from his plunge into the sea, Minos orders the ship to sail on (lines 87–89). The north wind provides Minos with a regular shipping route (lines 90–91); it is the reliability of this same wind that makes the Cretan Sea a *pelagos* for those who sail on its surface.[20] For Theseus, on the other hand, this same sea by which he is engulfed is a *pontos*; he has disappeared in "the unknown open sea . . . without any reference point to orient himself."[21] Fate (*Moira*) will have to make a new route for him (line 89), which cannot be the regular one followed by Minos as he sails with the north wind; Bacchylides explicitly contrasts (using the particle δέ) the route of Theseus with the more normal one taken by Minos (κατ' οὖρον, "by the favorable wind," line 87). Since Theseus is lost in the underwater world, it will have to be a very special one, a "different route" (ἑτέραν ὁδόν, line 89), and yet it is not an entirely unnatural one. Theseus is, after all, "in his element" (in the most literal sense of the expression) and is being welcomed to his real home under the sea (δέξατο θελημόν, "it gladly welcomed him," 84–85).

The sea is called the house of Theseus' father (lines 66 and 99–100), and even a *megaron* (line 101), or great hall of a palace, but it is significant that it is called not his father's *megaron* but rather the "*megaron* of the gods" (θεῶν μέγαρον, lines 100–101). The royal *megaron* always includes the hearth from which a king's child is born,[22] but Bacchylides shows that this underwater *megaron* is not a father's great hall, nor even a home in which any normal child could be born. When Theseus dives into the sea, he is welcomed home by the "grove of the *pontos*" (πόντιον ἄλσος, lines 84-85). The adjective πόντιον ("of the *pontos*"), reveals that the "home" Theseus is going to visit does not have any determined location, that he is of "no fixed abode," but the noun ἄλσος ("grove") tells us even more. If a Greek father acknowledged a child as coming from his own hearth, he raised the child from the ground and carried him round his hearth at the ceremony of the *Amphidromia*; if he rejected the child, he had him exposed, he had him placed on the ground in the mountains or in a forest. A nightmarish forest under the sea is where our hero originates from. Theseus' home does not just fail to be a proper *hestia* ("hearth" or "home"); it is a grove (ἄλσος), the complete antithesis of a *hestia*. Like Oedipus, whose real home is Cithaeron and not the royal *megaron* of Thebes,[23] Theseus comes from a place where no child could have survived. These heroes belong to the mountains and forests of those children who have been abandoned by their fathers, who have been denied their identity as legitimate sons.[24]

Bacchylides has led us to expect that Theseus in his unusual home under the sea will meet Poseidon, but in fact he is welcomed by Amphitrite and not by his father.[25] This sudden appearance of Amphitrite is very puzzling.[26] Segal remarks that Theseus' journey through the sea to find his father is similar to the search of Telemachus for Odysseus.[27] Like Theseus, Telemachus does not find his father; instead he meets Helen and Menelaus. Helen recognizes Telemachus immediately,[28] and she gives him a *peplos* for his future bride,[29] thus showing a concern for the survival of his household which his own mother Penelope may lack.[30] The absence of the father and his replacement by a female figure are not just quirks of Bacchylides' poem; they are important themes in Greek myth.[31]

Theseus, like Telemachus, has to go in search of a father, but he is obliged to do so twice, because he has two fathers to deal with. Before examining Bacchylides' rendering of the myth, I would like to look at the very first time that Theseus seeks out his father (a story which has come to us through later authors). This story tells how Theseus goes to Athens in search of his autochthonous father, Aegeus. When he reaches his home, Medea is living there with Aegeus. As in the case of Ithaca and Mycenae, the royal house is almost extinct and the king is endangered by rival claimants. Aegeus is having problems with the Pallantids because of his lack of children (ἀπαιδία),[32] and he is obliged to rely on the wiles of a woman.[33] Medea is an expert with drugs, and just like Helen's,[34] these drugs can be used for good or evil. If she puts them to a good use, they could solve Aegeus' problems: "she promised to cure Aegeus of childlessness with her drugs" (φαρμάκοις ὑποσχομένη τῆς ἀτεκνίας ἀπαλλάξειν Αἰγέα).[35] Put to an evil use, they could kill his only son, Theseus: "she persuaded [Aegeus] to entertain [Theseus] as a guest and kill him with drugs" (ἔπεισεν αὐτὸν ὡς ξένον ἐστιῶντα φαρμάκοις ἀνελεῖν).[36] These phrases expressing the contrary powers of drugs are juxtaposed in two succeeding sentences in Plutarch's *Life of Theseus*. The drugs that women possess are thus two-edged weapons: they may completely destroy a man and his household (which is what Medea tries to do when Theseus arrives) and yet they are necessary if a man wishes to preserve his household (which is why Aegeus has Medea living with him in the first place). Thus, in their effects, they are like women themselves, as Hesiod sees them, for they are both necessary and dangerous.[37] The connection between women and magic is not unexpected, especially in the case of Medea. The myth of autochthony, however, denies the role of sexual reproduction altogether, and in particular it refuses to recognize the role of women and their almost magical powers of reproduction. The myth of Theseus explores both theories of human reproduction, the sexual and the autochthonous. As a descendant of the autochthonous Erechtheus, Aegeus represents the mythical notion of autochthonous reproduction. It should come as no surprise, therefore, that the magic power of Medea succeeds neither in supplying Aegeus with a son, nor in killing Theseus; it has been made irrelevant to the course of the myth.

A fragment from Euripides' *Aegeus*, a play which may have included this very incident in the myth of Theseus, explicitly denies the bond of maternity:

> πέφυκε γάρ πως παισὶ πολέμιον γυνή
> τοῖς πρόσθεν ἡ ζυγεῖσα δευτέρῳ πατρί.[38]

> Somehow a woman is naturally hostile to the children
> of her first marriage when she marries a second father.

These lines may refer to Medea herself, perhaps explaining why she had no "natural" (πέφυκε) affection for her children by Jason, once she realized she would have to leave him, but its specific context is not of vital importance. Its real significance lies in its gnomic assertion about women in general, and it follows a trend in Greek thought that goes back to Homer. If a woman marries a second husband, the truth at last emerges that she was never anything more than a complete stranger to her children.[39] Euripides' *Aegeus* very significantly refers to the second husband as a second "father," thus implying that she remarries not to acquire a new partner, nor to have more children for herself, but rather to help a new father create his own family. Just as the previous children belonged to her first husband, with the result that she has no reason to show them any affection once he has gone from her life, so the new children will belong to the second father. Thus a woman's relationship to her children is merely an indirect and vicarious one that operates through their father. In effect, there is no such thing as a mother; there is only a father's wife. We find the same view presented by Athena in the *Odyssey*:

> οἶσθα γὰρ οἷος θυμὸς ἐνὶ στήθεσσι γυναικός·
> κείνου βούλεται οἶκον ὀφέλλειν ὅς κεν ὀπυίῃ,
> παίδων δὲ προτέρων καὶ κουριδίοιο φίλοιο
> οὐκέτι μέμνηται τεθνηότος οὐδὲ μεταλλᾷ.[40]

> For you know what kind of heart is in a woman's breast:
> she wants to promote the household of the man she marries,
> and as for her previous children and her dear husband
> she no longer remembers or cares once he has died.

Athena is warning Telemachus not to trust his mother, for there is no close bond between a woman and her children. Every woman cares only for her present husband and his household. Athena, just like the unknown speaker several centuries later in the *Aegeus*, is saying that a mother is but a father's wife, and that it is only through his father that a son has any relationship with her.

The myth of autochthony declares in an even more radical way that the father is the sole parent, the mother is irrelevant. She is barely even recognized as the one who has provided the embryo with a womb, since this role in the origin of the Athenians is transferred to the soil of Athens. Women merely imitate the maternal role which was played for the first time by the earth itself.[41] The child belongs completely to the father, and he may grant or deny the child a real identity by either giving it a name or rejecting it.[42] This is so much the case with Theseus that the very fact that he has been accepted and named by his father constitutes his name:

> Τεκούσης δὲ τῆς Αἴθρας υἱὸν οἱ μὲν αὖθις ὀνομασθῆναι
> Θησέα λέγουσι . . . οἱ δ' ὕστερον Ἀθήνησι παῖδα θεμένου
> Αἰγέως αὐτόν.[43]

> When Aethra gave birth to her son, some say he was
> named Theseus at once . . . others says it happened later in
> Athens when Aegeus declared him his son.

One version of the myth declares he was named Theseus as soon as he was born, and derives his name from the placement (*thesis*) of the recognition-tokens by Aegeus. The more significant version of the myth is the one that explains his name as deriving from his father's acknowledgment (*themenou*) of Theseus as a son. It goes against the logic of realism by suggesting that the hero was nameless until he became an adult, but this will also be the case, even if we accept the first etymology of his name. If he is named after the recognition-tokens, he will not really have earned his name until he reaches manhood and retrieves the tokens. The story that he was not named until recognized by Aegeus is a more explicit and doubt-less truer reading of the myth, for myths like other representations of reality are often the most illogical when they express what is most deeply felt. In another great myth exploring the nature of autochthony, the story of Ion, it is once again the meeting with his "father" that constitutes the hero's name.[44] These two myths about the naming of two archetypal Athenian heroes might seem no more than an exaggerated image of the normal process where the newborn child remained nameless until the tenth day. We might explain the myths by saying that this normal period has simply been expanded from ten days to almost twice as many years, but this would not exhaust their significance. The myths are correct quite literally, in that an Athenian boy does not really acquire his full name and identity until he has reached adulthood and has been officially acknowledged as his father's legitimate son by the phratry to which his family belongs. In democratic Athens, this late acquisition of one's name is quite obvious since a citizen's full name consists of his own name, his patronymic, and his demotic. He is not fully entitled to his demotic until he has been listed on the official records of the deme as an adult citizen, so in the most literal sense he does not acquire his full legal name until this event takes place. At this time, he joins the other male citizens, and it is to his father alone that he owes his identity as a man and as an Athenian.

And yet, if Athens is the land of autochthony par excellence, this image of human origins does not have a complete monopoly over Athenian ideology. Perhaps it is impossible for any myth to dominate completely the representation of reality, and if we look briefly at the myths of another land where this myth of autochthony was very powerful we shall find that this was clearly the case. The myths of Thebes, although they celebrate the birth of the first Thebans from the very soil of Boeotia, present autochthony as just one way of interpreting human origins. As Lévi-Strauss explained in his analysis of these stories, the Theban myths present us with two opposite poles. On the one hand, we have an insistence on literal birth from the soil without any role being attributed to women, and on the other hand, we have an exaggeration of sexual reproduction in the tales of Oedipus and Jocasta.[45] The myth of Oedipus is thus based on the conflict between these two theories of reproduction—the mythical one based on autochthony, where a father alone will suffice, and the realistic one based on sexuality, where both parents are necessary. These theories in turn are but particular examples of a more general dichotomy found in myth: does humanity derive from one original parent or from a couple?[46] In the case of Theseus, we shall likewise discover assertions of maternal filiation, even though he was the prototype of the autochthonous Athenian race.

If we return now to Theseus' search for his other father and to his underwater visit in Bacchylides' seventeenth poem, we shall see that his search is a failure. Instead of his father "he saw the dear wife of his father" (εἶδέν τε πατρὸς ἄλοχον φίλαν, 109). For us, the absence of his natural mother is odd, but for the Greeks, it would be the absence of his father, Poseidon, that was really striking. It is quite uncertain, however, who Theseus' father is, and Bacchylides deliberately maintains this ambiguity. Eriboea calls out to Theseus as the son of the autochthonous Aegeus: "offspring of Pandion with the brazen breastplate" (χαλκο- / θώρακα Πανδίονος ἔκγονον, 14–16), but elsewhere in the poem, his father is Poseidon.[47] By leaving the identity of Theseus' father in doubt, Bacchylides places all the more emphasis on the mother figures, Aethra and Amphitrite.

At line 34, Aethra is called "the daughter of rich Pittheus." This formula (Πιτθέως θυγάτηρ) reminds us that Theseus is a *thygatridous* (θυγατριδοῦς, literally "a son through a daughter"), the son of an *epikleros* (ἐπίκληρος, a sole heiress, a woman who is "attached" ἐπί to the "family fortune" κλῆρος). The fortune (κλῆρος) of Pittheus will pass on directly to Theseus. Aethra is significant only in that she gives birth to an heir for

Pittheus, and once she has performed this function, she is ignored. She appears once more in the myth of Theseus, when she is kidnapped by the Dioscuri as a reprisal for the abduction of Helen. This kidnapping removes her from the story of Theseus, and after that she is completely forgotten. A generation later, during the Trojan War, she is still with Helen, working for her as a servant,[48] and it is not until after the fall of Troy that her grandsons secure her release. Her one major action in the myth, that of giving birth to Theseus, is, however, a significant one, because the case of an *epikleros* is the one case in which the Athenians are forced to recognize "uterine filiation."[49] Even if she makes only a furtive appearance in the myth, it is one that undermines the autochthonous origins of the hero.

The surprising appearance of Amphitrite in Bacchylides' poem has a similar importance. Theseus has been heading for his father's house right up to line 100, but in a sense he never manages to get there, for at this very point we discover that he has arrived at the "*megaron* of the gods" (θεῶν μέγαρον, 101) These "gods" turn out to be not gods in general but the Nereids (line 102) and Amphitrite (line 109). Bacchylides uses this word (θεῶν) for gods once again in this poem, when he speaks of the gifts that Theseus has just received, the "gifts of the gods" (θεῶν δῶρα, 124). Once again, the "gods" turn out to be these same goddesses.[50] The home of Theseus is rather the *megaron* of these goddesses than that of his father Poseidon, and when Theseus meets Amphitrite (lines 110–111), Bacchylides once again suggests that the house really belongs to the goddess:

σέμναν βοῶπιν ἐράτοι-
σιν Ἀμφιτρίταν δόμοις.

the holy ox-eyed Amphitrite
in her attractive home.

Eratos ("attractive") is a very feminine word, and earlier in the poem Bacchylides has already used this adjective (in a compound form) to describe Europa: "the attractively named daughter of Phoenix (Φοίνικος ἐρα- / τώνυμος κορά, 31–32). That which is *eratos* belongs to the world of women, to their names, their dwellings, their surroundings. Theseus enters a world of "feminine presences" and thus finds himself in the same situation as the supremely autochthonous hero, Erechtheus, whose birth has been described as follows by Loraux:

Sometimes the father is absent. This happens with Hephaestus, "father" of the autochthonous child, whose absence entrusts feminine presences with the duty of surrounding the birth of the miraculous child.[51]

The father is absent, the mother is ignored, but it is the feminine presence that manages to reassert itself. Amphitrite and the Nereids replace Aethra, the natural mother of Theseus, just as the Cecropids replace Ge, the mother of Erechtheus. As a symbol of this replacement, Theseus wears the garland (πλόκος, 114) of Amphitrite rather than the wedding veil (κάλυμμα, 37–38) of his own mother, Aethra.[52] Amphitrite's function in this myth is to represent the feminine forces and to draw attention to the absence of the father.

The myth of Bacchylides' seventeenth poem thus undermines in several ways the myth of autochthony, which Vernant describes as "this dream of a purely paternal heredity."[53] It alludes to autochthony (at line 15) only to ignore it throughout the rest of the poem. It denies that Theseus is a child from his father's hearth, by giving his paternal hearth no fixed location, by placing it in a *pontos* where place has no meaning, and by questioning whether a hearth could belong to a male god in the first place, whether it is not by its very nature a focus of female power. Finally, it undermines the role of fatherhood since Theseus' quest for a father ends up in the discovery of a mother figure, and his identity as a hero is established by feminine powers.

The Metis *of the Sea*

The denial of Theseus' autochthony in this poem affects not only his birth but indeed an entire way of thinking. As we mentioned previously, democracy was admired by the Athenians not on its own merits but as a genuinely aristocratic form of government, and the proof of this lay in the noble autochthonous origins of every citizen. Democratic Athens was a house of lords, a land inhabited by noblemen alone, a state governed by strict adherence to the timeless principles of aristocracy. In reality, of course, it was probably the most changeable state in the Greek world, and the greatest virtue demanded of its statesmen was an exceptional adaptability to rapidly changing circumstances. In such a society, the art of government cannot be an exact science, as Plato noted with disgust. For him, democracy was anarchic and variegated (ἄναρχος, ποικίλη),[54] it was like a patchwork coat (ἱμάτιον ποικίλον);[55] it had all those characteristics that made the world of becoming and appearance so objectionable and unknowable. Its fluid, changing, and multiple nature was, however, subject to a very different kind of knowledge, one that Plato thought little of, for flexibility and multiplicity are the very essence of *metis* ("cunning intelligence").[56] *Metis*, the ability to conjecture about the future and to improvise rapidly, was the supreme gift of the great democratic leader, Themistocles,[57] who is specifically praised for this talent by Thucydides.[58] Democracy brings us into the realm of *metis*, and it was through their exploitation of such cunning intelligence that the Athenians rose to mastery in Greece.[59] Poem 17 was probably written in the time of the Delian League, and among other things it represents through myth the passing of the thalassocracy from Minos to Theseus and the Athenians.[60]

Minos is honored throughout the poem as a king and as the son of Zeus, and yet if his sovereignty is to be permanent, it cannot rely on power alone. Such power can always be undermined by the use of superior intelligence, and if Kratos (Power) and Bia (Force) have been reduced to the permanent followers of Zeus,[61] it is because he has absorbed the goddess Metis within himself.[62] Minos is one of the most royal of Zeus' sons, and even after death he continues to hold a position of authority in the underworld; nonetheless, his power is subject to the same limitations and the same dependency on *metis*. His use of this gift in our poem shows that he has a poor command over it, and that he has not advanced greatly beyond the primitive powers who rely on force alone, and inevitably fall to the more enlightened masters of *metis*.[63]

The major action of the poem is motivated by the two attempts of Minos to use *metis*. The first is his "heavy-handed *metis*," or "scheme" (βαρεῖαν ... μῆτιν, 28–29) to seduce one of the seven Athenian girls. Aphrodite is one of the great divinities of *metis*, and even Zeus finds it difficult to outwit her, but his son Minos is utterly incompetent. He shows no aptitude for persuasion or seduction, and his clumsy effort to win the girl is no more than an act of violence, a display of brute force (μεγαλοῦχον ... βίαν, 23). Bacchylides even describes it as that dangerous manifestation of human arrogance which draws down punishment from the gods, "grievous *hybris*" (πολύστονον ... ὕβριν, 40–41). A king who relies on such force alone will not be a king for very long, and Theseus openly defies him with impunity. It is highly ironic that an experienced ruler should resort to such a device and be rebuked for it by a young man.

Minos tries to use *metis* again, and this second time it is a genuine effort at real *metis*. Bacchylides emphasizes that this is a true use of *metis* by his very description of it: "he wove a new *metis*" or "scheme" (ὕφαινέ τε ποταινίαν / μῆτιν, 51–52). The metaphor of weaving is typical in such descriptions of cunning schemes,[64] and the adjective *potainios* is also loaded with significance. The word means "new," of course, but novelty and innovation are not concepts that the Greeks were very comfortable with. The ancient lexicographers gave two interpretations of this term, both of which are rather sinister. The first treated it as a Doric equivalent of *prosphatos* ("recently dead," hence "fresh" and "new") thus relating it to death, and the *metis* of Minos is of course a plan to bring about the death of Theseus. The second derived it from *ainos* ("story" or "riddle"), and the problem of retrieving the ring is indeed a puzzle that Theseus must solve. It is quite similar to the deadly riddle of the Sphinx, which Oedipus solved by realizing his own identity as a human being. Theseus fulfills the quest of Minos by asserting his own identity as the man from the sea, the child of Poseidon, of Amphitrite, and of the Nereids.

This new device of Minos would have succeeded against any normal person, but Theseus is more than that. The art of navigation, of orienting oneself in the middle of the confusing and ever-changing sea, is one that above all other skills demands the use of *metis*.[65] Minos, as ruler of the waves, is a master of this craft and quite comfortable sailing the Cretan Sea, but he is no match for Theseus, for if Minos can manage a *pelagos* Theseus can even overcome the *pontos*. To survive and indeed feel at home in such chaos is to be an almost invincible master of *metis*. His purple robe and crown of roses have been compared with the emblems of a triumphant Roman general,[66] but even if we do not make this connection, they certainly symbolize his mastery of the sea. The *pontos* itself congratulates him (127–128), and Minos, described with a touch of irony as the commander (στραταγέταν, 121, is the standard word for "general") receives a humiliating check that almost wins our sympathy ("Alas, what thoughts he put an end to!" 119–121).

Theseus has outwitted him in the realms of Aphrodite and Poseidon, where the gift of *metis* is especially required, and he will humiliate Minos even more in the future and put an end to the Cretan thalassocracy. Through the help of Aphrodite, he will seduce the daughter of Minos and end the tribute that Athens had to pay the king. He will openly defy Minos and escape across the sea, and according to Pherecydes' version of the myth, he will use his cunning intelligence again to destroy the great fleet of Cnossus.[67] But above all else he has shown himself to be the archetypal representative of the ordinary Athenians, "the people, the oarsmen, the saviors of our city,"[68] and in this respect at any rate a forerunner of Themistocles.[69] He has left behind the old, supposedly innate *arete* ("courage") of the aristocratic hoplite, which was celebrated by the official orators of Athens who dwelt so much on the myth of autochthony; he is instead a representative of the new and acquired *sophia* ("intelligence") of the democratic Athenian navy, a *techne* ("skill") that requires no mythical justification but relies rather on the proof furnished by its own success.[70]

Bacchylides 18: Ephebe and Foreigner

If Poem 17 questions the autochthonous origins of Theseus and the Athenian people as a whole, Poem 18 seems to assume and rely for its dramatic effect on the assumption that Theseus is the son of Aegeus. In Poem 17 he had proved himself to be the son of Poseidon; in Poem 18 he seeks out his autochthonous father, Aegeus, but although this poem accepts the myth of autochthony, it also raises some of the problems implied by it. The greatest of these is the embarrassing gap between a male child's birth and his entry into the world of men as an ephebe[71] eighteen years later. Men do not exist as citizens until this age, so when they are initiated into the adult world, they are in effect coming from nowhere, from a realm of nonexistence. Their ambiguous status, neither children nor citizens, means that they are in a state which, as van Gennep remarks, is equated with that of death in many societies.

> In some of these ceremonies, the novice is considered to be dead, and he stays dead for the duration of the noviciate. This noviciate lasts over a period that may be long or short, and it consists of a physical and mental weakening of the novice, intended no doubt to make him lose all recollection of his childhood.[72]

In the myth of Theseus, which Jeanmaire calls "the story of the Athenian ephebe system,"[73] the hero enters the adult world twice: on his first arrival in Attica, after he has completed his dangerous journey along the Saronic Gulf, and on his return home from Crete, after he has defeated the monster in the labyrinth. Since Athens is both a land power and a sea power, Theseus must prove himself in both realms.[74] In the first case, Theseus comes back from the no-man's land on the borders of Attica. In the second one, where he comes back from Crete, the coast has the same significance for a seafaring people as a forest or a mountain on the border of their country would have for an inland people. In each of his integrations into adult male society, Theseus, the model of the ephebes, comes back from the same type of place.[75] It is always a no-man's land on the margins of society, and even of life itself. This alone gives him a character that is ambiguous if not sinister, but it is one that he has in common with all young men at this marginal stage of life.

His very begetting is unusual and, whichever of the two versions we choose, it belongs to the world of ephebic initiation and *apate* ("deceit").[76] Aegeus, his terrestrial father, was in physical danger because of his childlessness. Since he was not a parent, he was not respected as a proper ruler of Athens.[77] His belated initiation to parenthood takes place not in Athens but in Trozen, an outlying marginal region that is neither fully Athenian nor completely foreign. There he is tricked (the verb used is derived from *apate*[78]) by Pittheus, who gets him drunk, and he sleeps with Aethra. In the alternative version of the hero's begetting, Aethra sleeps with Poseidon on the island of Sphairia, which as a result changes its name to Hiera ("the holy island"). She had been tricked into going to the island by Athena Apatouria,[79] the goddess of ephebic initiation, and tricks are in themselves typical of such initiations. Aethra's seduction is clearly felt to be an initiation, because after the event, she establishes the custom that all Trozenian girls should dedicate their girdles to Athena Apatouria when they get married.[80] Marriage plays the same role in a woman's life that formal initiation does in a man's, and in Athens it was on the occasion of these events that men and women were entered in the records of the phratries. Aegeus in the first version and Aethra in the second have to be tricked into a sexual initiation, and in each case the *apate* of Aphrodite[81] is closely associated with initiatory *apate*.

The strange birth of Theseus makes him a very peculiar and ambiguous person. His father is either the infertile Aegeus or the hyperfertile Poseidon. His mother is an immature maiden who is tricked into premature sexual intercourse, and is neither wife nor concubine to either of her lovers. Finally, Theseus is not born in Attica. His birth, therefore, goes against the laws of nature, of marriage, and of Athens;[82] and yet, he is the natural and legitimate heir of Aegeus, and will become the embodiment of Athens, as her king and hero. He is both the most outrageous example of an unnatural illegitimate foreigner, and the most perfect example of a natural legitimate Athenian. It is this ambiguous status of Theseus that makes him so suitable as an archetype of the ephebes.

Theseus is always presented as a young ephebe from the Classical period on,[83] and he is the role model for all male adolescent Athenians. Heracles, as the hero of the *palaistra* and of physical development, is also an important hero for them, and they dedicate their hair to him at the Apatouria. He is their model, however, only in so far as he inculcates in them the agonistic spirit that is a necessary aspect of life in the polis. This spirit must always be subjected, however, to the cooperation required of adult men as citizens and as soldiers.[84] Heracles is not so much a hero of the ephebes as a hero of the gymnastic training that plays so large a part of their lives. Theseus, on the other hand, is their prototype as ephebes, as young men who will soon be called upon to play a central role in the polis, just like Theseus himself. He is very clearly presented as such in Bacchylides' poem. He is a boy (παῖδα, 56) but he is starting to be a young man (πρώθηβον, 57),[85] he carries the spear (49) and wears the cloak (54) that were characteristic of Ephebes undergoing military training.[86] He is something more than an ordinary ephebe, however, and before we continue to examine his significance for young Athenians, we must consider his role as a young prince.

Initiation of a Prince

The poem of Bacchylides makes it quite clear that Aegeus is frightened when the unknown ephebe arrives: "I am worried how these things will turn out" (30). His fear is emphasized in the other accounts of Theseus' first arrival in Athens,[87] and is obviously an important element in the myth. Jason, another ephebe, has the same effect on Pelias[88] and on the people of Iolcus[89] in a poem by Bacchylides' great predecessor in epinician poetry, the fourth *Pythian Ode* of Pindar. Bacchylides may seem to have exaggerated the alarm caused by Theseus, since he has a herald running to the city (16–17), and Aegeus sounding the alarm (3–4) and calling an assembly of the people, as if the country were being invaded (5–7). It is unlikely that a young man, however heroic he might be, would be capable of defeating the entire people of Attica single-handed, so we must conclude that Aegeus fears not so much for his country as for his throne, and this is clear from other versions of the story.[90] His fear is well-founded because Theseus, like Jason, after being sent on a voyage and going through a series of endurance tests, returns and brings about the death of the old king.[91] Theseus must prove himself, not only as an adult Athenian, but also as a prince, and his initiation does not truly come to an end until he takes over as king of Athens and declares himself a hero by establishing the Theseion in Athens.[92] The myths of Theseus and Jason are rather special cases because the ephebe is also heir to the throne, but they are a mythical representation of a common practice which van Gennep found all over the world: "Sometimes indeed the succession only takes place if a special rite is performed in which the successor puts his predecessor to death."[93] This is an element that appears several times in the story of Theseus. When he kills Skiron, he does so by throwing him over a cliff. In so doing, he acts exactly as Skiron himself did, and becomes his replacement, his successor, just as the famous priest of Diana at Nemi attained his position only through the murder of his predecessor.[94] When Aegeus kills himself, his death is brought about, if indirectly, by Theseus who will succeed him. Once again the king dies at the hands of his successor by falling off a cliff, the Acropolis. Finally, when it is Theseus' turn to surrender his crown, he is likewise thrown off a height to his death, and Lycomedes, the ruler of Skyros, carries out this murder to please Menestheus, the successor of Theseus in Athens.[95] We do not, of course, have to believe that this was the mode of succession in Mycenaean Athens, or that the Greeks ever behaved in such a manner, but obviously the notion had crossed their minds. The resentment of the younger generation at the patriarchal family was projected onto the character of Theseus.[96]

The death of the king at the hands of the returning young prince is not simply the projection of a hidden desire. It also represents the initiation of an entire generation into manhood, and its significance has been noted not by psychologists working in private cases, but by anthropologists such as van Gennep working on entire societies: "Myth conflates the new king and the new generation. The death of the old king represents the destruction of the past."[97] A practice of an African people, the Masai, reveals the implied threat posed by the new generation: the young men of this people are initiated only if their fathers acknowledge that they are now "old men" and agree to be named after their sons (if the son's name is X, the father from now on will lose his previous name and be called "father-of-X").[98] There is a curious parallel to this particular custom in the *Iliad* where Odysseus, whose son Telemachus is another typical ephebe, is called "the father of Telemachus."[99] It also appears in the wish-fulfillment world of comedy, where Bdelycleon is the real head of the family and orders Philocleon about,[100] so that his father becomes in effect a minor.[101] In both these cases, the normal roles of father and son are reversed, and in the case of Odysseus, even the normal practice of naming a man, "Odysseus son of Laertes," is overturned, and he is renamed "Odysseus father of Telemachus."

The advent of a new generation does not just promise a renewal of society; it also threatens a revolution in society. The marginal position of these new adults means that they will not necessarily feel themselves bound by the rules of their society. As Vidal-Naquet has pointed out, the dubious status of the initiates is clearly expressed in Pindar's fourth *Pythian*,[102] where Jason is not just a prince and successor to Pelias, but, like Theseus, a representative of the entire age-group of ephebes. In this ode Jason is said to be "a stranger or a citizen,"[103] and thus occupies an ill-defined status which somehow lies between and partakes in both of these radically different conditions. To emphasize Jason's double status, Pindar describes him as wearing both a normal Megarian cloak and a strange panther skin, the garment of a citizen and the garment of an outsider to civilized society.[104] Similarly, in Bacchylides' poem, the behavior of Theseus mark him out as an external or internal threat to Athens, an "enemy" (δυσμενής, 6) or a "bandit" (ληισταί, 8). His marching "alone" (35 and 46)[105] marks him out as a "wanderer" (ἀλάταν, 36), who thus belongs to no society, and since he comes to Athens as "to a land of other people" (ἐπ' ἀλλοδαμίαν, 37), he clearly does not belong there either.

By the fourth century, the marginality of the ephebes was completely eliminated in Athenian law, for they were enrolled as citizens as soon as their Ephebic period of military training began at the age of eighteen.[106] This fourth-century practice was based on an earlier tribal initiation, of which an image survives in Athenian myth and ritual, where the young men are not even regarded as Athenians. They occupy an ambiguous status between citizen and stranger, and this marginality is emphasized by the very places where they are initiated, for these places are the frontier regions where the territory of the state merges into that of its enemies.

Places of Initiation

At the beginning of Pyanopsion, there were two festivals associated with the myth of Theseus and with his role as a young man being initiated into society, the Oschophoria and the Theseia.[107] The festival of the Oschophoria was celebrated on the seventh of Pyanopsion,[108] the same day as the Pyanopsia. The myth explaining the origin of the festival said that Theseus himself had founded the Oschophoria on his return from Crete,[109] and the cries of joy and sorrow made by the participants supposedly commemorated his joyful return and the sorrowful death of his father Aegeus, both of which occurred on the same day.[110] I suspect that these aetiological myths may have been created by Atthidographers in the fourth century, so I shall not base my argument on them. A direct link is established, however, between the Oschophoria and initiation by two of our sources, Proclus and Athenaeus, since they tell us that *epheboi* took part in foot-races during it.[111] They may, however, be referring to a later innovation, and it is not clear whether they mean ephebes in general, or Ephebes in the military sense of the word.[112] In spite of these doubts about the connection of the festival with the Theseus legend and with ephebes or the Ephebes, the Oschophoria are interesting in themselves because of the general themes of initiation and marginality that run through them.

The goddess at the center of the Oschophoria[113] was not the goddess of the city but Athena Skiras,[114] a goddess who was imported from Salamis, and the priests in charge of the festival belonged to the Salaminioi, a family which was deported from Salamis. Her original sanctuary, the Skiradeion, was on Salamis, and indeed the island itself had formerly been called Skiras. The goddess, her priests, and her home are, therefore, not quite Athenian, and yet not quite foreign. Her marginal status becomes even clearer when we consider the location of her temples in Attica. In addition to her original sanctuary on Salamis, she had only two temples. The first was her temple at Skiron on the river Cephisus,[115] and she shares this location with a non-Athenian hero. A mythical prophet called Skiros was buried here after he had died fighting for Eleusis in the war waged by Eumolpos against Athens. Skiron was, therefore, the no-man's land between Athens and Eleusis where the two armies met in this mythical war. Skiron is also a very important place in the myth of Theseus. It was here at the river Cephisus that the Phytalidai had purified Theseus from the murder of the bandits he had killed on his way to Athens.[116] He leaves behind his bloody past as a killer of bandits, and now that he has proved himself, he can enter the city and reveal himself to be his father's soon. The other temple of Athena Skiras was on the beach of Phaleron, and this temple was close to a sanctuary of the Salaminian hero, Skiros. The presence of the half-foreign, half-naturalized goddess and hero bring out the borderline status of Phaleron, and of Theseus who arrives there when he has once again proved himself as a hero by defeating the Minotaur.

Both these places are, therefore, very important in the myth of Theseus. Skiron is the point at which Theseus enters Athens after demonstrating his prowess on land, just as Phaleron is the point at which he returns to Athens after proving himself at sea. Both Skiron and Phaleron are places dedicated to Athena Skiras (herself an imported goddess) and to a hero (Skiros) who comes from a region once hostile but now integrated into the Athenian state (Salamis and Eleusis). They are both places where dangerous and threatening elements could be assimilated, a line over which those changing from the status of stranger to that of citizen would have to pass. These marginal places are sacred to mythical enemies who were taken over as heroes by Athens, just as Theseus is assimilated at these places and becomes a full Athenian. He makes this transition at Skiron when he first comes to Attica, and again at Phaleron when he returns from Crete.

In turning from myth to ritual, we find that these two places, Phaleron and Skiron, mark the frontier between the city of Athens (the *polis*) and the territory of Attica (the *chora*). The three sacred ploughings reveal the status of Skiron as midpoint between Athens and Eleusis, for they take place under the Acropolis of Athens, on the Plain of Rharos at Eleusis, and at Skiron itself.[117] Again, in the cult of the Eleusinian goddesses, Skiron is the point where they arrive in Athens by land. Every year, at the festival of the Skirophoria, the Athenian deities, Athena and Poseidon, welcome the Eleusinian goddesses, Demeter and Kore, at Skiron.[118]

Phaleron is, however, more interesting for our purposes, since it is not just a place where foreign gods and heroes might be assimilated, but also one where young Athenians took part in the Oschophoria, which has strong initiatory characteristics. A peculiar feature of the Oschophoria was that the procession at its heart was led by two boys disguised as girls.[119] This transvestism is a characteristic feature of initiation rites,[120] and it is also found in myths about young heroes on the verge of manhood. Theseus himself is mocked because of his girlish appearance and clothing when he first comes to Athens,[121] and Achilles dresses as a girl when he hides among the daughters of Lycomedes.[122] According to this primitive view found in myth and ritual, the status of the young men is so dubious that they may even be assimilated to women, a group that is completely excluded from the polis. At the Oschophoria, the two transvestite boys who lead the procession started from a temple of Dionysus in the city, probably the Limnaion,[123] and end up at the temple of Athena Skiras. The second part of the festival consisted of a race by young men from her temple back to the temple of Dionysus. It concludes with a sacrifice and banquet. The festival thus includes the three phases of an initiatory rite. First, it starts with the departure of the sexually ambiguous boys from Athens; second, the procession ends up in the marginal area of Phaleron; and third, we have the return, during which the procession led by boys is replaced by a group of young men who prove their prowess by running home to Athens. The departure is clearly marked off as a preinitiatory phase by the age of the young boys and their female clothing. The return is likewise marked off as a postinitiatory phase by the age of the young men, their nakedness, and even by the very fact that they run, because this in itself was considered a mark of virility by the Greeks.[124] Whatever we may think of the aetiological myths that explain this festival, or of the role played by the Ephebes in it, the Oschophoria is clearly a festival of initiation.[125]

In the more practical world of military service, the old religious city line represented by Phaleron and Skiron drops out of the picture altogether, but the world of the Ephebes is simply an expanded, secular version of the older one we have found in the myth of Theseus and the festivals of Athens. The Ephebes carry out their duties in the borderlands of Attica, and these marginal lands include not just its frontiers with Megara and Boeotia, but also the Peiraeus, which had replaced the old beach at Phaleron as Attica's frontier with the sea.

The other festival in Pyanopsion concerned with Theseus and male initiation was the great feast day of Theseus himself. The Theseia were celebrated on the eighth of Pyanopsion, and on the eve of the festival a ram was sacrificed to Connidas, his tutor.[126] This tribute must be paid to his childhood years, which he has left behind him forever, before the Athenians can celebrate his transition to the adult world on the day of the Theseia. The Theseia celebrate his new status as a mature warrior, a king, and a hero.[127] When the practice of Ephebic military service was introduced, the Ephebes competed in torch races, fights in armor, and javelin contests at this festival.[128] Their significant presence at the festival is yet another relic of the older tribal initiations that survived the transformation into the purely civic and military initiation of the Ephebes.[129] The festival is, of course, simply an elaborate version of a hero sacrifice, but the participation of the Ephebes reminds us that the myth of Theseus, from his birth abroad to his return from Crete, is indeed an Athenian story about initiation.

Marginality and Misbehavior

The ephebes are neither near enough to the center of society to be treated as true citizens, nor far enough from it to be rejected absolutely as if they were foreigners. Their marginal position is reflected not just spatially, but also through their irregular behavior in the martial and marital fields. In myth, Theseus and the other figures who represent the young initiates act in a flippant and antisocial way. Their behavior is sharply contrasted with the manner of the mature citizen-soldier, who is the responsible head of a household and a loyal comrade in the hoplite line of battle. The inherent ambiguity in the status of the young men is found in many cultures, and van Gennep records the dilemma they present to every society:

The novices are beyond society, and society has no power over them, all
the less so in that they are genuinely sacred and holy, and therefore intan-
gible, dangerous, just as gods would be. . . . Society is defenceless against
the schemes of the novices.[130]

The mixture of both trickery and force, which is characteristic of young
men, shows that they are still boys but that they are already mature warriors too. In Pindar's fourth *Pythian* the same ambiguity surrounds the
stranger who will one day kill Pelias. Just as he is both citizen and stranger,
so his tactics combine force (χείρεσσιν) and "inflexible trickery" (βουλαῖς
ἀκάμπτοις).[131] The same traits appear in the character of the young
Theseus, as he is seen by the Athenians in the Bacchylides dithyramb (Poem
18). They ask whether Theseus is a military commander (7) or part of a
group of bandits (8). A little later, they ask again whether he is a general
who is coming with an army, or rather a man coming alone with one or
two servants (33–36), a man wandering around like a merchant, a trickster
who is the antithesis of a disciplined soldier on the march. The description
is much more thorough here than in Pindar's poem: here Theseus is not
just a young man and a trickster; he is also a bandit, a loner, and a vagabond.

These features are found in yet another myth which examines the nature
of male initiation, the Athenian myth of Melanthios. Vidal-Naquet has
explained Melanthios as a mythical prototype of the ephebes, whose character he contrasts with that of a mature hoplite: "On one side we have single
combat, on the other loyal hoplite combat."[132] A similar contrast can be
made, as Vidal-Naquet has shown, between the young Spartan *kryptes*
(secret policeman) and the adult Spartan hoplite: "with the hoplite, everything is order, *taxis*; with the *kryptes*, everything is trickery, *apate*, disorder,
irrationalism."[133] This is an excellent parallel, since the Spartans had transformed an old rite of initiation (*krypteia*) into a period of service in the
secret police,[134] just as the Athenians had transformed their rite of initiation (*ephebeia*) into a period of military service. In both societies the behavior of the young men in the sphere of warfare is so far from the norm
that it is even more foreign than the conduct of an enemy. Once again, they
are shown to be neither loyal citizens nor open enemies, but rather members of an unsettling group that fits into neither category.

There is a second major domain in which the young initiate may be
contrasted with proper citizens, the domain of marriage. The panther skin
worn by the young Jason marks him out as a seducer.[135] He has succeeded
in overcoming the most cunning and seductive of all animals, and he now
wears its skin as a sign of his superiority in this area, just as Heracles wears
a lion skin to show his excellence in quite a different field. Jason will use
his pantherlike talents to seduce the daughter of his enemy and get himself
out of a dangerous situation. This is a characteristic that he shares with

Theseus. Plutarch gives us a list of the women with whom Theseus was involved.[136] The list includes the rape of young women, abduction, several marriages—it represents total disorder in the sexual realm.

This disorder is not, however, without its own primitive logic. Dumézil has analyzed four types of marriage in Indo-European thought, which are distinguished most clearly in the laws of India. First is the *brahmana* (corresponding to *confarreatio* in Rome), the type suitable for the caste of kings and priests. The father freely hands over his daughter to a suitable son-in-law. The next two types of marriage are typically found in the warrior class: *raksasa*, marriage by abduction (a form that was phased out in Rome[137]), and *gandharva*, where the daughter consents to run away with a young warrior (this last type is similar to the Roman *usus*); in these two forms the father is left out of the picture. Finally there is *asura*, which is characteristic of the class of producers. This is a marriage by purchase, where father and son-in-law act as buyer and seller, with the daughter being viewed as a product to be sold (this corresponds to the Roman *coemptio*).[138] In the epics of India, the heroes tend to go through all the forms of marriage with different heroines, with the exception of marriage by purchase, because it belongs to a class lower than theirs and is, therefore, beneath their dignity as warriors.[139] The sexual unions of Theseus follow the logic of Indian epic. He marries Phaedra as a king's daughter, and she is to produce his heirs as king of Athens. Hippolyta, along with several others, he abducts by force. This is the most common form in the myth of Theseus, and accounts for no less than five of the ten unions listed by Plutarch.[140] In Indian epic, this is "the most honorable for warriors."[141] Finally, there is the case of Ariadne, who goes away with Theseus of her own free will, without the knowledge or consent of her father. The apparent disorder of his relationships with women actually shows that he is a king and a warrior.

Ariadne is doubtless the most famous of the victims of Theseus. Plutarch judges that the abandonment of this woman was neither noble (*kalon*) nor seemly,[142] which means that the action was not that of a noble warrior (a *kalos*), and that it broke the laws of society. Plutarch views it not as a trivial error of youth, but as an offense that undermines all social conventions. His ephebic fecklessness will overthrow the authority of his father, the principles of the hoplite warrior, and the rules of marriage. Through the frightful example of Theseus, we see that the return of the ephebes threatens society with anarchy.

If society is to continue, the young men will have to become citizens, warriors, and husbands. They have not yet reached this stage, so they are looked upon in a negative light, as outsiders, bandits, and seducers. To be accepted into society and be looked upon in a favorable light, they must pass through that neutral state, that period of nonexistence which is their initiation. The myth of autochthony tries to bridge this gap in their lives by creating an illusion of continuity, by attributing a man's citizenship to his birth from the soil, and by overlooking the long period in which his status is quite ambiguous, in which he is neither a citizen nor a foreigner. This uncertainty about his status becomes a serious problem when an Athenian boy reaches the age of majority, for up till now it has been taken for granted that he is a potential Athenian, but at the age of eighteen he will have to prove this. He can no longer remain in the ambiguous position of a child who is provisionally accepted as an Athenian; he must be declared either a full Athenian citizen or a complete outsider. He must formally end his childhood by registering as a full member of his phratry at the Apatouria,[143] and then he must face the scrutiny of his deme. Under normal circumstances, he will be declared an Athenian citizen, but this is not always the case. The deme can declare that as far as Athenian law is concerned, he does not exist; he is a complete outsider who may even be reduced to slavery if he persists in his false claim to citizenship. Thus, he can change overnight from a potential citizen to a real slave. The marginality of the adolescent is not just a poetic fancy but a very serious legal reality.

The lack of continuity, the transfer of power and property to a new generation of young men who are regarded as strangers of uncertain status, gives rise to doubts and concerns that are explored through the myth of Theseus. Such myths enable the Athenians to come to terms with these problems, just as the anxiety of Aegeus in Bacchylides' poem will be overcome by the joy of meeting his long-lost son. The poem reflects the joy of the parents who will see their now-adult sons returning to the sound of the trumpet.[144] The repetition of rituals and of the myths that provide their aition has a calming effect, and the two were combined at the Oschophoria. The *Deipnophoroi*, the women who brought food to the young men taking part in the festival, used to tell them stories to reassure them.[145] These stories surely must have included the myth of Theseus himself, to explain that the ritual ordeal the young men underwent was simply a reenactment of the trials of Theseus and would end with the same success.[146] These myths, retold every year at the Oschophoria, reassured the young men and their parents that if their status as legitimate autochthonous sons and full Athenian citizens was now under question, they would soon be able to prove their *arete* as yet another generation of heroic Athenians.

Notes

1. "The attention given to the Heroic Age was a reflection of the alarming seriousness with which the early Greeks took it" (Snodgrass 1980, 68). He is speak-

ing of the Archaic Age in particular, but points out that the ritual of the Locrian Maidens, the most drastic case of this "alarming seriousness," survived beyond the Classical period.

2. Loraux 1986, 194.

3. "It is not only the aristocrats . . . who proudly claim this incomparable birth, this most ancient of origins, mythical in the strongest sense of the word, but all the citizens of the polis; all of them consider themselves to be theôn paîdes, sons of Gê and Hephaïstos, by virtue of their legendary heroïc filiations." (Bérard 1974, 35–36).

4. Loraux 1986, 193–194.

5. *Odyssey*, 1: 215.

6. Hesiod, *Theogony*, 603–607; Euripides, *Hippolytus*, 618–624; *Medea*, 573–575.

7. Hesiod, *Works and Days*, 235. Hesiod actually uses the phrase ἐοικότα τέκνα γονεῦσιν ("children resembling their *parents*"), but he means "children resembling their *fathers*." West comments on the phrase as follows: "the women bear children, and children of the most satisfactory kind, resembling their fathers and thus clearly legitimate" (West 1978, 215 note to 235).

8. ἐκ τῆς ὑγρᾶς τὸν ἄνθρωπον οὐσίας φῦναι δόξαντες (Plutarch, *Table-Talk*, Book 8, Q. 8, 730 e).

9. Ὠκεανόν τε θεῶν γένεσιν καὶ μητέρα Τηθύν (*Iliad* 14: 201 = *Iliad* 14: 302); Ὠκεανοῦ, ὅς περ γένεσις πάντεσσι τέτυκται (*Iliad* 14: 246).

10. Pythagoras thought fish were φίλοι and οἰκεῖοι (Plutarch, *Table-Talk*, Book 8, Q. 8, 729 e); the ancient Greeks (the Greeks before Plutarch's time) revered the fish as an animal that was ὁμογενῆ καὶ σύντροφον (Plutarch, *Table-Talk*, Book 8, Q. 8, 730 e).

11. Since human babies cannot survive on their own for many years, Anaximander concluded that the first men must have been born inside fish (Kirk and Raven 1971, 140–141).

12. Nilsson 1941, vol.1, p. 429.

13. Tod 1985, vol. 2, inscription 204, pp. 303–304.

14. Loraux 1986, 148.

15. Hesiod, *Theogony*, 117.

16. Détienne and Vernant 1974, 151–153 and 211.

17. Vernant 1985, 157.

18. Calame invents the word "autothalassie" (!) to describe the peculiar origins of Theseus in this poem (Calame 1990, 440).

19. The distinction between *pontos* and *pelagos* is a very important one in Greek thought (Détienne and Vernant 1974, 151–152).

20. The Greeks would have called this route a πόρος. The ability to traverse the Cretan Sea by such a familiar and reliable route is what makes it a πέλαγος as distinct from a dangerous and unknown πόντος (Détienne and Vernant 1974, 151–152).

21. Détienne and Vernant 1974, 151.

22. Gernet and Vernant have examined the evidence for the notion that a son

is born from the hearth. It is found in several myths as well as in the ceremony of the *Amphidromia* (Gernet 1982b, 286–287, and Vernant 1985, 164–165).

23. The Chorus quite correctly describe Cithaeron as his compatriot, nurse, and mother (Sophocles, *Oedipus Rex*, 1,089–1,090). Cithaeron welcomed him (Sophocles, *Oedipus Rex*, 1,391) just as the πόντιον ἄλσος welcomes Theseus.

24. Sourvinou-Inwood, from her examination of myths of matricide and patricide, concludes that "the hostility . . . originates with the parent" and that "if a father abandons and/or does not care for his son, disaster will follow" (Sourvinou-Inwood 1979, 17).

25. All of the literary versions of this myth agree in saying that Theseus did not meet Poseidon, and in Micon's painting of this episode in the Theseion Amphitrite appeared without her husband (Pausanias, 1: 17, 3). Poseidon does appear, however, on some vase paintings of Theseus' underwater visit. See Brommer 1982, 77–83.

26. Segal 1979, 29; Scodel 1984, 138.

27. Segal 1979, 23 and 32–33.

28. *Odyssey*, 4: 141ff.

29. *Odyssey*, 15: 123ff.

30. *Odyssey*, 15: 20ff.

31. As Segal remarks, "His narrative exploits an ancient mythical pattern . . ." (Segal 1979, 23).

32. Plutarch, *Life of Theseus*, 3.

33. Odysseus owes his restoration to the intelligence and loyalty of Penelope, Menelaus is quite dependent on Helen, and perhaps even Agamemnon had placed his hopes of survival in Cassandra.

34. *Odyssey*, 4: 230.

35. Plutarch, *Life of Theseus*, 12. She makes an identical promise in Euripides' *Medea* at lines 717–718: παύσω δέ σ' ὄντ' ἄπαιδα καὶ παίδων γονὰς / σπεῖραί σε θήσω· τοιάδ' οἶδα φάρμακα ("I shall end your being childless and I shall enable you to sow a crop of children: such are the drugs that I know").

36. Plutarch, *Life of Theseus*, 13.

37. Hesiod, *Theogony*, 600–607.

38. Euripides, *Aigeus*, fr. 4 *TGF*.

39. Apollo, presenting the orthodox view, declares that the mother is a ξένη, at Aeschylus, *Eumenides*, 660.

40. *Odyssey*, 15: 20–3.

41. Plato, *Menexenus* 238 a 4–5.

42. The exposition of a child is described in the following terms by Loraux: "This disavowal of legitimacy that the exposition of a new-born child constitutes, is above all a disavowal of paternity" (Loraux 1981b, 228). As for the naming of the child, "the name is the father's business" (Loraux 1981b, 202).

43. Plutarch, *Life of Theseus*, 4.

44. Euripides, *Ion*, 661ff.

45. Lévi-Strauss 1958, 236–239.

46. Lévi-Strauss 1958, 239.

47. Bacchylides, 17: 35–36, 58ff., 77ff., 99–100, and 109.

48. *Iliad*, 3: 144.

49. Vernant 1985, 178.

50. Perhaps we should take θεῶν to be a contraction of θεάων from θεά, "goddess," in which case we should translate the phrases as "*megaron* of the goddesses" and "gifts of the goddesses." The Greek is ambiguous, however, and I think that Bacchylides wants us to assume he is referring to male gods, and then to surprise us by bringing on Amphitrite and the Nereids.

51. Loraux 1981b, 225–256. Loraux is, of course, comparing Erechtheus with Ion, but the comparison applies equally well to Theseus.

52. Contrast Odysseus, who is saved from the sea by the veil of Ino-Leucothea (*Odyssey*, 5: 346–353). See Vox 1983, 93–94.

53. Vernant 1985, 164.

54. Plato, *Republic*, 558 c.

55. Ibid., 587 c.

56. Détienne and Vernant 1974, 25–28.

57. Ibid., 301–303.

58. Thucydides 1: 138, 3.

59. Détienne and Vernant 1974, 282–285.

60. Thucydides refers to Minoan Crete as the first great naval power in Greece (1: 4) and democratic Athens as the last and greatest of all time (1: 18, 2–3).

61. Hesiod, *Theogony*, 385–388. Their complete obedience to Zeus is brutally presented in the prologue of the *Prometheus Bound*.

62. Détienne and Vernant 1974, 102–103 an 106–107.

63. This is what distinguishes the victory of Zeus from that of Kronos over his father and ensures that the reign of Zeus will be permanent (Détienne and Vernant 1974, 100–102).

64. Μῆτιν ὑφαίνειν is the standard phrase in Homer (*Iliad* 7: 324, 9: 93; *Odyssey* 4: 678, 9: 422, 13: 303 and 386).

65. Détienne and Vernant 1974, 147–148 and 215–217.

66. Vox 1984a, 209.

67. Jacoby, *FGrH*, 3 (Pherecydes) fr. 150.

68. Aristophanes, *Acharnanians* 161–162.

69. I do not wish to imply that Bacchylides is a supporter of Themistocles, or indeed that he had any opinions on Athenian politics. Vox sees him as an opponent of the Athenian leader (Vox 1984b, 118–119). Barron, who believes our two dithyrambs honor Cimon, would doubtless agree with him (Barron 1980, 1–3).

70. The skillful nature of naval warfare, which can be learned by anyone whatsoever, was felt to be opposed to spirit of hoplite warfare, which supposedly required more aristocratic virtues. See Vidal-Naquet 1981, 138–139 and 142–143; Loraux 1986, 151 and 212.

71. The word *ephebe* is unfortunately ambiguous. It can mean either a young man on the verge of manhood (somewhere between sixteen and twenty years old) or a young man between the ages of eighteen and twenty who is being trained as a soldier. I distinguish between them by using a lower case *e* for the former, and

an upper case *E* for the latter. Often my arguments will apply to both, because the initiation of the Ephebes into the military world is a later (fourth century B.C., at the latest) and secularized instance of the initiation of ephebes into the adult world.

72. van Gennep 1909, 108.

73. Jeanmaire 1939, 245.

74. Calame 1990, 373.

75. "Mythology, which is rich in such distinctive initiation motifs as the exposure or sacrifice of children, seclusion in the wilderness and struggles with a dragon, seems to refer to older institutions" (Burkert 1985, 261).

76. Initiation and trickery were closely associated in Greek thought (Vidal-Naquet 1981, 157–160).

77. Plutarch, *Life of Theseus*, 3, 7.

78. διηπάτησε, Plutarch, *Life of Theseus*, 3, 5.

79. The Greeks (incorrectly) derived this epithet of the goddess from the word *apate* (Vidal-Naquet 1981, 157–158).

80. Pausanias, 2: 33, 1.

81. Hesiod, *Theogony*, 205.

82. See Calame 1990, 193.

83. In earlier works he is often shown with a beard, but it disappears at the end of the sixth century B.C. (Brommer 1982, 144).

84. Foley 1985, 174–175.

85. The ambiguity of this adjective, πρώθηβον ("at the start of youth"), can be seen from the fact that it is used to qualify both παῖς ("boy") and κοῦρος ("young man") in Homer (at *Iliad*, 8: 518 and *Odyssey* 8: 263, respectively).

86. Aristotle, *Constitution of the Athenians*, 42, 4–5. If the Ephebe system had not been set up by the time Bacchylides wrote his poem, we must assume that a cloak and spear were typical accoutrements of young men, and were later adopted as the official "uniform" of the Ephebes for this reason.

87. "Aegeus, not recognizing his own son and being afraid of him, sent him against the Marathonian Bull" (Apollodoros, *Epitome*, 1: 5). "Aegeus did not recognize him, being rather an old man and frightened of everything on account of the civil unrest" (Plutarch, *Life of Theseus*, 12).

88. Pindar, *Pythians*, 4, 97.

89. Ibid., 86.

90. Aegeus attempts to get rid of him by poisoning him (Plutarch, *Life of Theseus*, 12) or sending him against the Marathonian Bull (Apollodoros, *Epitome*, 1: 5).

91. Calame 1990, 122.

92. Ibid., 256.

93. van Gennep 1909, 156.

94. Brelich has studied the similarities between Theseus and the bandits he defeats, and makes the following comment on their deaths at the hands of Theseus: "It is not just in the case of Romulus that we have to deal with the murder of a brother" (Brelich 1956, 136). There is certainly a kindred spirit between the hero and the brigands, but I think that in the case of Skiron, at least, the story is rather modeled on the father-son relationship than on that between two brothers.

95. τῷ Μενεσθεῖ χαριζόμενος (Plutarch, *Life of Theseus*, 35). Brelich notes the connection between Theseus' death and that of Skiron: "He concludes his earthly existence with the same type of death that he had made Skiron undergo" (Brelich 1956, 139).

96. Needless to say, the new generation will one day find themselves in the same position of resented authority, and it is ironic that Dodds, who explored these tensions within the Greek family, should have used Theseus as an example of a threatened member of the older generation! (Dodds 1951, 45–47).

97. Jeanmaire 1939, 364.

98. van Gennep 1909, 122.

99. Τηλεμάχοιο πατήρ (*Iliad* 2: 260 and 4: 354). In both these passages, the status of Odysseus has been threatened just before he speaks these words. In the first he feels himself insulted by someone below him, Thersites, and in the second, by his commander, Agamemnon. In calling himself Τηλεμάχοιο πατήρ he is proudly asserting his right to be respected, that he is not simply an "old man" but also the "father of somebody."

100. Aristophanes, *Wasps*, 67–70.

101. Philocleon, "the old master" (*Wasps*, 442), is now so completely powerless that he "can represent himself as being a child not yet of age to perform legal acts" (Lacey 1968, 128).

102. Vidal-Naquet 1981, 154–155.

103. Pindar, *Pythians*, 4: 138.

104. Pindar, *Pythians*, 4: 140–144.

105. Two servants accompany him (46), but they do not count; he can still be described as "*alone* with two servants" (μοῦνον σὺν ὀπάοσιν, 35).

106. It is uncertain whether this practice of civic initiation and military training, as described by Aristotle (*Constitution of the Athenians*, 42, 2–5), was introduced before the fourth century.

107. Calame suggests that it was the proximity of the Oschophoria to the Theseia in the calendar that led to the former festival's being associated with the myth of Theseus (Calame 1990, 447). He believes that the festival was "resemantized" during the period of the Persian Wars (Calame 1990, 448).

108. Parke 1977, 77; Simon 1983, 89.

109. Plutarch, *Life of Theseus*, 23.

110. Ibid., 22.

111. Proclus 322 a 27; Athenaeus 11: 495.

112. Pélékidis believes that the Ephebes participated, but unfortunately there is no epigraphical evidence for this (Pélékidis 1962, 226).

113. Parke 1977, 79. Simon follows Deubner in making it a festival of Dionysus (Simon 1983, 91). Both Athena Skiras and Dionysus are involved in the Oschophoria, and I do not wish to decide which of them is the more important for this festival. I focus on the role of Athena Skiras because she happens to be more significant for my purposes, not because she was necessarily the primary deity of the Oschophoria.

114. Modern scholars explain the title Skiras as meaning "Gypsum or Lime Goddess" (Kock, *RE*, vol. III A, col. 535. See Jacoby, *FGrH*, note 77 to 328

Philochoros fr. 14–16, 202; Burkert 1985, 230 and 439, note 24). Her importance would therefore have derived from the use of lime as a fertilizer, but as far as the myth of Theseus is concerned, the fact that she is a foreign goddess who protects the borders of the city is of greater significance. See Calame 1990, 361–362.

115. Pollux, 9: 96; Eustathius on *Odyssey* 1: 107. Other references at *RE* vol. IIIA, cols. 534–535.

116. Plutarch, *Life of Theseus*, 12.

117. Plutarch, *Marriage Precepts*, 114 a–b. See Calame 1990, 343.

118. Burkert 1985, 230; Calame, 341–343.

119. Proclus 322 a 14–15 and 22–24; Plutarch, *Life of Theseus*, 23.

120. Vidal-Naquet 1981, 167–169; Walter Burkert 1985, 258–259 and 261. Calame believes that it is merely a Dionysiac element (Calame 1990, 335).

121. Pausanias, 1: 19, 1. See Calame 1990, 187.

122. Scholiast to *Iliad* 9: 668, Apollodorus, 3: 13, 8.

123. Parke 1977, 77; Claude Calame 1990, 324.

124. Vidal-Naquet 1981, 167.

125. Calame argues that the Oschophoria have nothing to do with initiation, since Phaleron is within the city limits, so no real departure or return takes place (Calame 1990, 335). Phaleron is, however, as close as one can get to the sea, without actually performing the festival under water! (This is not as absurd as it might seem. Anthropologists have found cases of initiatory dives, and some have felt that such a practice might lie behind the myth of Bacchylides' Poem 17).

126. Plutarch, *Life of Theseus*, 4.

127. Plutarch describes all three events as simultaneous: at the Oschophoria Theseus commemorated his return as a warrior and the death of his father, while at the same time he established his own hero-cult! (Plutarch, *Life of Theseus*, 23).

128. Pélékidis argues that the festival was organized like the Panathenaia, with Greater Theseia being celebrated every four years and Lesser Theseia taking place annually. The Greater Theseia might have been introduced after Athens regained Scyros in 166 B.C. (Pélékidis 1962, 229–230). He believes that the athletic events would only have taken place at the Greater Theseia (Pélékidis 1962, 230–231), but torch races and military reviews occurred with such frequency at the Theseia that these events cannot be limited to the hypothetical Greater Theseia.

129. Vidal-Naquet 1981, 152. Speaking more generally, Burkert notes that "tribal initiations tend to be preserved only in relics," but he points out that they are remembered in myth and that marginal situations remain important in ritual (Burkert 1985, 261).

130. van Gennep 1909, 161.

131. Pindar, *Pythians*, 4, 72.

132. Vidal-Naquet 1981, 160.

133. Ibid., 162.

134. Finley 1986, 165.

135. This seductiveness associated with the panther is not a trait of adult men, but it is characteristic of women and of the effeminate Adonis (Détienne 1977, 96–98).

136. Plutarch, *Life of Theseus*, 29.

137. Dumézil 1979, 25.

138. Ibid., 31–45.

139. Ibid., 82.

140. Plutarch, *Life of Theseus*, 26–29. If Periboia and Phereboia are the same person, the ratio would increase to five out of nine.

141. Dumézil 1979, 81.

142. μὴ καλὴν γενέσθαι μηδὲ πρέπουσαν (Plutarch, *Life of Theseus*, 29).

143. It was probably at this earlier stage that tribal initiation would have taken place, but in Classical Athens it is reduced to a religious formality. The military Ephebeia bears some similarities to the ordeals that would have preceded tribal initiation, but it occurs after the young men have been enrolled as full citizens. Relying on a study by Labarbe, Vidal-Naquet argues that the expression ἐπὶ διετὲς ἡβῆσαι ("to have been a youth for two years"), which refers to the Ephebeia itself, points to an earlier, tribal initiation, which would have taken place at the age of sixteen, and that the *Koureion* sacrifice at the Apatouria is a relic of this primitive initiation (Vidal-Naquet 1981, 155).

144. Merkelbach 1973, 62.

145. Plutarch, *Life of Theseus*, 23, 3.

146. Jeanmaire 1939, 371–373; Parke 1977, 78.

4

The Hero-King

Euripides' *Hippolytus*: Exorcising the Ghost of Monarchy

A considerable portion of the myth of Theseus is devoted to his image as a youth on the verge of manhood, someone who has yet to prove himself as a hero, but the death of his father makes him the king of Athens. As a young ephebe, he is ipso facto a marginal figure, but even when he is presented as a mature hero, Athenian myth must come to terms with the incongruity of having a king in a polis, especially in the eternally democratic polis of Athens. Even as an adult hero, he is still an anomalous figure who can only with considerable difficulty be integrated into the world of the polis.

One solution to this problem was to declare that Theseus was a democrat and thus distort his representation to suit the nature of his city, but this made him a very peculiar character who was both a king and a democrat. From the many plays that survive dealing with the myth of Theseus, it is clear that Euripides was intrigued by this contradiction in the Athenian hero. It is, however, the archaic Theseus, the one known only for his affairs with heroines and his battles against monsters and bandits, that is presented to us in the *Hippolytus*.[1] Theseus himself swears on his reputation as the killer of Sinis, Skiron, and the other bandits of the Saronic Gulf (976–980), and there is no trace in the *Hippolytus* of Theseus the democrat. When Hippolytus refers to Athenian "monarchy" (1015), he means neither more nor less than "tyranny," as he himself makes clear at 1013 and 1020, and yet, in a later play by Euripides, the *Suppliant Women*, we shall find Theseus himself vigorously denying the existence of monarchy in Athens. The opposition between these two aspects of Theseus' character, the democratic and autocratic, is one that is essential to this hero in Greek myth.

113

Plutarch, who depicts the democratic Theseus in chapter 24 of his biography,[2] presents us with quite a different personality in the following chapter. This other Theseus is afraid of a democracy that is not "mixed," and he grants his subjects only a semblance of equality.[3] So he sets up three classes, giving special privileges to the aristocrats, the *Eupatridai*.[4] This autocratic Theseus is the one we see in the *Hippolytus*, and he is called *eupatrides* twice in the play (151 and 1283). Outside this play, the title *eupatrides* is applied to a mortal only twice in the extant works of Euripides. It is used first in the *Alcestis*, where the married couple, Admetus and Alcestis, are called *eupatridai*.[5] This usage is quite a natural one, since they are the king and queen of Pherae. It is of no great importance for Athenian notions of *eupatridai*, but the second occurrence is. This time, the word *eupatrides* appears in the *Ion*, where we are told that Creusa, because she is born of a Eupatrid family (or rather *the* Eupatrid family, since the Chorus are referring to the Athenian royal family), will not bear to see an outsider in control of her patrimony, which is Athens itself.[6] The *Ion* is one of our major sources for the Athenian myth of autochthony, and this birth from the earth is, as we have seen, shared by all Athenians.[7] So went the democratic myth, but there were other versions of this myth that restricted the privilege of being a real Athenian to the small group of old families, the Eupatrids.[8] Only such a nobleman could claim that he was autochthonous, that his ancestors were of heroic stature, that he himself was, therefore, a true Athenian. Athenian democracy extended these aristocratic notions to all citizens, so that all Athenians were autochthonous, and all could thus look upon Theseus as their mythical archetype. The other Theseus is always there in the background, however, Theseus the Eupatrid, who cannot so easily conform to the world of the democratic city. In the *Hippolytus*, Euripides brings him into the foreground.

In this play, we find that Theseus is specially privileged in his relationship to the gods, as is his son. Theseus is, however, a little too confident in his assurance about what this proximity to the gods entitles him to, and he makes the same false assumptions that we shall notice in the later *Suppliant Women*. In the later play, tragedy is avoided because he listens to and is reformed by his mother's advice, but in the *Hippolytus*, he follows his principles to the end and is destroyed by their rigidity. After Theseus has cursed his son by appealing to Poseidon as his father, and sworn to see him punished by appealing to his own reputation as a slayer of bandits, the Chorus lament that human good fortune is nonexistent. Just as Aethra will do in the later play, they explain this by saying, "his previous fortune has been overthrown" (τὰ γὰρ δὴ πρῶτ' ἀνέστραπται πάλιν, 982).[9] By using his former courage to destroy his innocent and, under the circumstances, helpless son, by appealing to Poseidon as his father to help him murder his own son, Theseus is himself undoing all his previous glory (τὰ πρῶτα, 982). In this ironic and tragic case, it is not a jealous intervention by the gods that makes Theseus see the fragility of his success; he has called them in himself and is the author of his own punishment.

Theseus is, in short, abusing his privileges as a *eupatrides*, but he will learn that his claim to those privileges was dubious in the first place. Throughout the play Theseus often uses the expression "Father Poseidon," but he is also spoken of as the son of Aegeus.[10] Theseus himself does not seem to be quite sure about his paternity, but for him, the ambiguity is resolved when he hears that his curse has taken effect and that his son has been killed: "So you really were my father after all!" (1169–1170). The description of the accident of Hippolytus by the Messenger reveals the location where the curse was fulfilled. Places recalling the former victories of Theseus against the bandits who plagued the Saronic Gulf form the background to the death of his son. Theseus had called on Isthmian Sinis (977) and the Skironian Rocks (979–980) to witness his curse against his son. The giant wave concealing the monster that kills Hippolytus appears in this very region and blocks from view the Skironian Cliffs (1208) and the Isthmus (1209). It also hides the Rock of Asclepius (1209), and as we see in the *Suppliant Women* (714), Epidaurus was another major location in Theseus' first journey to Athens, and the "Epidaurian weapon," a club, was his characteristic weapon. The monster appearing from the wave is itself a bull (1214), twice the opponent of Theseus (Bull of Marathon, Minotaur). For Theseus, therefore, his former achievements and his divine birth join together to punish his son, as he had hoped they would (895–898; see 973–980).

Theseus, however, has gone too far. If the *Hippolytus* is the tragedy of a young man who presumed too much on the friendship of Artemis and thought he could neglect and even insult Aphrodite, it is also the tragedy of Theseus, who presumed too much on his affinity with the gods and on his own knowledge. The fatal similarity between father and son is brought up in the play at the point where they are most opposed to each other, where Theseus has already cursed his son and ensured his death. When, at this point in the play, Theseus accuses young men of licentious behavior (967–970), we must agree with Grube that he ought to know, if anybody does.[11] Indeed, when he is first mentioned in the play (apart from Aphrodite's reference to him in the Prologue), he is spoken of as a philanderer.[12] Ironically, this is also the first time that he is called *eupatrides*, so his claims to moral superiority are belied at the very moment he is granted by others the title on which those claims are based. His belief that he has a special relationship with the divine world, though he mocks the claims of Hippolytus to any such privileges (948–949), are undermined by his impi-

ety in scoffing at the omens sent by the gods (1059), and we shall see that
the gods do not forget this insult (see lines 1321–1322). In dismissing such
signs, he uses the exact same expression that Hippolytus had done in rejecting Aphrodite, "I bid them a hearty farewell!" (πόλλ' ἐγὼ χαίρειν λέγω,
1059).[13]

Theseus begins to suspect his mistake even before Artemis appears and
explains everything. He is ashamed of what he has done both before the
gods and before his son (1258–1259). He has already lost his confidence
that he was privy to what the gods might judge right or wrong, he has lost
his assurance that they would agree with his decision. He is already beginning to suspect that the three wishes were merely a gift, and that the fulfill-
ment of the first told more about Poseidon's sense of duty in adhering to
his promises than it did about the merits of Theseus himself or of his request.
As Artemis remarks, "[Poseidon] granted what he had to, since he had given
his word" (1321). The pronouncing of the curse against his son is not, however, the only way in which Theseus has risked the anger of the gods. When
he curses Hippolytus, he is appealing to his reputation in the sphere of battle
to punish his son for an offense in the sexual realm, the sort of offense from
which he himself, of course, had hardly abstained. This reputation of
Theseus as a warrior is not without blemish itself, for the *miasma* (pollution) of which he accuses Hippolytus in the sexual realm (946) is matched
by the *miasma* of which he himself is guilty as a warrior (the *miasma* of
the murder of the Pallantids, 35). Both these types of pollution are caused
by transgressions that are almost identical in nature. The polluted man has
wrongfully turned his power against members of his own family, Hippolytus
by seducing his stepmother, Theseus by killing his own cousins, with the
important difference, of course, that Theseus' offense is a very real one,
whereas that of Hippolytus exists in the mind of his father alone.

When Artemis suddenly appears on the stage, she shatters all the proud
illusions of Theseus. In the very first words that she speaks to him, she
addresses him as the son of his mortal father, Aegeus, not of Poseidon
(1282–1283), and she follows this immediately afterward by denouncing
him for impiously murdering his own son, Hippolytus.[14] She is making it
quite clear to him that he is no more than an ordinary mortal, and indeed
something less than that. His presumption that he was close to the gods
was as unjustified as his enmity toward his son. Artemis shows up the noble
Theseus for what he really is. She is being quite sarcastic when she calls
him *eupatrides*, for it is a title to which he has no claim; she on the other
hand is a genuine *eupatrides* (literally, "the offspring of a noble father")
since she dwells in the noble palace (εὐπατέρειαν αὐλάν, 68–69) of her
father Zeus. Theseus' pretensions become contemptible in the presence of
this goddess; he is not a noble man, he cannot even claim a place among

good men (1294–1295). Poseidon and Artemis are both angry with him for not using the curses against an enemy (1317), and for not appealing to seers (1321; see 1059). The way in which the two gods are paired in her speech (1320) contrasts their realm with that of mere mortals, of whom Theseus is at this point a particularly despicable example. Even if a temporary aberration of the god may happen to have made Theseus his son, Theseus remains no more than a human being, and he has no special claim to the approval of Poseidon or of any other god. When it comes to such moral issues, the gods are united in condemning those who do wrong (1339–1341).

The limitations of human knowledge and the fragile nature of any contact between man and the divine are not the only themes of the play; they would, in fact, leave a lot unexplained. In the third stasimon, the Chorus of Hunters indicate that there is much more than this to the sufferings of Hippolytus. They contrast normal human ignorance with the completely inexplicable nature of the extraordinary events they are witnessing. They sing of their faith in the gods; they have always believed that the gods play an active role in human affairs (1104–1105), although things that happen in the world have sometimes left them a little doubtful (1106). The fate of Hippolytus, on the other hand, is of a completely different order. It makes them doubt their own sanity (1190) and dashes their expectations (1120).[15] The Chorus of Hunters restrict themselves to such doubts and questionings, but the Chorus of Trozenian women go even further. This time, as far as they are concerned, the gods have gone beyond negligence. In a magnificent act of defiance, the women appropriate the awful anger that the gods unleash against mankind, the *menis* of the gods, and turn it against those very gods themselves: there is a world of human pride in those two words they cry out, μανίω θεοῖσιν ("I am filled with *menis* against the gods!"; 1146).

The Sins of the Father, the Sins of the Son

Hippolytus and Artemis conclude, rather calmly, that Aphrodite has destroyed Hippolytus himself, Phaedra, and Theseus (1404–1405), and they seem none too surprised at her outrageous revenge. We have known about the fate of the first two ever since the Prologue. Aphrodite must avenge herself on Hippolytus, even if this will entail the death of the innocent Phaedra, but she forgets that she will also be punishing Theseus. We are told why Phaedra must fall in love with her stepson, reveal this love to him, and die; we are not told why Theseus must murder his own son, or why he gets away with it so lightly. Phaedra had some kind of nobility to her (1300–1301), as Artemis is careful to point out to Theseus, but Theseus himself is most evil (1316), he will never be included among good men (1295–1296). Unlike Phaedra, he is not an innocent victim. Nothing can be learned from Phaedra's death; it is simply a regrettable side-effect of Aphrodite's revenge. Phaedra is swallowed up in the destruction of two men, Theseus and Hippolytus. Aphrodite herself acknowledges that Phaedra is innocent (47); Hippolytus (1034) and Artemis (1300–1301) absolve her of all guilt. The two men, on the other hand, are punished because their characters are flawed; Theseus and Hippolytus have committed offenses that are the opposite of each other, but their behavior is equally distant from and contrary to the normal order of things.

Hippolytus is practically an anti-Theseus, and between them lies the world of the polis, which each of them ignores in his own way. Theseus exceeds the status of a citizen, Hippolytus never quite attains it. He remains an adolescent forever, and never gets to practice warfare or to marry, the marks of the normal adult citizen. He spends his time in the "green wood" in the company of Artemis (17), away from his fellow men. The meadows he frequents are, to use his own expression, "undefiled" (73 and 76) by civilization. There is no agriculture and no stock-raising in his world (75–76); it is inhabited only by the wild animals he hunts (18). There was a legitimate place for hunting in the life of a normal adult, but with Hippolytus the sport becomes unusual. He practises it all the time (17), and if we can believe Theseus (952), he disdains to eat what he has caught. His hunting is as pointless and as all-consuming as that of Orion in the underworld, and it reflects the futility of his refusal to leave adolescence. Such occupations are contrasted, implicitly, with the more manly deeds of his father. Aphrodite tells us that Hippolytus "gets rid of wild animals from the land" (18), but there is a touch of mock-epic in what she says. The word she uses to characterize his activity is *exairein*, one which in this sense is used to describe the great fights of civilizing heroes against monsters.[16] These monsters are not, of course, the sort of animals that could be defeated with a little pack of swift hounds (18), such as Hippolytus possesses. They belong to the world of heroes, the primitive men who existed before the polis, who are too powerful and violent for the city-state. Hippolytus' actions, on the other hand, are completely ineffective; they lack all seriousness, his life-style is childish. Theseus is not so ridiculously wrong, therefore, when he mocks Hippolytus by calling him a Bacchant (954), an adherent of the religion that rejects the life of the polis, whose members neglect their duties and run off into the mountains, the region beyond the polis, the wilderness that Hippolytus prefers to live in. Like the Bacchants, Hippolytus wishes to remain with his select group of friends, and speak to them alone.[17] He knows quite well that he stands outside the polis, and is happy with this status.

The world Hippolytus has chosen to live in puts him beyond the pale of civilization. As far as the Messenger is concerned, these regions are the very limits of Trozen (1159),[18] the *eschaton* of Attica, as Phaedra herself says (372–373). In tribal society and in the relics of it that survive in myth, the *eschatia*, on the frontier of the polis, is where the young men are initiated; Hippolytus never leaves it, he never reaches manhood, and so he remains outside the polis. To remain an adolescent (ἐγκαθηβᾶν) is, for him, a way of achieving true happiness (εὐδαιμονία, 1096). He wishes his life to be frozen at this point and never to change, so that he may remain an adolescent forever (87). His celibacy and his friendship with Artemis are part of the same outlook. This wish is a perfectly natural one. The Chorus of Sophocles' *Oedipus at Colonus* share his view that happiness is only possible in youth, if at all on this earth (*Oedipus at Colonus* 1229–1238), and the Chorus in the *Hippolytus* itself indulge in similar daydreams. Faced with the incomprehensibility of life, they pray for a spirit "undefiled" by sorrows (*Hippolytus*, 1114), but the adjective they choose to describe such a spirit (ἀκήρατον, "undefiled") is used elsewhere in this play only by or of Hippolytus. Such divine purity from misfortune as Artemis enjoys may be unattainable, but it is certainly not undesirable, even in the eyes of those models of conformity, the Chorus. Similarly, the "easy" ways that change with the hour (1116), which the Chorus can only dream of but which Hippolytus actually tries to imitate, are once again the ways of the gods.[19] The last words of Hippolytus to Artemis make this quite clear: "You easily leave a long friendship" (1441). He says these words without any bitterness; they are, rather, a mark of his admiration (note "blessed virgin" in the preceding line) and a statement of his own loyalty to her (see 1442–1443).

For Hippolytus, however, the purity of his life lies above all else in his having no "contact" with sex; he is "untouched" (1002), he is "pure of intercourse" (1003). When Theseus mocks his claims to purity, Euripides makes him use precisely the same word that Hippolytus had in describing his "undefiled" meadows (ἀκήρατος, 949). For Hippolytus, "undefiled" means "chaste." He does not, however, pursue this virtue in a rational way, nor does he adhere to it because such behavior is required by society.[20] His chastity is, rather, "a matter of temperament."[21] It is, as Arbogast Schmitt has pointed out, a violent passion with him, and rather than being passionless and rational, he is in fact dominated by his peculiar passion to such an extent that it gives him an artificial appearance of freedom from all other ones.[22] Hippolytus' behavior is once again marked by a deliberate perversity.

For the Greeks, to have experienced marriage and warfare are the marks of an adult male and a full citizen, just as sacrifice and the eating of meat are what define man's position against that of the gods. Hippolytus chooses chastity and hunting instead, and dwells far from the polis. His alleged refusal to eat meat would be perfectly in keeping with his fastidious character.[23] In his pursuit of purity and of the happiness of unending youth, he is trying to emulate the existence of the gods, and denying his status as a mortal. He deliberately stays behind in the temporary phase of adolescence, a stance that allows him to escape from the realities of adult life and once again to imitate the eternal youth of the gods. He is, Aphrodite tells us, the *only* mortal who refuses to yield to her ways (μόνος, 12); but before we condemn him completely, we must remember that he is also the *only* mortal who is allowed to accompany Artemis and speak with her (μόνῳ, 84).

Hippolytus is not, however, the only man in the play who stands outside the polis and enjoys a special relationship with the gods. If the privilege (γέρας, 84) of being the companion of Artemis is a special one granted to him, it is matched by the privilege (γέρας, 45) that Poseidon gave to Theseus. Hippolytus is an outsider by his own free choice, since he has refused to advance to the level of citizenship, but Theseus is likewise an outsider, though for quite different reasons. He is too great to be a proper citizen, he is too much of a warrior, and the city cannot contain his fury.[24] His violence has turned against his own kin, he is tainted with *miasma*; he must, therefore, for the benefit of all, be expelled from the city (37), if only for a year. His special connection with Poseidon is actually a threat to the city also, and this threat is carried out in the play. He has come to Trozen to free himself from blood-guilt, but his semidivine wrath will lead him into even greater *miasma* by the end of the action. Hippolytus exerts his slight energies on ridding the land of its game (ἐξαιρεῖ χθονός, 18); Theseus will abuse the power he had exhibited in destroying monsters, and turn it against his own son (ἐξελῶ γῆς, 893). Theseus has to be broken if he is to be integrated to the polis, and by the end of the play, he is so overwhelmed by the sense of his *miasma*, as was Phaedra, that like her (401–402 and 723), he sees no outlet but death (1325, 1408, and 1410).

Undemocratic Language

In their use of language, the father and son are again similar, and belong to an older world than that of the polis. Hippolytus acts as an "exceptional" person (περισσός, 948), and as such he wants to put his behavior beyond discussion by ordinary people (ἔξω λόγου, 437). He is embarrassed at the thought that he must account for his actions in public (εἰς ὄχλον δοῦναι λόγον, 986), but such public discussion at an assembly of adult citizens is an essential feature of the polis.[25] Hippolytus would prefer to restrict his audience to a few friends of his own age group (987); he does not care to exercise his right to speak before an assembly. He disdains to do this because he regards himself as more intelligent (σοφώτερος, 987) and better educated. He does not have the superficial education of a public orator, trained only to speak (μουσικώτερος λέγειν, 989), but the truly superior education, the inspired wisdom (μουσικός in the literal sense of the word), that can only be appreciated by the wise (σοφοί, 988), not by a "mob" of citizens (παρ' ὄχλῳ, 989). Being such a person, he should only have to speak among those who share these merits, his spiritual equals. His language is more ancient than the dialogues of the polis, it is the "magico-religious language" of a poet inspired by the Muses, a speech whose truth can neither be doubted nor proved by lesser beings.[26]

Earlier in the play, there was considerable discussion on the nature of public and private speech. The Nurse had told Phaedra that her passion for Hippolytus was neither "exceptional" nor "beyond discussion" (περισσόν and ἔξω λόγου, 437), making it quite clear that if something is exceptional, it cannot be subjected to scrutiny by normal rational discourse. She was quite wrong, of course, in denying the extraordinary and private nature of Phaedra's suffering, but her contrast between rational discourse and the exceptional is still valid. Phaedra's passion is not a story for the general public (κοινὸς μῦθος, 609), nor a matter for discussion by the citizens (ἐν πολλοῖς λέγειν, 610). Because Phaedra's passion is exceptional in demonstrating the extraordinary power of Aphrodite, because Hippolytus is exceptional in completely denying Aphrodite's power over him, what they say should not be made public. The language of exceptional persons cannot be a story for the general public,[27] to be subjected to their deliberations during a public debate (κοινὸς λόγος). Their language is not suitable for an open assembly,[28] where one man speaks in public against another and may be refuted, where the final force of what one says lies in "the ratification of the social group" rather than in any power that lies in the spoken words themselves.[29] In short, their language is not that of the city; it is a secret one restricted to a small group. The Nurse carefully distinguishes between a public matter (ἔκφορος συμφορά, 295) that may be revealed to everyone, and a secret matter (τι τῶν ἀπορρήτων κακῶν, 293) that must only be revealed to other women, just as Hippolytus wanted to reveal his thoughts to his small group of friends alone (987). Both these special groups are excluded from the city, women completely, young men temporarily, but Hippolytus wants his exclusion to be permanent. His words are not for the polis and its "mob" (εἰς ὄχλον, 986), and he clearly looks upon his father as a demagogue who can no longer be clearly distinguished from his subjects. Hippolytus will neither rule them nor be one of them.

In answering his father's charges, Hippolytus also appeals to the power of his oath (1025–1030), and the Chorus beg Theseus to accept this

(1036–1037), but such "oaths that decide an issue by their religious force" are yet another case of the "magico-religious language" that belongs to the period before the appearance of the polis.[30] Theseus realizes exactly what forces Hippolytus has been appealing to and accuses him of being a magician and a spellmaker (γόης, ἐπῳδός, 1038). Theseus ought indeed to know, because he has just been casting spells against Hippolytus; he too has been appealing to a primitive language from an age that preceded the polis. He is obliged to deride the force of Hippolytus' words, because two forms of magic speech are being opposed to one another here; to acknowledge that Hippolytus was anything but a charlatan would be to admit the religious nature of his words. To admit this, however, would be to own defeat, because the important point about such language is not whether it is convincing, but whether it is powerful, whether it has magic force.[31] Theseus himself had spoken like an archaic king whose words are automatically efficacious, whose power is equal to that of a seer,[32] whose scepter is also a magic wand.[33] Hippolytus acknowledges that the curses of Theseus are "oracles" (χρησμοί, 1349), equal in power to the pronouncements of Artemis' brother, Apollo. Theseus attacks his son with one form of magico-religious language, he speaks with the divine voice of the king; Hippolytus answers him with other forms of this language, the poetic speech of one who is inspired by the Muses (988–989), and the religious ritual of the oath (1025–1031). What both of them would prefer to ignore, what Hippolytus finds distasteful (986) and what Theseus rejects (1055–1059; see 1322), is the language of political debate.[34] Such dialogue is the characteristic form of speech in the polis, and by leaving this form aside, they reveal once again that both of them are outside the city, that neither of them can participate in its communal life.

There are, however, hints that if Theseus belongs to this primitive world that existed before the polis, he stands at the end of this period, that the magic power of the king is beginning to wane. There is no doubt that his words took effect (1255), but this is to be the last manifestation of his power. He feels some shame at what he has done, and realizes that the gods may not be too pleased with him, that he does not really possess the power of efficacious language himself. He sees that there is a considerable gap between his words and their effects, on the one hand, and the truth and power possessed by the gods alone on the other. In this doubting mood, he decides to grant Hippolytus a belated investigation (ἔλεγχος), but it has a double nature, corresponding to his own confusion at this point. He is standing on the dividing line between semidivine monarchy and the polis. As a primitive king, there can be only one way of testing the truth of his own words. The only question to be asked is whether they were effective or not; they are to be measured by their results alone, by the response from the gods (δαιμόνων συμφοραῖς, 1267). He is, however, no longer sure of his semidivine power, or of the correctness of such a procedure, so he proposes in addition a completely different test, the only one recognized by the polis, an investigation through public discussion (λόγοις ἐλέγχειν, 1267).

Phaedra had understood the power of such an investigation, and was in fact very frightened of it (1310), so she escaped it by persuading Theseus with her false letter (ἔπεισέ σε, 1312; σὴν πεῖσαι φρένα, 1337). Persuasion (Πειθώ) is a major factor in the new language of public debate that comes into being with the city,[35] but Phaedra's persuasion is rather different. Her letter has been written in accordance with the plans of Aphrodite, and the very fact that it has been written by her hand convinces Theseus that he must follow whatever it says (προσσαίνουσί με, 863), even before he has any idea of what it might contain (856–859). Its persuasiveness lies not in the merits of what it may say, but rather in the power it will have over him as a letter from his wife. Her persuasion is, therefore, the archaic magico-religious persuasiveness that accompanies Aphrodite,[36] rather than that of a public speaker. The investigation she is trying to avoid is one in which she would have to face a refutation of her words by an opposing speaker in a public setting (λόγων ἐλέγχους, 1337). She does not try to defeat such an opponent through greater rhetorical persuasion; instead she tries to evade such a debate by using a different, magico-religious type of persuasion; she is using the power of Aphrodite. Thus she avoids the sort of public debate to which Theseus challenges Hippolytus half-heartedly and far too late (1267). Hippolytus and Theseus relied on the magic power of special types of language; they were both surpassed by the all-powerful persuasion that attaches to words inspired by Aphrodite. Ironically, Phaedra, who is the only one who has always been aware that they could have resorted to open dialogue, is also the one with the power to ensure that such a dialogue never takes place, the power to overcome both Hippolytus and Theseus in the type of speech that they themselves have chosen to use.

Had they chosen instead to use the public discussion of the polis, Theseus and Hippolytus could not have been destroyed by Aphrodite, but then there would have been no tragedy. Magico-religious speech is caught up in the world of the gods, and takes effect immediately in ways that do not lie within the control of the men who use it. The laicized language of the polis, on the other hand, is restricted to the world of human actions; it usually precedes such actions and is designed to prevent tragic happenings. The dialogue of the polis is by its very nature opposed to the powerful language of the tragic heroes: "The city, with its deliberative and executive organs functions . . . like an anti-tragic machine."[37] It is to this quieter world of the polis that Theseus must submit, a world to which Hippolytus had refused to conform.

At the beginning of the play, we hear that Theseus has probably been unfaithful to Phaedra. We never find out whether this is true or not, but both the Chorus (151–154) and the Nurse (320) take it for granted that he has, and that his misbehavior is the source of Phaedra's illness. Although it was more forgiveable for a Greek man to err in this respect than it was for his wife to do so, the lengths to which Theseus has carried such misbehavior are characteristic of a hero from an earlier age, like Heracles, or of a tyrant, a ruler who in effect reverts to such an earlier age, who returns to prepolitical times.[38] The polis does not approve of such multiple liaisons, especially if they are contracted with an outsider. Creousa, in Euripides' *Ion*, would rather die than allow Athens be ruled by a foreigner, and in saying this, she echoes the feelings of the average Athenian. Hippolytus, as the illegitimate offspring of Theseus, poses a real threat to the stability of Athens. Technically, he may be illegitimate (309), but he thinks like a true-born legitimate son (φρονοῦντα γνήσια, 309), and in the disorder of Theseus' many liaisons, this might be the factor that would prevail. Both Phaedra and her nurse have quite legitimate fears that this might prove to be the case (307–308, 314, 423, and 717), and they are rightly concerned about the future of her children.

Phaedra does not, however, want her sons to be like Theseus, to be lone heroes fighting monsters on the outskirts of the civilized world. She wants their future to lie in a postheroic world, within the structures of the polis (422). In fact, it would be difficult to guess from her words that Acamas and Demophon are to be kings and not just ordinary citizens in Athens. Phaedra postpones till the next generation what Euripides in the *Suppliant Women* will depict as happening in Theseus' own lifetime. Her sons will not be semidivine rulers whose words will possess some special power; they will be free men (421) and enjoy the privilege of free speech (422). All these hopes are threatened by Theseus, who belongs to the older world, and by Hippolytus, who because of Theseus' misbehavior has as much right to succeed him as her sons. Even if she were to die honorably, he might manage to do so, since her sons would be left behind as helpless young orphans (305–306). Hippolytus would thus become their master (308), and they would be reduced to slavery (424). If she were to die in disgrace, however, this would naturally increase his chances of succeeding to the throne. Her disgraceful death would become public, it would dishonor her sons, and it would probably render them ineligible as Theseus' heirs, for they must have an impeccable reputation to live in Athens (423 and 717). In her hopes that her children will enjoy the privileges of living in Athens, Phaedra proves to be a better Athenian and a better democrat than either her stepson or her husband.

I have concentrated on those aspects of Theseus' character that make him stand out as a hero king, remote from the everyday life of the polis.

This does not, of course, account for the richness of Euripides' portrayal, and it neglects many aspects of the character. In many ways, Theseus is a very domesticated, family man. When he discovers that something is wrong, he starts to worry about his old father and his children (794–796 and 799). When he learns that his wife has died, his reaction is very similar to that of the quite unheroic Admetus.[39] Euripides revealed this side of Theseus' character quite deliberately, for the murder of his son is all the more horrifying when seen against this calm background. It is as if all his heroic fury has to break out for one last time and be spent in a violent *katharsis*, before he can be tamed and absorbed into the new order of the polis. In effect, Euripides has constructed a tragedy based on the double nature of Theseus as both a hero king and a model Athenian. For the tragedy to reach a stable dénouement, the hero king must be exorcised, and we are left with a good citizen and family man. Artemis sees to it that the family is reunited in the end, and orders Theseus to embrace his son, and Hippolytus to forgive his father (1431–1436). If Artemis in the heat of the moment had denied Theseus any place among good men (1294–1295), the last words of Hippolytus before bidding farewell restore Theseus to the civilized world. He absolves Theseus of the blood-guilt he has fallen into (1448), and directs his attention to the legitimate children of his marriage with Phaedra (1455). The violent disorders of the tragedy end in the calm acceptance of the civic norms that Phaedra had desired for her sons.

The Hippolytus Veiled

Euripides' first version of the play, *Hippolytus Veiled*, does not seem to have dealt with the same themes. There is no trace of any civic concern in Phaedra or of any development in the character of Theseus, such as we have seen in the later *Hippolytus Crowned*. In fact, both of them seem to come from a more primitive world than their counterparts in the surviving play, and it seems that they stayed that way throughout the play. The major difference between the two plays lies in the characterization of Phaedra. In the *Hippolytus Crowned*, Phaedra has a strong civic spirit, although as a woman and a foreigner she can experience this attachment to Athens only through and because of her sons. It is her concern for the reputation of her sons and her hopes that they will be able to function as normal Athenian citizens (quite unlike Hippolytus or Theseus) that makes it so important for her to play the role of a proper Athenian woman, which is, of course, no role whatsoever. She will stay silent (*Hippolytus Crowned* 394) and not be spoken of (*Hippolytus Crowned* 403), even though this might entail her death.[40]

In the *Hippolytus Veiled* Phaedra is quite different.[41] Euripides used the play to "expose the shamelessness of women,"[42] and Aeschylus accuses

him in the *Frogs* of turning Phaedra into a whore.⁴³ She plays the part of
the Ancient Greek femme fatale to the full, and she even invokes the moon
in a magic charm, as does the woman in Theocritus' second *Idyll*.⁴⁴ The
only hint of such magic elements in the *Hippolytus Crowned*, and it is a
rather weak one, is the suicide note of Phaedra. This letter has been sanctioned in advance by Aphrodite, and it proves to be an irresistible charm.
Theseus feels its seductive effect before he opens the letter, and he was
doomed to be convinced by it even before it was written. In the *Hippolytus
Veiled*, the theme of magic seems to have played a considerable role, and
its presence in the play is part of an onslaught against women in general.
Thus, in a lyric passage, a woman says of her own sex that they are a fire
more difficult to fight against than a real one (*TGF*, fr. 429), a notion which
goes back to the misogynist remarks of Hesiod.⁴⁵ In another fragment (*TGF*,
fr. 430), it seems to be Phaedra who claims Eros as an excellent teacher of
rashness and daring,⁴⁶ and she says he is the "most difficult to fight against,"
recalling the expression used of women elsewhere in this play (*TGF*, fr.
429). As a result, Phaedra, who wins the sympathy of every audience in
the *Hippolytus Crowned*, is denounced severely in the *Hippolytus Veiled*.⁴⁷
At one point in the *Hippolytus Veiled* (*TGF*, fr. 440), a friend urges Theseus
never to believe a woman, even if she speaks the truth! In this play, Phaedra
was presented as a violator of all human decency, a model of female vil-
lainy. Her behavior would thus justify Greek misogyny and the exclusion
of women from civic life, and she clearly was not someone who could have
upheld the values of the polis.

Theseus himself is not much better. There are hints at his infidelity in
the *Hippolytus Crowned* (151–154 and 320), where it is suggested that this
might be responsible for Phaedra's illness. When it is discovered that she
herself is in love, those around her ignore the possibility that Theseus'
philandering has anything to do with her problems, and the question is not
raised again. Of course, it is always there in the background in the person
of Hippolytus and in the references to his illegitimacy. These allusions become more important as the play goes on, and they reach a climax at 1,083
where Hippolytus prays that the fate of being illegitimate may fall on none
of his friends, and Theseus responds by ordering his removal. In the
Hippolytus Veiled, on the other hand, the archaic nature of Theseus' character and his misbehavior are essential to the plot. His "wronging" of
Phaedra is the reason for her falling in love with Hippolytus,⁴⁸ and thus he
becomes responsible for the tragedy that results from her passion. The evils
that follow are not just brought on by the gods (θεήλατα, *TGF*, fr. 444,
line 2), as they were in the later play; they are also a direct result of the
natures of the main characters (ἔμφυτα, *TGF*, fr. 444, line 2).

The atmosphere of the whole play is therefore quite different from that of the *Hippolytus Crowned*, because Theseus and Phaedra are completely beyond the civilized order of the polis. They are more primitive and almost Cyclopean in character than their later counterparts, and they are driven by their basic desires; they are not complex people who happen to get caught up in a quarrel between two divinities. Their rough independence, their lack of concern for the gods and the laws of the city, come out at several points in the play. Thus (*TGF*, fr. 432), a male character is advised to act first, and then he can call on the gods if he wishes. Elsewhere (*TGF*, fr. 433), we are advised not to respect the law when in dire straits, but to do whatever is needed. But respect for the laws and the magistrates is essential for the survival of the polis, and it this type of subordination that marks the transition from the heroic ideal to that of the citizen. Finally, a speech (*TGF*, fr. 434) brushes piety aside and commends the use of effrontery and superior force as the only means to pursuing and achieving any human goals. The characters in the *Hippolytus Veiled* reject all the values of the polis, and they live in a much more brutal world. The *Hippolytus Crowned*, on the other hand, shows the transition from such a world, a world only lightly suggested so as to make its disappearance seem all the more natural, to the new world of the city-state.

This contrast between the two plays may be seen in the difference between the short anapaestic passages at the end of each one. In the *Hippolytus Veiled* (*TGF*, fr. 446), the youth is hailed as a hero, and the Chorus admire the honors he has received; they see him as exceptional among mortals (*TGF*, fr. 446, line 4). They consider him on a cosmic scale, as one who has advanced beyond ordinary mortals, and has gone nearer to the gods. There is no question of trying to make him fit into some political category. In the *Hippolytus Crowned*, on the other hand, the hero has, in death, been assimilated to the world of the polis, and the grief of Theseus, now also assimilated to this world, is joined by the tears of many others (*Hippolytus Crowned* 1464). This communal grief is felt by everyone in their capacity as citizens of Athens (πᾶσι πολίταις, *Hippolytus Crowned* 1462), and it is from the new world of the polis that Theseus and the Chorus bid farewell to his son.

Euripides' *Madness of Heracles*: An Old-fashioned Hero

Theseus, "Another Heracles"

Theseus plays a very different role in the *Madness of Heracles*; in this play he is the tame civic hero whom we saw at the very end of the *Hippolytus Crowned*. The development undergone by the main character in the *Madness of Heracles* is, however, remarkably similar to that of Theseus in the second *Hippolytus*. The Doric hero is brought around to the worldview of the Athenian ruler who makes his appearance at the end of the *Madness of Heracles*. The problem in each of these plays is that of integrating the hero into the polis. Heracles' labors are now a thing of the past, and it is difficult to see what function such heroic deeds could have in the polis.[49] The same is true of the deeds of Theseus, which in part were modeled on those of Heracles and in part derive from the same stratum of primitive myth. It might seem strange that we should compare these two heroes, since Theseus in Classical Athens was presented as a young man and deliberately contrasted with the more rugged Heracles. Euripides, however, was not particularly interested in this clichéd opposition between Dorian strength and Attic grace, but rather in the contrast between the contradictory images of Theseus. For him, the heroes bore a remarkable and disturbing resemblance to each other, and it comes out quite clearly in these two plays.

In each of the plays, we first hear of Theseus and Heracles as men who have performed a series of mighty labors, but are now coming toward the end of their careers. They have murdered a rival to the throne who threatened their own family, and they must be purified of this killing (*Hippolytus Crowned* 34–37; *Madness of Heracles* 922–930); but in each case, the process of purification is interrupted by the intervention of a goddess, Aphrodite in the case of Theseus, Hera in that of Heracles. This poses a considerable moral problem. The hero genuinely tries by ritual means to put an end to his former existence and become a normal member of the community once again. Euripides makes it perfectly clear that the hero has done everything possible to achieve this reintegration, and presents him as someone surprisingly quiet and domesticated.[50] Yet in each play, the gods intervene to turn him into the murderer of his own offspring. The pious act of integration becomes instead an opportunity for the gods to drive the hero into even greater pollution.

No real explanation for their suffering is offered, and even some gods are driven to condemn what has happened. Artemis criticizes the evil deeds (*Hippolytus Crowned* 1338) and plans (*Hippolytus Crowned* 1406; see *Hippolytus Crowned* 28) of Aphrodite, and Lyssa denounces the evil plans (*Madness of Heracles* 854) of Hera, which she herself will have to carry out. In Theseus' instance, the problem is resolved by divine intervention. Artemis appears as a dea ex machina, and there is a last-minute reconciliation with his dying son, who releases him from all blood-guilt. Heracles' situation is quite different. The normal myth does not present a Heracles who changes his ways; he dies, or achieves immortality, when he is burnt alive on the pyre on Mount Oeta, and this ending is a direct result of his own violent deeds. He remains the same type of hero till the end, and the termination of his earthly existence is as violent as the life he has led.

Euripides twists the legend to produce the same sort of dramatic structure and character development that he had unfolded in the *Hippolytus Crowned*. The murder of his wife and children is put at the end of Heracles' labors (1279), rather than at the beginning, so that it may become the climax of his violent deeds, instead of his immolation on Mount Oeta. Thus his remorse for what he has done may act as a *katharsis* of his violence, and it will be as effective as the flames that purify him in the normal version of the legend. Because this change takes place and Heracles himself rejects his heroic career, even to the point of asking himself whether he should discard his weapons (1378–1385), he can endure to go on living (1351).

Euripides still has to find a place for Heracles to end his days in, so he transports him to Athens, and Heracles changes from a Theban hero, a "problematic and aristocratic figure from the past,"[51] into a hero who can play an important role in the democratic city. There is no question of his being or becoming divine. When he dies he will go to Hades (1331), and he himself has deliberately rejected the fatherhood of Zeus (1265). He is reduced from a superman to mere humanity, but that change is presented as a great improvement on the old Heracles, just as the human friendship offered by Athens (1404–1405) is preferable to any relationship with the unreliable gods. Heracles refuses to acknowledge that he even knows who Zeus is (1263), and he cannot see how anyone could recognize Hera as a proper goddess (1307–1308). This rejection of divinity makes it impossible for the plot to be resolved by the appearance of a god at the end of the play. The gods have already appeared on the stage, in the persons of Iris and Lyssa, but only to destroy Heracles.

In the *Hippolytus Crowned*, the young hero may have committed an offence against a goddess, but divinity itself is never called into question as it is in the *Madness of Heracles*. When the Nurse exclaims that Aphrodite is not a goddess (*Hippolytus Crowned* 359), it is only to assert that she must be something greater still. What happens to Hippolytus arises in part because he finds it incompatible to serve both Aphrodite and Artemis, so it is not so surprising that Artemis should intervene at the end of the play on his behalf. In the *Madness of Heracles* such an apparition would make no sense whatsoever. None of the gods is prepared to do anything for Heracles; even his father, Zeus, will not intervene; Hera is given unlimited power to destroy him (1253). The entire Olympian system is being cast aside by Heracles; he wishes to have nothing to do with their divinity, even at the price of going to Hades and forfeiting his own immortality.

The play cannot end with a deus ex machina. This role is played instead by a mortal, Theseus, and the social bond between human beings replaces the claims of nobility to divine origins. The "yoke" of friendship between two mortals (ζεῦγος φίλιον, 1403) is modeled on the horizontal relationship of marriage. This is the model suggested by the word *yoke*, ζεῦγος, which is commonly used of marriage. Like marriage, friendship is social rather than natural, and it is a union that is chosen deliberately. It surpasses in importance the vertical line of descent, even if, as in the case of Heracles, this descent is a direct one from the king of the gods himself. When Heracles defies the gods at 1243, Theseus has to play the same calming role that Artemis does when she warns her dying favorite to be careful about what he says (*Hippolytus Crowned* 1416–1419). Theseus also argues against Heracles' condemnation of Hera, and does so in a speech that is based quite closely on the Nurse's speech to Phaedra in the earlier play. He tries to argue that Heracles' recent misfortunes are things that could have befallen anyone; no one, he claims, is "undefiled by fortune" (1314). This phrase recalls the tranquillity of the gods that the Chorus of the *Hippolytus* had dreamt of ("a life undefiled by sorrows," *Hippolytus Crowned* 1114), and that Hippolytus himself had hoped to achieve by living a life that was undefiled by human desires. Theseus, like Phaedra's nurse, says that such hopes are completely futile and that even the gods do not enjoy so peaceful an existence. Like her, he appeals to the authority of the poets ("the words of the poets," *Madness of Heracles* 1315; "the writings of previous generations" read by those who are "always among the Muses," *Hippolytus Crowned* 451–452). He points out in practically the same words that the gods put up with their misfortunes and continue to live on Olympus ("But yet they live / on Olympus and tolerate making mistakes," *Madness of Heracles* 1318–1319; "But yet they live in heaven / and, I imagine, tolerate being overcome by misfortune," *Hippolytus Crowned* 456–457). Such arguments are rather aristocratic in their emphasis on the closeness between humanity, or rather a small sector of the human race, and the gods. Euripides seems to enjoy placing such arguments in the mouth of the democratic Athenian and having them refuted by the hero of the oligarchic Dorians. It is as if Sparta were to acknowledge the moral victory of Athens and everything she stood for.[52]

A Farewell to Heroism

Heracles makes a remarkable answer to the speech of Theseus, in which he denies that the gods, if they were proper gods (ὀρθῶς θεούς, 1345), could commit adultery or other such offences, and he says that such stories are merely "wretched inventions of poets" (1346). His claim that the gods should be moral and his blaming the poets for misrepresenting them is similar to the theory of Xenophanes,[53] but there is an important difference between the philosopher's views and those of the tragic hero. Heracles knows only too well, and has said quite clearly only a few moments earlier, that Zeus is perfectly capable of seducing someone else's wife (1263–1264; 1308–1309) and that Hera would destroy someone who had never done her any wrong (1303–1310). He says they are immoral, but does not deny that they are gods or that they really exist. What he is saying here goes along with his earlier remarks about these two divinities, when he dismissed Zeus with the brusque phrase, "whoever he may be" (1263), and wondered how anyone could ever think of praying to a goddess like Hera (1307–1308). He acknowledges that the Olympians are gods, but they are gods who abuse their power and behave in a completely immoral way. They are not his kind of gods (1345), so he will have nothing further to do with them. A hero is semidivine, he enjoys a special proximity to the gods; Heracles chooses instead to distance himself from them and deny his heroic nature.

This is why Theseus' appeal to the Olympians is completely irrelevant to Heracles' problems (1340). We must not, however, cut off this part of Theseus' speech from its context and its rhetorical purpose. He is not a preacher. His aim, like that of the Nurse in the *Hippolytus Crowned*, is to offer Olympian consolation for earthly misfortunes, but he is really just as dismissive of the Olympians as Heracles himself. As Bond has remarked, Theseus' famous statement (at 1232) that Heracles as a mortal cannot be thought to pollute the gods "exhibits a new rationalistic spirit. . . . Such speculation . . . leaves little room for divinities who take offence."[54] The thought lying behind this statement is therefore exactly the same as that which lies behind Heracles' denunciation of the Olympians; and just as Heracles will choose human friendship above that of such gods, so Theseus justifies his ignoring the danger of pollution by denying that any such religious scruples should come between friends (1234).[55] Both Heracles and Theseus leave the world of the Olympians behind them and concentrate on human values instead.

The Olympians have only one characteristic that men might be tempted to envy: they have no need of friends, and neither does anyone who enjoys their favor (1338–1339).[56] When the Chorus of the *Hippolytus* wished for an easy life "undefiled by sorrows" (*Hippolytus Crowned* 1114) they wanted above all the "easy ways" (*Hippolytus Crowned* 1115) that are peculiar to the gods. Even Hippolytus, in spite of his suffering, must wistfully admire the "easy way" in which Artemis says farewell and leaves him there to die (*Hippolytus Crowned* 1441). But it is this very immunity of the gods to the bonds of friendship that makes them so irrelevant to Heracles. The friendship of the gods is worthless, because it cannot be based on any need on their side (1345–1346), so for Heracles, the conduct of those gods who befriend mortals is just as meaningless as the persecution of those gods who decide to harm them. There could be no exchange in their friendship such as might guarantee it some stability. An exchange of favors can only occur among mortals (χάριν . . . ἀντιδώσω, 1336–1337). Heracles rejects both the parentage and the friendship of the gods, he rejects everything that would mark him out as a semidivine hero, everything that might distance him from his fellow men.

Like Sophocles' Ajax, Heracles cannot respect the gods who have humiliated him, but he differs from him in consenting to go on with life. He accepts the ebb and flow of life that had exasperated Ajax so much, and he accepts the friendship of Theseus. He does not stand alone to face death at the end of the play. Theseus had pointed out that mortals must put up with changing fortunes (1314 and 1321), so Heracles consents to serve fortune alone (1357). He will put up with life as it is and go on living (1351), but there is more to his decision than that. He will live with and for other people.

Heracles bases his decision on his past reputation as a hero. He is leaving this past behind, but there is still some value in his heroic virtues, a value that can be recognized even in the very different world of the city-state. He has carried out countless hard tasks in the past (*Madness of Heracles* 1353), and he will not risk being charged with cowardice in the future (*Madness of Heracles* 1348) by refusing to face this new world. His courage, which was always very admirable, will now be displayed in the world of human warfare (ἀνδρὸς . . . ὑποστῆναι βέλος, *Madness of Heracles* 1350). It is as a companion and not as an independent fighter that he is going to Athens, and he now dreads being left alone (μονούμενος, *Madness of Heracles* 1388).[57] He will no longer be the wild hero who faced monsters in single combat; he will be integrated into the city as one who is a role-model for the hoplite warrior.

Joining the Citizens

This development had been prepared for earlier in the play. When he hears of the danger his family had been in, he says good riddance to his previous achievements (575) and states that his first duty is to his household. This obligation to children is half of what a good citizen is supposed to do, according to the Theban Herald in the *Suppliant Women* (506); the second half is to love one's parents and country (*Suppliant Women* 507). The shock of seeing his family in danger had gone a long way toward making a good citizen of Heracles, but he had actually served as a hoplite on one previous, if very unusual, occasion. Amphitryon points out indignantly to Theseus that his ill-treated son had fought for the ungrateful gods as a "shield-bearing warrior" (ἀσπιστάς, 1194) in their war against the Giants. This term (ἀσπιστάς) marks Heracles out as a hoplite, for the distinguishing feature of the hoplite warrior in the polis is that he bears a shield (ἀσπίς).

This is his specific weapon, his *hoplon* (ὅπλον); this is what makes him a hoplite. In the battle against the Giants, Heracles was already acting as a hoplite, and not as the lone combatant who rid the world of so many monsters.[58]

He had, however, joined the wrong kind of army. Hoplite warfare requires that all the soldiers be "equals" (ὁμοῖοι), and Heracles could never fight as an equal side by side with the gods. He discovered this to his cost after he had obliged the gods in this battle, because he received no acknowledgement for what he had done. The disastrous misfortunes that befell him show how far he always was from being even "similar" to the gods. He is half-man and half-god by birth, so it was natural that he should have joined the gods when they fought against the Giants on the Phlegraean Plain, but the sufferings he has endured and the disgraceful ingratitude of the gods show that his real place is with his fellow mortals.

Theseus, from the moment he walks onto the stage, acts as a new model for Heracles' behavior. The schemes of Hera (855) are not opposed by any of the gods and seem to have met with their active approval, since they are executed by Iris, the messenger shared by all the gods as a group. Hera drives Heracles to the point of suicide, and it is the arrival of Theseus that alone is capable of putting an end to his suicidal plans (1153). Theseus says that he has come as an ally (1165), that he wants to repay Heracles for saving him previously (ἀμοιβάς, 1169), but he can only save Heracles by transforming his character. Heracles will change from an old type of civilizing hero, who from a sense of his own worth never refused to undergo any labor (1354). Then he had been the friend and benefactor of all mankind, but to be everyone's friend is to be the friend of no man. Heracles found that this friendship had been of as little use to him as that of the gods; mankind too had yielded to Hera (1253). The model of behavior proposed by Theseus is quite different; he offers Heracles a friendship based on exchange (1169) and gratitude (χάρις, 1223). This is the code of a city of equal hoplites, where the *aristeia* performed by a noble warrior to further his own glory is replaced by the mutual protection of the phalanx, where each man's shield defends his neighbor and no one stands out as a better man than the rest. In this egalitarian form of warfare it is vitally important that if one part of the phalanx falters, the other members must rush to its aid, rather than pressing ahead to display their superiority over the men of the weaker wing (*Suppliant Women* 707–709). So, because of Heracles' misfortunes, not in spite of them, Theseus insists on helping him out: "He shares in his suffering" (συναλγῶν, 1202); "he sails with his friends when they are in trouble" (συμπλεῖν δὲ τοῖς φίλοισι δυστυχοῦσιν, 1225).

Heracles is won over to Theseus' way of looking at things, and when he decides to go on living and to accept Theseus' offer to move to Athens, he does so because he accepts the principle that friends should exchange favors (1352). Amphitryon tells him that this type of friendship is peculiar to those who have been brought up as Athenians, a "land that produces fine children" (πατρὶς εὔτεκνος, 1405). The equality of the contributions made by each party is stressed at the end of the play. Heracles will receive "countless gifts" (1352) but he has performed "countless services" (1353). Heracles is downcast now (1413), but Theseus is acting in gratitude to Heracles for saving him from the underworld (1169–1170), and at that time he himself was equally downcast, as Heracles reminds him (1415). Theseus acts as a mere oarsman to Heracles (ὑπηρέτῃ, 1398); Heracles is merely a small boat being tugged by Theseus' ship (ἐφολκίδες, 1424).[59] Each one is in turn subordinate to the other, but such mutual service is the hallmark of the democratic polis, where the citizens rule and are ruled in turn.[60] To serve each other in turn is the only way for them to sail together as equals (συμπλεῖν, 1225).[61] Heracles follows Theseus as his children had followed him (1424 and 631), but he in turn adopts Theseus as his child (1401) to replace the loss of his own children. All these reciprocal relationships bring out the real similarity between Heracles and Theseus in their new role (new for Heracles, at any rate) as equal and interchangeable citizens of the democratic city. By adopting Theseus, Heracles has turned his back on the old dynastic world of the heroes, in which his children would have become kings in various cities as members of a Panhellenic dynasty.[62] Through this artificial parenthood, Heracles binds himself to the new world of democratic Athens.

There is, however, a strange twist in this mutual adoption of each other by the two heroes. Heracles is, after all, being led by the hand to his new adoptive city by a hero whose own Athenian nature is shrouded in ambiguity. It is quite clear that Heracles has accepted the values of the hoplite city, and that he can play a meaningful role in it, but he will not be accepted in Athens as a hoplite. The weapons he is bringing there, as his contribution to the defense of the city, are ambiguously called *hopla* (ὅπλα, 1377 and 1382, which is normally used of a hoplite shield), but they are, in fact, his bow and arrows. He will play a marginal, if essential, role in Athens as the protector of the ephebes.[63] Theseus himself goes through the opposite development, from marginal ephebe to central ruler. Most of his adventures take place while he is an adolescent, and after his father's death his only exploits are his escapades with Peirithous and the war against the Amazons.[64] It was only quite late that Theseus began to occupy a more central place at Athens, and it was not until Euripides' *Suppliant Women* that he became the founder of Athenian democracy. Heracles will take over the ancient sanctuaries of Theseus in Attica, but he will also take over the previous marginal character of Theseus, thereby leaving him free, as it were, to occupy the center of the city. Only four of these sanctuaries were with-held from Heracles, as Philochorus tells us,[65] and these four were the sanc-tuaries of Theseus in and around the city of Athens. Euripides' *Madness of Heracles* brings us to the point in Athenian history where the center of the stage (in every sense of the word) will now be completely taken over by Theseus.

Three Lost Plays

Euripides devoted two other tragedies, which are now lost, to stories from the Theseus Cycle that seem to depict him in his old image. These are *Aegeus* and *Theseus*, and both of them treat exploits he performs as a young hero rather than as a mature monarch. These are, of course, the sort of themes that were especially popular in the archaic version of the Theseus myth. As we have seen, *Aegeus* told the story of Theseus' first arrival in Athens and Medea's attempt on his life, and it probably also included the episode of the Marathonian Bull too.[66] There is an atmosphere of the archaic age about the fragments that survive. One passage remarks that even he who stays at home to avoid trouble will still have to die (*TGF*, fr. 10), and this seems to be a direct echo of Pindar.[67] Elsewhere, we find praise of tyranny: it is noble provided that the tyrant is a good man (*TGF*, fr. 6). This is presumably said in praise of Aegeus, but sounds rather odd coming from Euripides. To make up for this, perhaps, he calls Aegeus cowardly at another point in the play (*TGF*, fr. 3), where he condemns the loud-mouthed wives of such henpecked rulers. *Aegeus* was, of course, set in a mythical era when there was no question of claiming that Athens was anything but a monarchy, however much you juggled with the mythology. There is, however, a fore-taste of the new world that Theseus will one day bring in. When Theseus has not yet been recognized, though perhaps after his victory over the Bull of Marathon, someone says with reference to him that success is better than noble birth (*TGF*, fr. 9).[68] This is only a small point, of course, but already it takes us far from the world of heroic monarchy or Pindaric aristocracy.

The second tragedy, *Theseus*, deals with the defeat of the Minotaur and Theseus' affair with Ariadne. Someone speaks a few moralizing lines (*TGF*, fr. 388) saying that men should "fall in love with" (ἔρως, line 1; ἐρᾶν, line 5) a good soul and with pious people, and should forget about Cypris. This strange use of *eros* (which normally refers to erotic love) and its correspond-ing verb recalls Pericles' appeal to the Athenians to fall in love with their city,[69] though the play was produced around 440 B.C.[70] and therefore pre-dates the famous speech of Pericles. There is also an interesting passage (*TGF*, fr. 389) which says that a man who is poor but strong will not refrain from taking by force the possessions of the rich. This statement, which is

typical of antidemocratic propaganda, may, however, have come from the
Aegeus instead, and Webster suggests that Medea spoke these words to
Aegeus against the as yet unrecognized Theseus.[71] In any case, specula-
tions about democracy are found in both these plays, and are a foretaste of
what is to come in Euripides' *Suppliant Women*.

In addition to these two tragedies, Euripides also wrote a satyr-play,
Skiron,[72] in which our hero must have appeared. He was probably presented
as the old-fashioned slayer of monsters, not very different from Heracles,
but more than this we cannot say.

All these tragedies based on the myth of Theseus come from Euripides'
early period (455–428 B.C.) They can be divided into those that present
Theseus as an archaic hero who performs various labors (*Aegeus, Theseus,*
and the two *Hippolytus* plays), and those that show him as the enlightened
ruler of Athens (*Madness of Heracles*). This newer image of Theseus
reaches its apogee in Euripides' *Suppliant Women*, to which we shall turn
in the next chapter. The division between the two very different presenta-
tions of the Athenian hero is not, of course, something that Euripides was
responsible for; it is a result of the double nature of Theseus himself.
Euripides never tries to play down this ambiguity or to explain it away.
His tragedies are an examination of the difficult transition an archaic hero
will have to go through before he can be accepted and internalized by the
Athenian democracy.

Notes

1. Speaking of the role of the gods in this play, Conacher describes Euripides'
approach as "neo-Homeric primitivism" (Conacher 1967, 28). Blomqvist has a
similar view: "The manner in which the 'gods' act would remind the Athenian
audience of what was regarded as an archaic or barbaric stage in the development
of mankind, a stage that civilized man had passed through and raised himself
above" (Blomqvist 1982, 413). Their words might be applied to Theseus, especially when he uses the curses of Poseidon to kill his son (though Blomqvist himself believes that the human beings in the play are much more advanced than the
gods).
2. "Offering a kingless constitution and democracy," Plutarch, *Life of Theseus,*
24, 2.
3. "He did not allow democracy to become . . . disorderly or confused, but
he established it fairly by assigning certain functions to the Eupatrids . . . and others to the other citizens." (Plutarch, *Life of Theseus*, 25, 2).
4. "Theseus thus becomes . . . responsible for the extensive privileges of the
favored class in cult, in the political constitution, and in the administration of jus-

tice" (Herter 1973, col. 1,216). Ampolo and Manfredini argue that this division into functional classes reflects antidemocratic theories of the fifth and fourth centuries (Ampolo and Manfredini 1988, 238, commentary on 25, 3–4).

5. Euripides, *Alcestis*, 920.

6. She is "one born from a *eupatrid* home" (Euripides, *Ion*, 1,073).

7. Bérard 1974, 35–36.

8. "Those who lived in the city itself and were members of the royal family and took care of sacred rituals were called *Eupatrids*" (*Anecdota Graeca*, 257, Bekker).

9. See *Suppliant Women*, 331, where the same verb and adverb are used: ὁ γὰρ θεὸς πάντ' ἀναστρέφει πάλιν.

10. "In our play Th. is Poseidon's son only where the curse is in question. . . . at 1283 and 1431, where the curse is not in question, he remains the son of Aigeus" (Barrett 1964, 334, note to line 887).

11. "He knows too well the power of Aphrodite over young men (and so he should! Hippolytus is there to prove it)" (Grube 1941, 188).

12. This is at 151–154, where the Chorus are trying to guess what may be afflicting Phaedra, and ask whether it is that her husband is keeping another woman.

13. See 113: "I bid that Cypris of yours a hearty farewell!" (τὴν σὴν δὲ Κύπριν πόλλ' ἐγὼ χαίρειν λέγω). This point was remarked upon by Grube: "It is no accident that the king here uses the same words—πόλλ' ἐγὼ χαίρειν λέγω—which Hippolytus used against Aphrodite in the earlier dialogue with his slave (113). They are hubristic here also" (Grube 1941, 189). Schmitt also notes that "Phaedra's personality and real wishes are so irrelevant to him that he gives them as little scrutiny as Theseus will later give his" (Schmitt 1977, 40–41 and 41, footnote 94).

14. Αἰγέως παῖδα (1282–1283) . . . παῖδα . . . σὸν (1287) and τέκνον Αἰγέως (1431) . . . σὸν παῖδα (1432).

15. Note the contrast between ἐλπίδι and λεύσσων in lines 1105–1106, which is repeated in line 1120, ἐλπίδα and λεύσσων.

16. See Euripides, *Madness of Heracles*, 154, where ἐξελεῖν is used of Heracles strangling the Nemean Lion, and Herodotus 1: 36 where the expression ἐξαιρεῖν χώρας refers to the killing of a wild boar that is ravaging Lydia.

17. He wishes "to be happy always with his excellent friends" (1018), where τοῖς ἀρίστοις φίλοις ("excellent friends") implies social as well as moral superiority. Hippolytus will only "answer to the select friends of my own age" (986).

18. Notice how he contrasts this border region with the polis itself: Ἀθηναίων πόλιν (1158) and γῆς τέρμονας Τροζηνίας (1159).

19. "This desire to remain unchanged, unpolluted by experience, to retain a child's innocence and virginity, is, as it were, a death wish—or a wish to be like a god: only the dead and the gods remain forever unchanged" (Luschnig 1980, 94).

20. Berns argues that, lacking this rational component, Hippolytus has got αἰδώς but not true σωφροσύνη. He rejects human Nomos which is necessary to complete his Physis (Berns 1973, 172–173). Schmitt raises a similar objection to Hippolytus' self-control (Schmitt 1977, 25–26).

21. Winnington-Ingram 1960, 184.

22. Schmitt 1977, 28 and footnote 48 to that page. The analysis that Schmitt makes of Hippolytus' παρθένειος ἡδονή supports the view of Kovacs and Orban that αἰδως is included among the ἡδοναί mentioned by Phaedra at 382–383 (Kovacs 1980, 288; Orban 1981, 11–12).

23. When Phaedra refuses to eat, the Chorus very significantly say that she is "keeping her body pure from food" (Δάματρος ἀκτᾶς δέμας ἀγνὸν ἴσχειν, 138). The purity of someone that is ἀγνός covers three areas that we have mentioned in the case of Hippolytus: food (137–138), sex (by implication of Phaedra at 317, and explicitly of Hippolytus at 102, 655, and 1,003), and bloodshed (316–317). To fail in any of these is to be guilty of μίασμα, and both Theseus and Phaedra are guilty of this offence (Theseus, 35; Phaedra, 317).

24. See Vernant 1962, 59–60, for the change of attitude that moves the polis to condemn warlike fury and the striving after personal glory.

25. Détienne 1967, 89–93.

26. Ibid., 27.

27. Ibid., 90–91.

28. Ibid., 98–99. See Détienne 1967, 98, note 71, for expressions such as κοινῷ λόγῳ χρησάμενοι.

29. Ibid., 102.

30. Ibid., 100–101.

31. Détienne points out that kings and poets are not absolute "Masters of Truth," and that their language may also be deceitful. Pittheus, though a king, and thus a man who possessed the power of magico-religious language, is also the inventor of rhetoric (Détienne 1967, 72). It is this deceptive form of language, this imitation of magico-religious speech, that Theseus now accuses Hippolytus of using, and Hippolytus was, of course, the great-grandson and pupil of Pittheus (Πιτθέως παιδεύματα, 11).

32. Détienne 1967, 43–44.

33. Ibid., 56–57.

34. Hippolytus might seem to be appealing to such an ἔλεγχος at 1055–1056, but he is asking Theseus to consider not the force of his arguments, but rather the magico-religious power that lies behind the words of someone who has taken an oath and behind the pronouncements of a μάντις. Theseus rejects these appeals as he did at 1038–1039.

35. Détienne 1967, 94.

36. Ibid., 95.

37. Vidal-Naquet 1986, 156.

38. See Gernet 1982b, 231–232 for polygamy among heroes, and 230–231 and 232–233 for bigamy in the case of a tyrant.

39. His house is deserted (ἔρημος οἶκος, *Hipp.* 847; ἐρημία, *Alc.* 944); his children are orphans (καὶ τέκν' ὀρφανεύεται, *Hipp.* 847; καὶ παῖδας ὠρφάνευες, *Alc.* 297); he will never remarry (*Hipp.* 858–861; *Alc.* 304–307 and 328–335).

40. See Thucydides 2: 45, 2 where Pericles says that it is best for a woman if men never say anything about her, whether good or bad (ἐπ' ἐλάχιστον ἀρετῆς πέρι ἢ ψόγου κλέος, "the least reputation for virtue or blame")!

41. Webster suggests that Phaedra, far from being concerned about the proper succession, actually suggested to Hippolytus that he should sieze the throne from Theseus. He bases this view on a few fragments (432, 433, 434) which encourage bold action (though its nature is left quite vague) and, rather more convincingly, on the presence of this theme in Seneca's *Phaedra* (Webster 1967, 67).

42. The expression comes from the *Life of Euripides*, which finds the motivation for this attack on women in Euripides' discovery that his wife, aptly named Χοιρίνη, was guilty of ἀκολασία (*TGF* p. 491). The first Hypothesis to the *Hippolytus Crowned* insists, by way of contrast, that Phaedra in that play was not ἀκόλαστος (εἰς ἐπιθυμίαν ὤλισθεν, οὐκ ἀκόλαστος οὖσα).

43. Ἀλλ' οὐ μὰ Δί' οὐ Φαίδρας ἐποίουν πόρνας (Aristophanes, *Frogs*, 1043).

44. This parallel was remarked upon by the Scholiast to Theocritus. See *TGF*, p. 491.

45. Women, according to Hesiod, burn men up (*Works and Days*, 586–587 and 704–705), and are thus a fitting punishment for man's theft of fire (*Works and Days*, 57–58). Note the parallel between "something bad in exchange for fire" (ἀντὶ πυρὸς . . . κακόν, *Works and Days*, 57) and "another fire in exchange for fire" (ἀντὶ πυρὸς γὰρ ἄλλο πῦρ, *TGF*, Euripides, fr. 429, 1).

46. It is possible that someone else speaks the lines of *TGF*, fr. 431, where the desires of others, including the gods, are used to prove the power of love and the futility of resisting his power, but *TGF*, fr. 430, where someone speaks of the power of Eros over herself must be attributed to Phaedra. See Webster 1967, 67.

47. Webster makes the following remark about the difference between the portrayal of Phaedra in the two plays: "But sympathy for Phaedra is bought at the expense of sympathy for Hippolytus. . . . In the second play when he denounces all women to the nurse . . . our sympathy for Phaedra is already won and all we think of is that he completely misunderstands her" (Webster 1967, 74).

48. "He had Phaedra blaming Theseus on the grounds that it was because of his crimes that she had fallen in love with Hippolytus" (Plutarch, *On Listening to Poetry*, ch. 8, 28A). See *TGF*, 491.

49. Foley 1985, 150–151.

50. Foley makes the following remarks on this unusual presentation of a gentle Heracles and on the sudden change that occurs after the hero appears in this light on the stage: "Instead Euripides provides an untraditional Heracles, a model of paternal concern, piety, and justice. In descending into madness he seems to be pushed arbitrarily into his own literary reputation for violence and instability . . ." (Foley 1985, 161). The same remarks could be applied to the Theseus who appears in the middle of the *Hippolytus*, the concerned family man who suddenly turns into the murderer of his son, and thus reverts to the archaic Theseus who was guilty of shedding the blood of his kinsmen, the Theseus he was trying to bid farewell to by undergoing a purificatory period of exile.

51. Foley 1985, 195.

52. Thucydides does something similar at 1: 70 where the Corinthian "condemnation" of Athens is in fact the highest praise.

53. Xenophanes B11 and A32, lines 23ff. See Bond 1981, 400.

54. Bond 1981, 376, note to 1232–1234.

55. "Human friendship is a surer guide for conduct than the doctrine that pollution offends the gods" (Bond 1981, 376, note to 1232–1234).

56. Bond remarks that "the combination of irrelevance with a near-repetition from another play may suffice to justify Nauck's deletion." He therefore brackets the two lines in his text; but even if we could prove that these two lines are irrelevant, we should be saying no more than Heracles himself says about them, and that certainly would not justify us in deleting them. The irrelevance to human beings of the friendship of the gods is, in fact, a major theme at the end of this tragedy (Bond 1981, note to 1338f).

57. Note the two occurrences of compound verbs with συν- in the previous two lines: συγκάμ' ("join me in performing this task," 1386), συγκατάστησον ("join me in settling this matter," 1387).

58. Curiously enough, the Giants are presented in hoplite formation in the reliefs depicting this battle on the frieze of the sixth century Siphnian Treasury at Delphi (Boardman 1978a, illustration 212.1, groups 10 and 21–22; Schefold 1992, plates 67 and 69).

59. The word is the same one used to describe the way his children hang on to Heracles (631), and it indicates his helplessness and his dependance on Theseus.

60. "One characteristic of freedom is being ruled and ruling in turn" (Aristotle, *Politics* 1317 B 2–3).

61. Bond says of the use of the verb συμπλεῖν: "The metaphor is appropriate here for it was well known that one must not sail with the impious if one valued one's skin." This aspect of the metaphor fits in nicely with Theseus' refusal to be worried about the possibility of acquiring μίασμα from his contact with Heracles (1234 and 1400) (Bond 1981, note to 1225).

62. See Foley 1985, 174 and 192. Foley argues that Heracles wishes "to found a Panhellenic dynasty, to create a source of Greek unity" (Foley 1985, 192). In the same work she remarks, "Tragedy presented and interpreted the myths of a Panhellenic past for a democratic society in Athens" (Foley 1985, 149). The *Madness of Heracles* not only interprets this past, but converts one of its representative heroes to the ways of a democratic society. The Panhellenic past was not so very distant that it could not still threaten the democratic city. As far as the aristocrats were concerned, this past had never died. See Gernet 1982b, 227 for the Panhellenic nature of Greek aristocracy.

63. "The young men who are about to cut off their fringe . . . fill a great cup of wine (which they call an *oinisteria*) and offer it to Heracles, and after making a libation, they give it to those who come with them to drink from it" (Athenaeus 494 f). Photius defines οἰνιστηρία as "a libation made to Heracles by the young men before they cut their hair" (Photius, *sub voc.* οἰνιστηρία). See Foley 1985, 174–175 and Burkert 1985, 211.

64. Even this "war" was originally just another wild escapade, since the rape of Antiope is found in works of art from about 520 B.C. on, whereas the bowdlerized story that Theseus was involved in a proper war with the Amazons only appears in the fifth century B.C.

65. *FGrH*, 328 (Philochorus) 18. See the commentary, on p. 309, for details on the four sanctuaries.

66. It would thus follow the version of the myth that had Aegeus send Theseus off to fight the bull, in the hope that he would never return. It is only after he is successful, and to the dismay of Aegeus and Medea, returns safely to Athens, that Medea tries to poison him. According to an earlier version of the story, Medea attempted to poison him immediately on his arrival at Athens. See Sourvinou-Inwood 1979, 22–25 and 51.

67. "Even he who sits at home away from trouble must die" (Euripides, *Aegeus, TGF*, fr. 10). "Since we must die, why should anyone / sit in the dark and cherish in vain an inglorious old age / deprived of all fine things?" (Pindar, *Olympians* 1, 82–84).

68. See Webster 1967, 78–79 for the inclusion of the Marathonian Bull episode and the interpretation of the fragments this enables us to make.

69. Thucydides 2: 43, 1.

70. Webster 1967, 102–103.

71. Ibid., 78. The manuscripts of Stobaeus that provide us with this fragment differ in its attribution, some saying that it is Αἰγεῖ, others saying Θησεῖ Αἰγεῖ (!). See *TGF*, p. 480.

72. In *TGF* fr. 675, someone offers Corinthian prostitutes to an Athenian for various prices expressed in "horses." I think the reference to "horses" might be poking fun at the Homeric way of reckoning the value of women in terms of farm-animals, though it could also be a reference to the figure of Pegasus on the coins of Corinth. The passage resembles the Aristophanic parody on the causes of the Peloponnesian War (*Acharnians*, 524–529), which in turn is based on Herodotus' account of the reasons for the rivalry between Asia and Europe, but there is no way of telling when this play was produced.

5

The Democratic Ruler

The Royal Democracy

In his work, *The Republic*, Cicero tells how Cato often used to compare the constitution of Rome with those of the Greek states.[1] Cato would criticize the latter because they were created at one moment in time by a single legislator, whereas the Roman constitution developed little by little through the ages, and it grew like an organic being while remaining always the same. But the Athenian constitution is the worst of all. The others may be a bit simplistic, being the work of one man, but Athens has had dozens of constitutions so that it is practically impossible to name all the legislators who were involved in it. Although these changes in the Athenian constitution might seem to be the same thing as the gradual and natural development that, according to Cato, characterizes Roman institutions, the Athenian constitution has not developed in the right way. It is rather a series of botched attempts (and each attempt is the work of just one legislator) to achieve a good constitution, a series of changes that threatens to go on forever.

This criticism was well aimed. The Athenians knew only too well that their constitution had gone through quite a number of changes, or at any rate this knowledge was always readily available to them, though they were not so eager to possess it. It has been rightly said that "the men of the fourth century B.C. were not unaware of this evolution but . . . they dreaded its ultimate consequences."[2] The men or rather certain men of the fourth century are loud in their praises of an "ancestral consitution," which they claim is the real constitution of Athens. They do not seem to be able to agree whether this constitution is that of Draco, Solon, or Cleisthenes, but they have in common the belief that the Athenian constitution should have

143

stopped developing at some point. The democratic system was, however, a very lively one and refused to stop changing. The process of democratization went on. They feared, therefore, that this evolution, of which they were only too aware, would have no end; and they feared perhaps even more that it could only have one end. So they chose to repress their awareness of it. This tactic of deliberately forgetting the dramatic changes in the constitution and of pretending that it had always remained the same was even adopted by the democrats, who in this, as in so many other matters, took over the ideology of the aristocrats rather than developing an independent one of their own.

They knew, of course, that things had not really been this way, and this realization, which disappoints their longing for a past that would have known no such disturbing changes, often comes to the surface. So we find that Lysias, who had no reason to be a friend of Sparta or oligarchy, actually reveals a certain envy of the Spartans, "the only people who have never experienced *stasis* or defeat, and who have always used the same customs."[3] This is an important passage since it shows that the continuous victories and the absence of stasis so wished for by the Athenians were associated in their minds with the enjoyment of a constitution that would always remain one and the same. Hence their wish to imagine their constitution as one that had never changed, and to root it firmly in the distant past. They even went so far as to attribute its inception to Theseus.

This story about Theseus and the beginning of democracy actually became an official myth. There was a fourth-century painting by Euphranor in the Stoa of Zeus Eleutherios that showed Theseus in the company of Demos and Demokratia.[4] This painting infuriated Pausanias when he saw it during his travels: the ordinary people (the πολλοί), he says, believed that Theseus had established their democracy and that this system had lasted up to the age of Peisistratus. This version of Athenian history is only an old wives' tale (a φήμη) that they heard when they were children and still hear in tragedies;[5] they are stupid enough to continue to believe in it. This credulity, he tells us, comes from their complete ignorance of history, from which they could easily have learned that Theseus had been and remained a king, and that his dynasty had lasted for another four generations after his death.

If we turn to the historians, we shall see that Pausanias was only partly right. His remarks about the ordinary Athenians may well be correct, but the true version that he opposes to their uninformed beliefs was not followed by every historian. If we turn to the tradition of what Jacoby calls Great History (as distinct from local history), it is certainly true that Theseus has nothing to do with democracy.[6] Herodotus ignores the theory that Theseus had founded democracy, and attributes this achievement to

Cleisthenes without even hinting that there were different accounts of the origins of democracy.[7] Thucydides likewise betrays no knowledge of a democratic Theseus; for him, Theseus is simply a monarch. Thucydides could not, however, simply have been unaware of the democratic version of Theseus' career. Euripides had already presented it in his *Suppliant Women*,[8] so Thucydides must have ignored it deliberately. The version of Thucydides was taken up by the first historian to devote an entire work to the history of Athens, Hellanicus. He had established a list of the Athenian kings, and he knew that there had been kings after the reign of Theseus.[9] Theseus appears once again as an absolute king in the work of the last historian of Athens, Philochorus.[10]

The opposite version, according to which Theseus was the founder of Athenian democracy, seems to have been invented by Euripides, but it is also found in some *Atthides*.[11] The political implication is, as Jacoby has said, obvious;[12] it gives Athenian democracy a royal pedigree. This is the version that wins out in the fourth century B.C. in the popular imagination, if not among all the historians; but it created problems for those who had decided to accept it, because it contradicted the list of kings that everyone had accepted as being genuine. The Marmor Parium, the only *Atthis*[13] we know that clearly made Theseus the founder of democracy, simply refuses to solve the problem. After saying that Theseus handed over "the constitution and democracy" to the people, it continues to list events by the reigns of the kings of Athens, including Theseus himself![14] According to the Marmor Parium, the archons only begin in 683/2 B.C.,[15] so the monarchy somehow continued to exist throughout all those centuries after the foundation of democracy. This contradictory account, however exasperating we may find it, is actually an ideal one as far as the Athenians were concerned. It conveniently glosses over the various changes in the development of the constitution, and would thus enable the Athenians to claim that their constitution had always remained the same. Oddly enough, it is actually its unhistorical nature that is the great attraction of the story that tells of a Theseus who had established Athenian democracy.

By transforming the establishment of democracy into an act carried out by order of the king, by modeling this transfer of power on the royal succession, any elements of stasis and of force are eliminated. The words used to describe this transfer by those authors who attribute the creation of democracy to Theseus are παραδοῦναι ("to hand over") and παραδέξασθαι ("to receive" or "take over"). These are the technical terms normally used to describe the peaceful and orderly succession from one king to the next, from father to son. So, when Isocrates talks about the succession of kings, he describes it as follows: "They handed over their personal possessions and their power to their own children up until Theseus" (τὰς κτήσεις τὰς αὐτῶν καὶ τὰς δυναστείας τοῖς αὐτῶν παισὶν παρέδοσαν μέχρι Θησέως).[16] He distinguishes between their *kteseis* (κτήσεις), which are their personal properties, and their *dynasteiai* (δυναστεῖαι), their royal pre-rogatives. The royal power of the king is, however, an ancestral power (πάτριος ἀρχή).[17] So the distinction between the personal property of the king and his royal power boils down to the more basic distinction between *ktemata* (κτήματα) and *patroa* (πατρῷα), between disposable personal property and ancestral possessions, these last being hereditary and inalien-able.[18] The heir to the king has an absolute right to this second category of goods because the king cannot give them away as a gift to anyone. What Theseus does, in effect, when it is his turn to bequeath his goods, is to declare the Athenian people his heirs, in exactly the same way as the pre-vious kings used to name their own children as their heirs: Theseus "passed them on to the people" (παρέδωκεν τῷ δήμῳ), Isocrates says, whereas the other kings "passed them on to their own children" (τοῖς αὐτῶν παισὶν παρέδοσαν).[19] So it would not be completely accurate to take up Jacoby's formula and say that in the story that Theseus founded democracy we are dealing with a gift made to the people, because the most important characteriztic of royal power is that this power, being ancestral (πάτριος), cannot be given away as a gift; it can only be inherited.

The same term for "handing over" or "bequeathing" (παραδοῦναι) is found in the other accounts from the fourth century B.C. onward that make Theseus the creator of democracy. On the Marmor Parium it is said of Theseus, "he handed over democracy" (τὴν δημοκρατίαν παρέδωκε). Likewise, in the story criticized by Pausanias,[20] the event is described as follows: "he handed public affairs over to the people" (παρέδωκε τὰ πράγματα τῷ δήμῳ).[21] The other versions of the foundation of democracy, the ones which do not claim that Theseus was its founder, speak of force: the people snatch power from the kings,[22] and expel them.[23] The version that attributes democracy to Theseus, on the other hand, removes all ele-ments of force and disagreement from the story, and Theseus passes on his power to the people voluntarily and peacefully.[24] The king is succeeded by a royal people.

The Democratic Monarch of Euripides
Suppliant Women

This particular version of the establishment of democracy is, as we have seen, first found in Euripides' *Suppliant Women*, and it is quite clear from the play what exactly is involved. Theseus says at line 351, "I established [the people] into royal power" (κατέστησ' αὐτὸν ἐς μοναρχίαν). If καταστῆσαι ("to establish") carries with it a trace of tyrannical power, of a return to a monarchist past, it is perfectly harmless and in place here, because Theseus is indeed a king. On the other hand, Theseus has not introduced a revolutionary change; he has not even abolished the monarchy. He has simply organized the royal succession so that the next monarch will be the people. The nature of this democracy is not completely clear from his brief description of it, but it is significant that the references to it occur only after Theseus has been persuaded to help the mothers of the Seven. The change that occurs in him at this point in the play is not just based on the difference between the two opposite policies that the king must choose from, between pity[25] and reason,[26] between a rigorously logical notion of justice and a humane sympathy for misfortune. He has changed his whole outlook on the world, and turns out not to be a king at all; for the audience, it is at this point in the play that Theseus becomes a democrat.

There is nothing humane or democratic about his attitude earlier on in the play; he is self-centered and authoritarian. For Euripides these predemocratic views, which he imagines the ancient hero to hold, are identical with the antidemocratic views of some of his own contemporaries. Sophists like Thrasymachus were notorious for their belief that certain men were vastly superior to others, and that these supermen were not to be bound by the laws of common decency. One of the hallmarks of the city-state is, however, that there should be no supermen; the city-state is a republic of equals. During the era of the city-states, the possibility of a semidivine king or leader is strictly denied; such beings preceded the city-state and will return to destroy it.[27] The only exceptions to this clearly drawn line between gods and mortals are the heroes, and they, rather obligingly, are dead. Euripides is honest enough to acknowledge that if such a hero were to return from the dead, he would be a menace to the state. So he does not present us, at the beginning of the play, with a Theseus who just happens to be a democrat. He does not present us with an Athenian Servius Tullius who, out of the goodness of his heart, wishes to free his people,[28] for goodness of heart is not a particularly heroic virtue. He presents us instead with a very believable portrait of a highly unpleasant, highly undemocratic leader.

Theseus the Sophist

Theseus is surprisingly harsh, considering that we are dealing with a suppliant play, and that he is the leader of the country the suppliants have appealed to. Instead of pitying Adrastus and welcoming him, which is what we should expect, or pointing out regretfully that he could not oblige him at this particular time, which we might have forgiven, he actually goes out of his way to condemn him in a rather smug speech at 195ff. The Chorus have, just before this, asked him to look on their misfortunes with compassion (194). He answers their emotion with a clever *sententia* (γνώμην, 198) and the sight of their misfortunes with the airy and hardly appropriate statement that, on balance, the good always outweighs the bad in life (199), and that they have no cause for complaint (214–215). In his list of the benefits that come to man from the gods, there is one that is especially significant for this play: nourishment from grain (τροφή τε καρποῦ, 205). As we learn from the first line, the scene is set in Eleusis, and shortly afterward we are explicitly reminded that Athens was the first place where grain appeared (31). This was one of the great boasts of Athens, and it is used in the *Menexenus* to prove that the Athenians are autochthonous: the Attic soil gave birth to humanity, and like all mothers provided its offspring with food (τροφὴν ἀνθρωπείαν).[29] The wording of Theseus' phrase recalls this notion, because the word for food here (τροφή) is especially used of the nourishment provided by a parent. Theseus is completely absorbed in a facile chauvinism, and chooses to boast about his own country rather than to address himself to the problems of the suppliants. Athens has indeed been very fortunate, but Theseus, unlike his mother, draws the wrong conclusion from this.

Theseus is almost incapable of sympathy. He declares that all misfortunes are either insignificant (215–216), or else deserved and sent as a punishment by the gods (248–249). These sententious remarks are pitiless, but consistent in their own perverse way. His grounds for saying that on the whole life brings more benefits than troubles is that otherwise the gods would not have put us here (200). They are benevolent, life is good, and therefore any serious blow of fortune must have been deserved. He even supports the primitive idea of guilt by contagion. By not restricting your circle of friends to fortunate people alone (εὐδαιμονοῦντας . . . κτᾶσθαι φίλους, 225), you are inviting disaster. Theseus has an answer for everything, including the commonplace that no man can know what tomorrow holds. This issue was first brought up by the ever-perceptive and ever-sensitive Aethra (1–11); it is raised again by Adrastus, when he pointedly reminds Theseus that he too was once a fortunate ruler (166), and by the Chorus, when they remind Theseus that all human happiness is short-lived (265–270). Theseus, however, has no time for such thoughts; he simply points out that if one is worried about the future, one can always resort to a prophet (211–213); and here Theseus does have a reasonable argument against Adrastus, whom he accuses shortly afterward of deliberately ignoring the advice of his seers (229–231).[30]

The goal of Theseus in this speech is to show that men bear complete responsibility both for acquiring happiness and for retaining it. It is not enough to be virtuous (εὐψυχία, 161; οὐδὲν ἠδικηκότα, 228); you must also put your good principles into action according to a rational plan (εὐβουλία, 161).[31] Without such a plan, your behavior is merely haphazard (ἔσπευσας, 161), and can no longer be looked upon as truly virtuous. He is not just saying that rational virtuous behavior is sufficient for happiness, and that one should ignore external misfortunes. He is making the further claim that such behavior will automatically bring along those external goods that are also necessary for happiness. If, then, your luck is bad (249), that is your fault and your problem. Athens, for Theseus, is just a great success story, the clever country that got it right. Aethra will later come up with a different conception of the city.

Theseus' self-righteousness leads him to attack the young at lines 232–237, which is rather ironic, since he is nearly always depicted as a young man in Athenian art and literature. He has, in fact, just been addressed as a youth by Adrastus (190–191). This strange inability of Theseus to see that his own speech could be turned against himself, or that he could ever undergo what the Argives have suffered, is an irony that pervades everything he says, and indeed the whole of this scene. In appealing to Theseus as a young leader, Adrastus was explaining why he had turned to the eternally young city of Athens rather than to some other state. The sophistry of Theseus' answer belies his hopes. Theseus has already had quite a lot of experience in splitting hairs (ἀμιλληθεὶς λόγῳ, 195), and he uses it to the full. His attack on the young shows that he is old in experience, and he refuses to pardon faults to which Adrastus felt he would, as a young man, be more susceptible and more sympathetic.

The Chorus, in the same way, had appealed to Aethra as a mother to sympathize with them (ἔτεκες καὶ σύ, "you too have given birth," 54), and they had appealed to Theseus as a son (τέκνον, 282) to have pity on their sons (τέκνοις, 285).[32] Aethra sees their plight (ἐσιδοῦσ' οἰκτρά . . . δάκρυα, "seeing our pitiful tears," 48), and her reaction had been to recognize their common humanity (ἐς τάσδε γὰρ βλέψασ' ἐπηυξάμην, "looking at these women I prayed," 8); but Theseus, though their situation is obvious to him and the city of Athens (οἰκτρὰ δέδορκε, "it has looked at pitiful events," 190), denies any similarity between himself and the youth of Argos. Theseus completely avoids the main issue, the common humanity that binds him to those less fortunate than himself. He does not wish to associate with them (225, 228, 246); he does not even want to form any connection in his thought with such people.

Euripides seems to believe that there should be a close connection between democratic institutions at home and an enlightened policy abroad. Like all of his contemporaries, he was later to receive a rather unwelcome enlightenment on this particular point, but we may grant that at the time the *Suppliant Women* came out, his belief was not so entirely absurd as to be unworthy of serious attention. The harsh attitude of Theseus toward the suppliants is, therefore, a reflection of his political attitudes, which are quite undemocratic. Aethra was capable of reacting to the sight of misery (1–11), and Adrastus shows that this ability to react to the circumstances of other citizens is essential for the survival of a democratic state (176–179). The poor, he argues, should look at the rich and be filled with emulation (the good *Eris* of Hesiod) and with the desire (ἔρως, 178) to succeed; the rich, at the sight of misery (οἰκτρά, 179),[33] should be filled with fear of failure. He deliberately refuses to call the rich happy, or anything like that; he calls them instead "such as are not (yet) unlucky" (τοὺς μὴ δυστυχεῖς, 179). Theseus, on the other hand, as one modern scholar puts it, "notices only greed and envy: he believes in class struggle."[34] According to Theseus, the only people who desire (ἐρῶσ', 239) prosperity are the rich, but they already have more than enough. The poor, if they look at the rich, are only filled with jealous hatred (the bad *Eris* of Hesiod) and with envy (φθόνος, 241), not with any healthy desire to improve themselves.[35] The rich, it would appear, do not consider the unfortunate at all, and neither does he.

He reserves his praise, not that there is much of it, for the middle classes, whom he calls those "in the center" (ἐν μέσῳ, 244). The center in a democracy should not, however, be occupied by anyone; it should be the empty point to which all may contribute (ἐς μέσον φέρειν, 439), it should be common to all citizens. Theseus has put one class in there to act as the guardians of the city. He is doing, in fact, precisely what Aristotle was to recommend a century later. Aristotle declares that the city should set up a "mixed" constitution, avoiding both democracy and oligarch; it should have a large middle class and hand over power to them, because it will not survive otherwise.[36] Athenian democracy, on the other hand, was supposed to ignore such class distinctions;[37] it deliberately refused to grant political power to any one group. Theseus in this speech is neither egalitarian nor a loyal democrat.[38]

Theseus is presented, rather, as a defender of the narrow-minded, middle-class, and not very democratic patriotism that the Athenians were often guilty of. It is the type of patriotism that prides itself on the common genealogical origins of all citizens. Right at the start of the play, we are told that Theseus is the grandson of Pandion (6), which is an assertion of his racial purity. Shortly afterward, in his argument with Adrastus, Theseus assumes that the king had found Argive husbands for his daughters (τῷδ' ἐξέδωκας . . . Ἀργείων; 133). Theseus is shocked, as many Athenians would have been, to hear that Adrastus has defiled his household by marrying his daughters to foreigners.[39] By the time that this play was produced, Pericles had yielded to such sentiments by introducing his citizenship law, which made all children illegitimate except those born of two Athenian parents.

The spirit of Cleisthenes' reforms was quite different. He had insisted that there be no investigation into the status of Athenians, but that all be accepted as citizens.[40] Theseus, the introducer of synoecism and dweller in the Theseion, is also quite different.[41] As we see him in this play, however, Theseus is disappointingly familiar. The thought behind the whole speech (195–249) is simply a feeling of confident superiority based in part on the ancient privileges granted to the Athenians as sons of the earth. His attitude is summed up by what he says to Aethra after his clever speech. When she weeps for the suppliant women, he anwers curtly, "You should not cry for the misfortunes of these people!" (291); "you were not naturally born to be one of these" (οὐ σὺ τῶνδ' ἔφυς, 292). Theseus seems to believe that by the laws of nature and by virtue of their superior birth,[42] Aethra and he are exempt from such misfortunes, and even from feeling sympathy. Perhaps the most fitting comment on the ironies that pervade this speech is the very existence of a scholarly controversy over the lines of the Coryphaeus that follow it. The leader of the Chorus charitably remarks, "He made a mistake; but this is a common fault among the young; one ought to forgive him." There is still some doubt about the identity of the man who has done wrong (ἥμαρτεν, 250),[43] the young who do so habitually (νέοισιν, 250), and who should be forgiven (τῷδε, 251). Some readers, not without reason, suspect that all three of the designations in these lines may refer to Theseus rather than Adrastus and his young followers.[44] Theseus would not have been amused.

The Conversion of Theseus

Aethra wants to persuade Theseus to change his mind, but he has made it quite clear that any appeal to sympathy will not work (292). He coldly admits that he did feel some emotion on seeing these poor women, but that is as far as it goes; he will not act on this emotion.[45] Aethra must answer him in his own language. He had criticized Adrastus for his errors and lack of careful planning; she now turns these charges against Theseus. In neglecting to defend a divine law, he has shown himself to be strangely lacking in wisdom, just as Adrastus, according to Theseus, had failed to plan carefully.[46] Theseus has made a serious mistake (μὴ 'σφαλῇς, 302, and 'σφάλης, 303), one just as bad as that of Adrastus (ἐγὼ 'σφάλην, 156, and ἐσφάλη, 336).

She also picks up on his remarks about the middle class being the one that upholds the city (σῴζει πόλεις, 244; κόσμον φυλάσσουσ', 245) and argues that it is loyal citizens, whatever their class, who keep a city together by obeying its laws (συνέχον πόλεις, 312; νόμους σῴζῃ, 313). He should not rely on any one class, but rather on the average citizen, on anyone (τις, 313) who is prepared to uphold the laws of the city. The state may be an amalgam of different groups,[47] but the answer to any problem the city might have is not to entrust its government to one of these groups. The city belongs to the people as a whole. In the present case, it is not just a matter of saving Athens, but of preserving a custom that is necessary[48] for the survival of the whole of Greece (νόμιμα ... πάσης Ἑλλάδος, 311; πάσης Ἑλλάδος κοινόν, 538).[49] In the long run, it will hurt Athens to allow this custom to be broken in the case of the Seven, even if she owes Argos nothing. No social group can run the city alone, no city in Greece can afford to ignore the plight of its fellows.

Aethra concludes with an argument against Theseus personally: no warrior can survive on his own either. He may have acquired a certain amount of fame for having defeated a wild sow, she says, deliberately choosing the most paltry of his opponents, but such achievements are insignificant. What really counts is the courage a warrior displays in battle (316–319). She is not just questioning the value of pig-sticking; she is casting doubt on the merits of single combat in general. Theseus' adventures with the bandits on the Saronic Gulf were performed when he was a lone warrior, outside the framework of the city; Aethra is upholding the values of the polis, and her advice aims at benefiting the polis as well as her son (σοί τε καὶ πόλει καλόν, 293). These values are based above all else on the principle that all men are of equal worth, both as citizens and as hoplites, and if this principle appears quixotic, it has nonetheless served Athens very well.

Her advice, she realizes, may not seem very sound, but this apparent lack of logic has always characterized Athenian policy. Theseus may often have used impressive sophistic arguments in trying to maintain that no man could justifiably complain of his lot (195–196), but Athens has been prepared to lose the argument, to be mocked, to be called "ill-advised" (ἄβουλος, 321) for upholding higher principles (321–323). This "charming simplicity" of Athens, as the sophist Thrasymachus might have said,[50] goes against all the premises of Theseus' previous arguments against Adrastus. Aethra exposes his good planning (εὐβουλία, 161) for what it is; it is, she says, merely an over-cautious timidity, and it is quite un-Athenian. As Adrastus had remarked, Sparta may be devious and ruthless, but this is how she conceals her weakness (187–188); Aethra repeats this condemnation of Sparta by telling her son that Sparta's caution has deprived that city of any glory it might otherwise have won.[51] The root cause of Sparta's failure is that it has followed the disgraceful precepts that Theseus had upheld in his speech. Athens, by her naive and altruistic policies, is able to face the world (ἀναβλέπει, 322) with a bold look that turns all opposition to a stony silence (γοργὸν ὄμμ', 322).

The timid and cautious behavior that Theseus proposes and Sparta disposes is not only ignoble, it is pointless. The gods do not reward such mean-spirited calculation; in fact, they deliberately mix up all the figures (πάντ' ἀναστρέφει πάλιν, 331), so that life is more like a game of dice than a computation. It was not for being unjust that Adrastus was punished, as Theseus himself had been forced to admit (228), nor for being careless either. He simply suffered an inexplicable blow of fortune, and the same thing could happen to anyone. Likewise the Thebans, who are clearly behaving unjustly (328), are not being rewarded for their misbehavior, nor for being clever either. They can only attribute their success to an equally inexplicable stroke of good luck. Aethra is starting out from the same premises as Jocasta in *Oedipus the King*, who declares that fortune rules everything (*Oedipus the King*, 977–978), but she comes to the opposite conclusion. Jocasta infers that we might as well act as we please (εἰκῇ, *Oedipus the King*, 979); Aethra concludes that we might as well behave justly. This is a far cry from the meritocracy that we find in Pericles' funeral oration and that Theseus outlined earlier in the play. Theseus has very little to say in response to Aethra's speech. He mumbles a few words about his previous statements being factually accurate and their intention being merely to point out how Adrastus had made some errors in his plans (334–336). What Aethra's reaction might have been had he pursued this train of thought, or what exactly it was in her aspect that persuaded him not to do so, we shall never know, but the phrase "a Gorgon's glare" (322) does stick in one's mind. All we can say is that he rather quickly changes his tack and declares with moving conviction that his mother is absolutely right, and that he is awfully glad she brought these matters to his attention (337).

It is only after this abrupt change in his outlook that he makes his famous declaration that he invented democracy and set up the Athenian people as monarch in his place (352–353). The meaning of this phrase is quite clear, and it is in no way different from the definition he provides in the next episode, when he speaks of the power that is wielded by the people alone (μοναρχίαν, 352; δῆμος δ' ἀνάσσει, 406), a passage in which he is clearly describing the "radical" democracy of Euripides' time. He points out that they rule in succession to one another (διαδοχαῖσιν, 406). This is the proper word to describe the succession from one king to the next, and was used of the successors of Alexander the Great (the Διάδοχοι). The changeover from king to people is no less tranquil than the smooth transition from one set of annual magistrates to the next, and considerably more so than the accession of a prince to the throne.

Some readers have been unduly worried by two expressions that Theseus uses immediately afterward: "They will decide in your favor since I wish it" (δόξει δ' ἐμοῦ θέλοντος, 350), and "I will convince them of these things" (καὶ πείσας τάδε, 355). Goossens, for example, says that "the meetings of the assembly are no longer anything but formalities."[52] Theseus' confident attitude suffers from a comparison with the fear of Pelasgus in Aeschylus' play of the same name that the people will throw out his proposals (μηδ' ἀπορριφθῇ λόγος / ἐμοῦ, Aeschylus, *Suppliant Women*, 484). We must not, however, forget the context of these situations. First, the claim of the Danaids is much more dubious, and in the end they will give it up and accept marriage with their Egyptian cousins. Pelasgus is, therefore, not quite sure that his proposals are right, or that the people of Argos should accept them. Second, the Danaids openly resort to blackmail instead of appealing to the feelings of the Argives; it is not a conflict between right and might, but between two equally just claims that have been pursued in a wrong and forceful way. On the one side, the sons of Aegyptus have been promised their cousins in marriage, but they are trying to use force now to keep them to that promise; on the other side, the Danaids are genuine refugees and deserve sympathy, but they are forcing the hand of the Argives. Third, we are dealing with Argos in Aeschylus' play and Athens in the drama of Euripides. Who knows how the Argives may decide? But if someone, in a patriotic Athenian tragedy, appeals to the generosity of the Athenians, there can be no doubt about the answer.

Theseus is indeed very confident in his predictions at 350 and 355, but this does not make him "a subtle tyrant," nor does this make his Athens any the less democratic. In fact, he is paying a compliment to the generosity of the ordinary Athenian, and his confidence might have been shared by any member of the audience in a suitably patriotic mood. The phrase "they will decide in your favor since I wish it" (δόξει δ' ἐμοῦ θέλοντος, 350) is not at all undemocratic. In fact, it is modeled on the words that begin laws made by the people in fifth-century Athens: "the people decided during the archonship of X" (ἔδοξε τῷ δήμῳ ἐπὶ τοῦ δεῖνα ἄρχοντος). Furthermore, the word used for "wish" (θέλειν) implies considerably less than to command or even to will that something might occur (βούλεσθαι); it is merely the consent that accompanies an action. The Chorus themselves realize that the wishes of Theseus do not mean very much. They anxiously wonder, "Whatever will the polis decide concerning me?" (τί μοι πόλις κρανεῖ ποτ'; 375). They know only too well that the real power to accomplish anything (κραίνειν) belongs to the polis, which may or may not follow his suggestion. Theseus may be a strong leader like Pericles, but his confidence that the Athenians will heed his advice is based on the justice of his request and not on any power he holds over them. This is why he is going to bring Adrastus along with him to the assembly. He is more like a nervous defendant at a trial who decides to bring along his wife and children to win the sympathy of an Athenian jury, than a monarch who will impose his wishes on a respectful and obedient parliament.

Oligarchic Sophistry and Democratic Nobility

In the following episode, Theseus restates this definition of democracy and is led into an argument with the Theban Herald about the merits of this constitution and those of the monarchy at Thebes. This "notorious debate" has been condemned as a "flagrant irrelevancy,"[53] but it is necessary because it explains Theseus' change in attitude. It was by relying on a kind of social Darwinism, both on the individual level and on the level of the state, that he reached his first decision not to help the suppliants. Now he reaches the opposite conclusion, by paying more attention to the common good both of the state (439) and of Greece (538). The Theban Herald, on the other hand, draws the previous views of Theseus to their illogical conclusion, by asserting the right of the successful man to pursue his goals as far as he pleases. There is a lot of the former Theseus in what the Herald admires and in what Theseus now condemns.

Aethra and, naturally, the suppliants had warned Theseus that the success arising from careful planning, which he admired so much, was really a matter of luck to a large degree. He should look to the misfortunes of others, and not count on his own prosperity being permanent. No man, however carefully he may plan his life, is free from the blows of fortune, so we ought to help each other out (267–270). The Herald sticks firmly to Theseus' original views and holds that even if the victories of Thebes are due to "the luck of the game" (ἐν πεσσοῖς, 409), they are quite content with this type of superiority (κρεῖσσον, 410) and intend to push their luck all the way.[54]

When the Herald goes on to condemn democratic politicians, it is almost as if he has overheard Theseus' earlier speech and is plagiarizing from it.[55] Democratic politicians, he complains, only think of making money for themselves (πρὸς κέρδος ἴδιον, 413), just as Theseus had accused them of being motivated by profit alone (κέρδους οὕνεκ' at 236). They harm the people says the Herald (ἔβλαψ', 415); the people are harmed said Theseus (βλάπτεται, 237). They make blunders (σφάλματ', 416) claims the Herald; they led Adrastus astray, argued Theseus,[56] so that he blundered ('σφάλην, 156). The Herald argues that ordinary people should have no say in public affairs since they are incapable of judging arguments (417), or rather they do not reach the "right" answers. Theseus had argued that they could not be trusted, since they are too obsessed with their own poverty (240) and their envy of the rich (241–243) to be truly patriotic. The Herald continues by remarking that the democratic politicians such people will follow care only for the present (αὐτίχ', 414), they do not care what harm may lie ahead (εἰσαῦθις ἔβλαψ', 415). Once again, he is echoing the words of Theseus who had said that democratic politicians do not look ahead (ἀποσκοπῶν, 236) and consider whether the people may suffer harm (εἴ τι βλάπτεται, 237). Theseus, in his former state of mind, had declared that Aethra had no natural (ἔφυς) connection with the Argive suppliants,[57] and the Herald now declares that Athens is not naturally related (προσήκοντ') to Argos.[58] Both these expressions refer to the concern that you might have for a member of your family (your ὁμοφυεῖς and προσήκοντες), but that you do not owe to anyone else. Both of them concluded that Athens should not, therefore, get involved.

The Herald then goes on to condemn the poor, who are allowed a say in running a democracy. He does not bother with the issue of their bias against the rich, the one Theseus had dwelt on (240–243). His objection is a more fundamental one. First, they, like their leaders, are incapable of looking to the future, because they lack any real understanding of public affairs (μάθησις, 419). Second, and more importantly, they cannot even look to public affairs at all (422) because they are too poor and too busy trying to scrape together a livelihood (420–422). Euripides, however, makes the words of the Herald undercut what he wants to say. When the Herald argues that the people are incapable of governing, the verb he uses is "control" (εὐθύνειν, 418). A democracy is the only system, however, that imposes any "controls" (εὐθύναι) on its leaders, the only one where you have public offices that are "subject to control" (ἀρχαὶ ὑπεύθυνοι). It is essential to the power of a dictator that it be free from such checks (ἀνυπεύθυνος, "without controls"),[59] that no one may dare to speak out against anything he does. Again, the Herald says that the people will not have the leisure to look to the common good (κοινά, 422), but as Theseus points out, there is practically no common good under a dictatorship (οὐκ εἰσὶν νόμοι / κοινοί, 430–431). The ruler keeps political power all to himself (αὐτὸς παρ' αὑτῷ, 432). He turns this power into a personal possession, a *ktema* (κεκτημένος, 431), or to use an expression of the Herald, a private good (ἴδιον, 413) rather than a common one. The only reason a king will not try to gain private profit from his office is that he already owns everything.

The answer of Theseus is to be seen as a refutation both of the Herald's speech and of what he himself had said in the previous episode. He had developed his previous theories of optimistic individualism in the course of arguments with other people (ἁμιλληθεὶς λόγῳ, 195). The elaboration of his new, more democratic and egalitarian views[60] are elicited by this argument with the Herald (ἄμιλλαν λόγων, 426). In a democracy, he now argues, all political power is pooled together in the center (ἐς μέσον, 439). It is common property (κοινοί, 431) belonging to nobody in particular and yet belonging equally to every citizen. Everyone has an equal share in legislation (ἴσον, 432, refers to their equal share in making laws, the γεγραμμένοι νόμοι of 433), in deliberation (ἰσαίτερον, 441, refers to their equal share in proposing policy, the βούλευμ' of 439), and in the judicial process (δίκην ἴσην, 434). The poor are no longer the discontented rivals of the rich (240–243), but people who share equally in the government of their state and may well have some good advice to contribute to the city (πόλει καλόν, 293; πόλει χρηστόν, 438–439). Theseus answers the Herald's main point about the poor being too busy to acquire a sufficient knowledge of politics. He replies that they are not obliged to formulate policy (440–441), but having a share in the governing of the city, they will both want and be able to judge the merits of policies proposed by others.[61] It was only by hearing his own views put forward in an extreme form by the unpleasant Herald, that Theseus was able to analyze them properly and expose their errors.

Theseus similarly reverses his previous criticism (232–237) of the young, and claims that suspicion of the young is not only a bad thing in itself, but the mark of a tyrant (446), a statement that shows the distance he has traveled since the last episode, for it is the distance that lies between monarchy and democracy. The tyrant cuts down the young like a man mowing crops in a field in the spring (448–449). Euripides is referring to the anecdote about the tyrant Thrasybulus and the silent advice he gave to his fellow tyrant Periander,[62] when he cut down any ear of grain that was higher than the others.[63] Euripides changes the whole tone of this image by speaking of youth and springtime.[64] Tyranny is considerably less glamorous when seen from the viewpoint of its victims, and youth seems less rash and exasperating when the young people in question are lying dead.

Euripides' image of human crops has wider connotations within this play and in the works of Euripides in general, for it brings up the myth of autochthony once again. The very first crops appeared in Attica (31), because humans were created there first. In the *Erechtheus*, in a passage that gives the main elements of the myth of Athenian autochthony, Erechtheus refers to male children as a "masculine crop" (στάχυς ἄρσης).[65] This myth of men coming from the earth was not just an Athenian one; the founding myth of Thebes also started with the growth of men from the earth, the armed *Spartoi* who were born from the dragon's teeth sown by Cadmus. Euripides refers to these *Spartoi* several times throughout his work as the "earth-born crop" (γηγενὴς στάχυς) or the "crop of sown men" (στάχυς σπαρτῶν).[66] Theseus will allude to the Theban myth again in the play,[67] but here he hopes it will make a special appeal to the Herald, because the thought of young men being mown down by a tyrant is not just a poetic fancy. It is a reminder that the young men of Thebes and Athens have a special relationship with the earth itself, that they are the finest crop of men that Greece has produced: they deserve better treatment than this.

Theseus makes a final defense of Athenian democracy, which reflects an argument found in Herodotus. He points out that whether or not the poor will have time for political activity or not, they will still have political interests. Under a tyranny, they will have no incentive whatsoever to do any work, because all their labor to acquire wealth and a livelihood for their family (πλοῦτον καὶ βίον . . . τέκνοις, 450) will simply go to benefit the livelihood of the tyrant (τυράννῳ . . . βίον, 451). Similarly, Herodotus remarks that under the Peisistratids the Athenians did absolutely nothing, but with the establishment of democracy, they prospered because now each man was working to benefit himself.[68] In short, Theseus acknowledges that it would indeed be possible to establish a state in which the ruler was subject to no control, youthful energy was frowned upon as a dangerous force, and nobody had any incentive to work or achieve anything, but who on earth would want to live there? And after earnestly asserting that he certainly wouldn't (μὴ ζῴην ἔτι, 454), Theseus brings his defence of Athenian democracy to an end.

War and Peace

The Herald realizes from Theseus' response that he will have to find some other means of persuasion. He appeals instead to the force that Thebes could exert. He forces Theseus, and the audience of the play, to examine what role heroic *arete* can play in Athens. Must not a democracy automatically be inclined toward appeasement rather than heroic military adventures? The Herald seems determined to put the Athenians to the test, since he demands that Theseus should "untie" the holy garlands (λύσαντα, 470) and "expel" the suppliants from Attica (ἐξελαύνειν, 471). Earlier in the play, when Theseus decided to deal firmly with the Argive women, to act as their judge and punisher (253 and 255), they were allowed to leave their garlands at the altar to bear witness to their plea for mercy (259–262), although Aethra insisted on continuing to wear hers as a sign of protest (359–360). To take away their garlands, as the Herald demands, would not, of course, release Theseus or the Athenians from their obligation to help these refugees. It would simply mean that the Athenians were utterly shameless, that they could neither fulfill their obligation nor even admit to themselves that such an obligation existed. The Herald is asking them, therefore, not only to act dishonorably but even to abandon the very notion of honor.

It is quite obvious that the Herald's demand is outrageously unjust, but he does not argue for it on the grounds of its justice. Instead he seeks to impress the Athenians with a sense of the horrors of war, for if they refuse to give in to his demands, that is what they will have to face. He concedes that Athens is a wonderfully free and democratic state (ἐλευθέραν πόλιν, 477), but these great blessings can be enjoyed in times of peace alone. The Athenians have much more to lose by going to war than people who dwell in less happy lands. But even though every Athenian knows this in his heart, he may still be led astray by a rash and illogical optimism (ἐλπίς, 479). When it comes to voting on the issue (εἰς ψῆφον, 481), he may conveniently forget that he is voting for his own death (θάνατος ἐν ψήφου φορᾷ, 484). The Herald would like to bring them back to reality.

The Herald is arguing from the opposition Theseus had established between a good head (εὐβουλία) and a high spirit (εὐψυχία), or as Burian puts it, between *logos* (reason) and *pathos* (emotion).[69] The Herald clearly delineates this opposition by almost paraphrasing the words of Phaedra at *Hippolytus* 380–381. There the heroine had said, "We understand and know what is right (τὰ χρήστα), we just don't do it." The Herald's words are very similar: "We all know the better (τὸν κρείσσονα) of two plans, and what is right (τὰ χρηστά) and wrong (κακά) . . . but we wrongly ignore this" (486–487 and 491). The Herald is not making the absurd claim that the Athenians and their leaders are naturally irrational; he is simply pointing out that even an intelligent politician like Theseus might be led astray by his emotions and by fine-sounding phrases. Good plans (εὐβουλία, 161), and ideas (γνώμη, 198 and 336) and arguments (λόγοι, 334) are not enough.[70] In practice, careful reasoning turns out to be of little value, not just because of the role of Fortune, who undoes all calculations, but also because of human passions.

Euripides has the Herald finish up his speech with a clear echo of Theseus' arguments against Adrastus in the first episode. According to the Herald, the Seven against Thebes were justly punished by the gods, and Theseus should not, therefore, intervene to mitigate this punishment. To attempt to correct the judgment of the gods against Thebes would be to assert arrogantly that he knew better than Zeus himself (φρονεῖν ἄμεινον ἐξαύχει Διός, 504). This is precisely what Theseus had said to Adrastus, when the Argive king had dared to lament his lot and beg for help: "The human mind wants to be more powerful than god, and in our mental arrogance, we imagine that we are wiser than the gods" (216–217). The Herald has once again taken over the former persona of Theseus, so that the Athenian king may now argue against his former self. The Herald condemns the errors of rash leaders (508), just as Theseus had condemned the error of Adrastus (128 and 156) in allowing rash young men to act as leaders (160–161, 232, and 234). He praises quiet behavior (ἥσυχος, 509) and cautious foresight (προμηθία, 510), but Aethra had been quick to perceive that these very principles were the ones that led Theseus astray (ἥσυχοι . . .

εὐλαβούμεναι, 324–325), and she angrily denounced them as Spartan vices. The Herald's speech does not, of course, convince Theseus that he was right when he first decided to deny the appeals of the suppliants. On the contrary, its primary effect is to show the audience how foreign to Athenian values are the principles on which Theseus had based his denial. When they came from the mouth of a Theseus, we might perhaps have given such views some credence, but when we hear them from a Theban herald, we recognize them for what they are. They are the principles of foreign tyrants and must be rejected by all good-thinking Athenians.

Democratic Laws, Panhellenic Laws

In the final part of this verbal battle between democratic and oligarchic values, Theseus shows that when properly applied, Athenian principles will automatically entail the defense of Panhellenic ideals. Her democratic values will not oblige her to pursue a policy of appeasement or isolation. Theseus now focuses on the particular point of dispute here, the Panhellenic custom that an army should always be allowed to bury its dead. He rather ingeniously shows that the same principle lies behind the custom itself and behind the decision of the Athenians to risk their lives in what they be-- lieve to be a just cause. Our bodies, he starts off, are not our own at all (οὔ τι γὰρ κεκτήμεθα, 534), so by refusing burial to the Argive dead, the Thebans are not dishonoring them in any way (537). The real victims of the Thebans are Greek public opinion as a whole and even the very Earth itself and the Air, to whom these bodies rightfully belong.[71] In distinguishing between the body and the personality, Theseus is abstracting inner qualities from all outward success, and even from such physical goods as health, beauty, or a fairly long life.[72] To cultivate their inner personality and perform moral actions is the only success and happiness that people can know. It is by performing many such tasks that Athens has won great happiness (πονούσῃ πολλὰ πόλλ' εὐδαίμονα, 577). Aethra had, in effect, made the same argument when she told Theseus that the performance of such tasks had led to the greatness of Athens (ἐν πόνοισιν αὔξεται, 323), and that she would not be afraid to see him rushing out to fight for a just cause (328–329). She was not saying that he would meet with complete success if he did so, because she added shortly afterward that the gods confuse everything (331). In fact, the word she used there, "to rush out" (ὁρμᾶσθαι), brings to mind the rash and unfortunate haste of Adrastus (ἔσπευσας, 161). He had also been fighting for victims of injustice (152), and this reminds us that such fighters are not always fortunate. She was simply saying that to act justly is the only course open to us. If the gods do their part too, and reward us with success, so much the better, but such an outcome is far from guaranteed and should not affect our behavior. After all, fortune and success are rather unreliable things, and so are the gods for that matter. Theseus now sees that it is not mortals who are self-indulgent if they denounce the gods for neglecting their misfortunes (ἆρ' οὐ τρυφῶμεν; 215), but rather the gods themselves for ignoring us (τρυφᾷ δ' ὁ δαίμων, 552).

In standing up to the Thebans, Theseus will be defending his own honor (338–339, 342, 343), but this is not enough. His honorable deeds must also benefit others, as Aethra had told him (327). He is no longer a primitive hero who fights monsters and obeys his own laws; the principle he is now upholding is a law repected by the Athenians and by the Greeks as a people. If the Athenians are prepared to die in defence of their country's laws because they are common to all citizens (νόμοι / κοινοί, 430–431), then every Greek should be ready to defend the custom of granting burial to one's enemies because it is a custom that is common to all of Greece (πάσης Ἑλλάδος κοινόν, 538).

Such laws and customs are "common" in every sense of the word: they are established by everyone, they are for the benefit of everyone, they must be obeyed by everyone. If this particular law about allowing the vanquished to bury their dead were done away with, everybody would lose out. Nobody would wish to risk death on the battlefield if they thought they might be denied burial (540–541). Even those who denied them burial would also be less brave, because such abuses are a surrender to "evil and empty fears" (548), and for this reason should not be encouraged. By refusing to obey this custom, Thebes is behaving toward the other states of Greece just as a despot (δεσπόζοντ', 518) behaves toward the other citizens of his polis. The Thebans are demanding that they should be allowed to ignore the laws common to all Greeks, that they should be allowed to make special laws for themselves (οὗτος ἦν τεθῇ νόμος, 541), just as a monarch treats all the laws as his private possession (αὐτὸς παρ' αὐτῷ, 432). In each case the offenders against the common laws of the state or of Greece as a whole are trying to establish a system that might indeed benefit them, but that nobody else could endure. Theseus, by contrast, does not demand such unjust privileges for himself or for Athens. He has acquired the insight of the Argive women that no country is so invincible as not to depend on the cooperation of others (πόλις δὲ πρὸς πόλιν, 268). He has come to accept Aethra's view that life is more a matter of chance than of calculation (329–331). She had compared it to the throws of dice; he now compares it with "wrestling" (παλαίσματα, 550). He does not simply mean that it is a series of "struggles"; he is referring, like Aethra, to its ups and downs, to its alternations, and he is comparing it with the throws of wrestling, where first one man, then the other will be beaten to the ground. In the face of our common helplessness, he argues, we must rely on mutual aid and on laws that are common to all, both in our state and in Greece as a whole. The Athenians finally decide to go to war with the Thebans, not because Athens is strong and expects to win, but because Argos is weak and Athens might one day share her fate.

The Return of the Hero

Throughout the battle itself, which we hear about from a messenger,[73] Theseus behaves like a model general (707, 726). Toward the end of the description of the battle (714–717), however, he is given a Homeric *aristeia* and suddenly appears in a very different light. To quote a recent scholar, "At this stage of the battle he becomes the hero of legend, taking up the 'Epidaurian club' and reaping the enemies' heads."[74] We have seen this aspect of Theseus only in Aethra's speech at 316–317, where she disparaged his killing of the Crommyan sow and contrasted such deeds with the greater courage necessary on the battlefield. The grotesque image used by the messenger at lines 716–717, where he describes how Theseus was "reaping" and "snapping off" heads, has been objected to on stylistic grounds,[75] but it echoes line 449 with its description of the tyrant who lops off the heads of suspected opponents. These images are indeed grotesque and violent, but they are not poor or inappropriate, since that is precisely how a hero or a tyrant would come across in the world of the city-state. Euripides has reminded us for a moment that Theseus is a heroic figure, but this strange vision from the past vanishes as quickly as it had appeared. By 723, when we next hear of him, Theseus is once again the model general, who follows the principle he had announced at 555–557 by refusing to sack Thebes.

The very strangeness of Theseus' *aristeia* on the battlefield tells us a lot about his character in this play. He had spoken to Adrastus in the manner of a sophist with rather high illusions about his own importance, his intelligence, his invincibility. But the essential point that Euripides brings across in this play is that these are nothing more than illusions. Aethra quickly brought Theseus back to reality, and he recalled that he was not a sophistic superman, that he had handed over all power in the state to the people. For the rest of the play, he reflects on the significance of this new democratic world that he himself enabled to emerge. His political discussions with the Herald may seem irrelevant, and they may seem to render the play somewhat static, but the essence of this play is that Theseus as a king is largely irrelevant, that he cannot act on his own behalf. His only function is to speak on behalf of the people, to remind Euripides' audience what their rule entails, to inspire them like a good citizen speaking before the assembly, not to rule or command them.

It takes quite an effort to remind ourselves that Theseus and Adrastus are epic heroes, that the man who mows down his enemies with a club is in fact closer to the normal image of Theseus the hero. But Theseus refuses to push his heroic successes too far, and Adrastus' reaction to his victory is quite remarkable too. He does not gloat over his enemies, but rather laments for the lot of humanity in general: "O Zeus, why do people say that we wretched mortals can think (φρονεῖν) at all?" (734–735). Just as Theseus' view of wisdom has changed radically, so the implications of the verb "to think" (φρονεῖν) have altered in the course of the play. It had been used by Theseus to describe the excessively high notions of those who could find something to complain of in the gods' dispensation. Such thoughts (φρόνησις, 216), he had complained, were arrogance (γαῦρον, 216–217). Later in the play, his words were turned against him by the Herald (by this time Theseus had, of course, changed his own opinions entirely). The Herald had denounced the thoughts of those who might have such a high opinion of their own intelligence as to question the justice of the punishment that the gods had meted out to the Argives. Such thoughts (φρονεῖν, 504), he argued, were boastfulness (ἐξαύχει, 504). Now, at the end of the play, this same notion is used in a much more modest way, not of confidence or arrogance, but simply of human thought in general. Adrastus wonders whether such a thing can even be said to exist. It is not for rash behavior alone that the gods will send misfortunes to men. Even if men plan as carefully as they are able to, their feeble efforts will still be of no avail. The gods will attach whatever results they please to all these labors. Conversely, if a man is fortunate (εὐτυχής, 741), if his affairs go well for him, he must not congratulate himself on this (747). No mortal can ever trust the course of events, or assume that he has any real knowledge of them. In our common ignorance, we should therefore acknowledge that we must rely on one another as friends (φίλοις, 747). The lesson that Adrastus draws from the course of events is a humbling but very humane one.

Theseus has learned this lesson to the full. He had said earlier that the defeat of the Seven had been a disgrace for them (530), but now he even abandons this last vestige of his old self-righteousness. He performs the humble task, which even slaves would have performed only with reluctance (πικρῶς, 762), of cleaning the bodies of the Seven and preparing them for cremation. This he does on the grounds that there can be no disgrace in human misfortune (κακά, 768), since it is something that no one has any control over, something that is common to us all (ἀλλήλων, 768). The only disgrace is not to act virtuously, because that is the one thing that is under

our control. Adrastus and Theseus have both come to reject the smug confidence that Theseus once placed in the efficacy of good planning
(εὐβουλία). It is a measure of the change undergone by Theseus that, at
the end of the play, Athena criticizes him for being too trusting, too altruistic (1185–1188). This almost amusing intervention by the wily goddess
does not, however, in any way undo all that has gone before. She is after
all a dea ex machina, binding these mythic events to the course of history,
and she possesses knowledge of the future and the ability to put her plans
into effect; the absence of these powers is, we have learned, the distinguishing characteristic of humanity.

The play, as Gamble has shown, leaves us not knowing what to think
about a number of important issues within it, but this very ambivalence is
one of the main themes of the play.[76] It is this ignorance of what our actions
entail, an ignorance common to the audience, the personages on the stage,
and mankind in general, that proves the value and the necessity of the sympathy that induces Theseus to fight for the afflicted mothers of the Seven.[77]
It is equally essential to see that this same principle is related to Athens'
being a democracy. If careful planning does not guarantee the results projected, if the prosperity of the successful man is not really the direct result
of his own schemes and efforts, then it will be pointless to put political
power into the hands of such a man or a social class composed of such men.
There are no natural winners and no natural leaders; there are only equal
citizens. If some are occasionally a little luckier than others, this is merely
a temporary aberration to be corrected by a democracy rather than exalted
into a fundamental principle of human society. Success and failure lie in
the hands of the gods, and belong to no one man; they are common to all.
If Theseus is a representative of the Periclean age, his characterization has
not been inspired by the ideals of the Funeral Oration, which upheld success as the basis of the Athenian constitution. He has been modeled rather
on that other side of Pericles, he represents that Leader of the People
(προστάτης τοῦ δήμου) hated by the aristocrats, for "of the entire gallery
of pseudo-historical Theseus', this one is precisely the most radical."[78]

Notes

1. Cicero, *Republic*, 2: i, 2.
2. Mossé 1979, 436.
3. Lysias 33 (*Olympian Oration*) 7.
4. Pausanias 1: 3, 2; Brommer 1982, 146.
5. Pausanias follows Aristophanes (*Frogs* 1054–1055) in looking upon the
tragic poets as the replacement for adults of their childhood teachers.

6. Jacoby 1949, 221.

7. Herodotus, 6: 131, 1.

8. Jacoby, *FGrH*, note 4, p. 225 to the commentary on 328 (Philochorus) fr. 19.

9. *FGrH*, 323a (Hellanicus) fr. 23, sections 2 and 3.

10. Ibid., *FGrH*, commentary on 328 (Philochorus) fr. 19, 310–311. His Theseus is quite a reactionary figure and sets up a system of social classes based on occupation. Philochorus may have been the source of Pausanias' diatribe against the notion of a democratic Theseus (Jacoby, *FGrH*, note 36, p. 56, to the commentary on 323a Hellanicus fr. 23).

11. Ibid., commentary on 328 (Philochorus) fr. 19, 311.

12. Ibid., note 50, p. 58, to the commentary on 323a (Hellanicus) fr. 23.

13. Jacoby shows that the Marmor Parium is, in effect, an *Atthis*: "the backbone of the work was formed not just of Attic fasti . . . but an Atthis, if not several" (Jacoby, *FGrH*, introduction to the commentary on 239 Marmor Parium, 668).

14. See the formula βασιλεύοντος 'Αθηνῶν Θησέως at *FGrH*, 239 (Marmor Parium) fr. A21 and A22. These two occurrences of the formula appear *after* Theseus has handed over power at *FGrH*, 239 (Marmor Parium) fr. A20.

15. *FGrH*, 239 (Marmor Parium) fr. A32.

16. Isocrates 12 (*Panathenaic Oration*) 126.

17. Aristotle, *Constitution of Athens*, 3, 1.

18. Vernant 1962, 23.

19. Isocrates 12 (*Panathenaic Oration*) 126.

20. This story was probably based on the *Atthis* of Demon, just as its condemnation was probably based on that of Philochorus. See Jacoby, *FGrH*, note 36, p. 56, to the commentary on 323a (Hellanicus) fr. 23.

21. Pausanias 1: 3, 3.

22. "The people took away most of their power from the Medontid kings" (Pausanias 4: 5, 10).

23. ἐκβαλόντες, Lysias 2 (*Epitaphius*) 18.

24. The use of the verb ἀφῆκε ("gave away") to describe the action of Theseus in the late account of Libanius (*Declamation* 1: 152) clearly shows the difference between this peaceful version and the other ones, because it contrasts nicely with the expression ἀφείλετο ("took away") in Pausanias (4: 5, 10).

25. Pity is a major theme at the beginning of this play. We find seven occurrences of οἶκτος and related words in the first 200 lines alone: οἰκτείρειν (Aethra at 34, Admetus at 168), οἶκτος (Chorus at 194), οἰκτρός (Chorus at 48 and 68, Theseus at 96 and 104).

26. Reason, presented by Theseus as the opposite to pity, is also an important theme at the beginning of the play. Theseus speaks again and again of his γνώμη (198, 336) and his λόγος (195, 334).

27. Gernet 1982a, 20–21.

28. Livy 1: 48, 9.

29. Plato, *Menexenus*, 237e7–238a1.

30. "The conclusion of this list of blessings with the mantic arts is certainly not accidental . . . Adrastus' initial error was his disastrous failure to heed omens and prophecies" (Burian 1985, 132).

31. See 248–249: "For if you have not planned well (βεβούλευσαι καλῶς) / you should endure your misfortunes and leave us alone." In line 248, καλῶς βουλεύειν is a paraphrase of εὐβουλία.

32. The word τέκνον literally means "child" and is related to the verb "to give birth." They see their sons not as warriors but as the helpless infants they gave birth to.

33. The same word occurs at 48 and 190 in the same context of reacting to the plight of the unfortunate.

34. Goossens 1962, 431.

35. Goossens notes that a similar condemnation of the poor, not very common in Euripides who "is nearly always very severe with the propertied classes," occurs in the almost contemporary *Theseus* (Goossens 1962, 430). The relevant fragment is *TGF*, fr. 389:

> ἀνὴρ γὰρ ὅστις χρημάτων μὲν ἐνδεής,
> δρᾶσαι δὲ χειρὶ δυνατός, οὐκ ἀφέξεται
> τὰ τῶν ἐχόντων χρήμαθ' ἁρπάζειν βίᾳ.

> For, whatever man is short of money,
> but strong enough to act with his hands, will not refrain
> from taking away by force the possessions of propertied men.

36. Aristotle, *Politics*, 4: 1295 B 35–39. In the *Aeolus*, which appeared four or five years earlier, Euripides had one of his characters promote the idea of the "mixed" constitution, but in less bitter terms: ἀλλ' ἔστι τις σύγκρασις, ὥστ' ἔχειν καλῶς, "but there is a certain mixture that will enable things to be well" (Euripides, *Aeolus*, fr. 21). In the *Suppliant Women*, Theseus is saying that "to re-establish harmony in the state, you can rely neither on the rich nor the poor," so he puts the middle class in charge (Goossens 1962, 431–432).

37. It honors ἀρετή alone and pays no attention to μέρος, "class" (Thucydides 2: 37, 1).

38. Goossens remarks that Theseus' criticism of democracy and his political recommendations are "only removed as much as is necessary from an oligarchic profession of faith." (Goossens 1962, 426–427).

39. Note the contrast between "foreign men" and "Argive women" (ξένοις . . . Ἀργείας, 135); it is picked up by the later contrast between a "sparkling" household and a "muddied" one (λαμπρὸν . . . θολερῷ, 222).

40. According to Aristotle, Cleisthenes introduced the new system of tribes, "because he wished to mix people together, so that more people would share in government: hence the phrase, 'Do not distinguish people by their tribe.'" (*Constitution of Athens*, 21. 1). See also Lévêque and Vidal-Naquet 1964, 43–45.

41. There is an implicit reference to the Theseion at 268. The Chorus com-

plain that even animals have a place of refuge under a rock, and slaves too can run to the altars of the gods. The Theseion was especially famous for its function as a sanctuary for ill-treated slaves, who could stay there until they acquired a new master. See Christensen 1984.

42. The notion of rights by nature and by birth are combined in the word ἔφυς (292).

43. Elmsley emended it to ἥμαρτον, so that it would clearly refer to the Seven.

44. Grube 1941, 232 n. 2.

45. Note the use of τι, "somewhat," in the phrase κἀμὲ γὰρ διῆλθέ τι, "yes, it even affected me somewhat," 288.

46. Aethra remarks of Theseus, "You are wrong in this alone, though thinking wisely (εὖ φρονῶν) in other instances" (303). Εὖ φρονεῖν, like εὐβουλία and βεβούλευσαι καλῶς, is something on which our sophistic Theseus prides himself, and he had, of course, denounced Adrastus for the lack of this characteristic (εὐψυχίαν ἔσπευσας ἀντ' εὐβουλίας, 161, and μὴ βεβούλευσαι καλῶς, 248).

47. Note the συν- of συνέχον πόλεις (310). Aethra is moving from Theseus' model of a natural state where all the citizens are homogeneous and descended from one common race of men to the idea of a state that has been created by men and where citizens from various backgrounds have gathered; she is changing from a model of identity and autochthony (with its emphasis on τὸ αὐτό) to one of diversity and synoecism.

48. Theseus realizes why this is the case, and explains it at 541–542.

49. Note the play on συγχέοντας and συνέχον in lines 311–312. Συγχεῖν is to mix things up indiscriminately, to liquidize everything into mush; συνέχειν, on the other hand, like συμμιγνύναι (222, 224), is to join things together in a suitable mixture. Ironically, the only way to save Greece from the former is to resort to the latter, to join up with the unfortunate, instead of avoiding them as Theseus would do. The same applies to citizens within a state if they wish to save their polis.

50. Plato, *Republic* 1: 348c12.

51. By peering darkly and suspiciously at the world outside (σκοτεινὰ βλέπουσιν, 325), Sparta's actions have been covered with darkness in the outside world (σκοτεινὰ πράσσουσαι, 324).

52. Goossens 1962, 423.

53. "This notorious debate on democracy is always quoted as one of the most flagrant irrelevancies in Euripides" (Grube 1941, 234).

54. It was precisely this element of "the luck of the game" (ἐν κύβοις, 330) that had enabled Aethra to expose the flaws in Theseus' view of the world.

55. Goossens has noticed this too: Theseus makes "criticisms against the 'demagogues' that are remarkably similar to those of the herald" (Goossens 1962, 425).

56. "You were led astray by young men and destroyed your city" (231–232). Compare Adrastus' statement, "the clamour of young men confused me" (160).

57. Οὐ σὺ τῶνδ' ἔφυς, "you were not naturally born (ἔφυς) to be one of those" (292).

58. Προσήκοντ' οὐδέν 'Αργείων πόλει, "you are in no way related (προσήκοντ') to the polis of the Argives" (472).

59. Aristotle, *Politics*, 4: 1295a20.

60. Goossens does not believe that Theseus changes his views in the play, so he is surprised "that the régime of Theseus, opposed to radical democracy, should, however, be so radical itself" (Goossens 1962, 435).

61. Compare Finley's distinction between technical knowledge and political understanding. (Finley 1973, 20–22 and 31).

62. Herodotus, 5: 92, 2.

63. He may also be alluding to an even more recent event at Megara where the returning oligarchs had committed just such a massacre (Goossens 1962, 422).

64. The reference to spring goes back to the image of Pericles that the Athenians in losing their young men in the war were like "a year that had lost its spring" (Aristotle, *Rhetoric*, Book 1, 1365 a 31–33). This reference would be all the more natural if we were to follow Goossens in his belief that the character of Theseus throughout this play is based on Pericles (Goossens 1962, 435–440).

65. Euripides, *Erechtheus*, fr. 360, lines 21–22.

66. ὁ γηγενὴς σπαρτῶν στάχυς, *Madness of Heracles*, 5; γηγενῆ στάχυν, *Bacchants*, 264; χρυσοπήληκα στάχυν σπαρτῶν, *Phoenician Women*, 939. The word is used in similes for mankind in the *Hecuba*, at 593, for life in the *Hypsipyle*, fr. 757, line 6, and for an enemy line in the *Eurystheus*, fr. 373, line 1. In all, 5 out of the 12 occurrences of στάχυς in Euripides refer to autochthonous men rather than agricultural crops.

67. Lines 545–546 and 578–579.

68. Herodotus 5: 78.

69. Burian 1985, 130–131.

70. The correct reasoning of Theseus (λόγοι . . . ὀρθῶς ἔχουσ' and γνώμην, *Suppliant Women* 334–336) is contrasted with the bad βουλεύματα of Adrastus (*Suppliant Women* 336). Such correct reasoning is not enough; it is, in fact, too easy to acquire. Everybody knows the correct λόγος (πάντες ἄνθρωποι . . . τὸν κρείσσον' ἴσμεν, *Suppliant Women* 486–487); it is not because of a false γνώμη that people do wrong (οὐ κατὰ γνώμης φύσιν / πράσσειν κάκιον, *Hippolytus* 377–378).

71. τὴν θρέψασαν, "the [earth] that nourished it," (536) is another reference to the myths of autochthony shared by Thebes and Athens. Theseus, however, mocks the literal belief that the Thebans have in this myth (545–548, and again at 579).

72. To be happy, a man will also need "external goods" of this kind, such as "good birth," "good children," and "beauty" (Aristotle, *Nicomachean Ethics*, 1099a31–1099b7).

73. This messenger seems to be based on the Guard in the *Agamemnon*. He is perched on top of a tower (652; see *Agamemnon* 3: στέγαις) and claps and shouts at the victory of his master (719–720; see *Agamemnon* 25 where the Guard shouts out and *Agamemnon* 31 where he dances for joy).

74. Shaw 1982, 10.

75. ". . . and some very poor imagery in 715–717" (Grube 1941, 235 n. 2).

76. "This doubleness is conceived rather as part of the whole import of the play" (Gamble 1970, 394).

77. Speaking of Euripides, Gamble says, "It might be said that his very sense of our ignorance led him to feel that sympathy and mutual help was essential" (Gamble 1970, 405).

78. Goossens 1962, 435.

6

Theseus at Colonus

King and Country in Sophocles' *Oedipus at Colonus*

A Suppliant Play

Theseus plays a major role in Sophocles' *Oedipus at Colonus*, and to some extent this play could almost be seen as a response to Euripides' *Suppliant Women*. Sophocles is, of course, a very different person from Euripides, and a suppliant play written at the end of the Peloponnesian War will naturally be very different from one written at its beginning. In Sophocles' play there is no conflict between Theseus the adventurer and Theseus the reformer, between Theseus the king and Theseus the democrat. His past is alluded to at 562–568, but it is presented in a very favorable light: we hear only that Theseus endured exile and many dangerous toils. He is a civilizing hero who has suffered greatly in his efforts to benefit mankind, and there are no blots on his record. And he is, quite simply, a king; a very good one, no doubt, but one who is in no way obliged to account for his actions to the people. He leaves the stage several times, but it is never to consult with the Athenian people, unlike Euripides' Theseus in the *Suppliant Women* or King Pelasgus in the *Suppliant Women* of Aeschylus. The only person he listens to is Oedipus, in whom he can recognize a kindred spirit. Theseus represents the aristocratic spirit of Athens, its nobility. He is not a democrat but represents a higher authority whose demands must be obeyed by the people of Attica in the mythical world of the play, and whose ideals should be respected by the audience in the real world of Sophocles.

It is probably no coincidence that Thucydides, who favored the moderate oligarchy of the Five Thousand,[1] and Sophocles, who had his doubts about the spirit of Periclean Athens,[2] should present Theseus as a king, and thus undermine the myth of the democrats that their system was a very

171

ancient one, the natural and ancestral constitution of Athens. We cannot prove that Thucydides knew about this democratic myth, although it is rather likely that he did, as it had been around since Euripides produced the *Suppliant Women* in 429 B.C. Thucydides simply fails to mention this myth, but Sophocles deliberately refutes it. When Oedipus meets the Coloniate, Sophocles has him ask a very strange question. Oedipus asks the local inhabitant whether his country is a monarchy or a democracy, and he answers that it is ruled by a king. Since, however, Athens was the only state that anyone suggested had been a democracy in the heroic age, it follows that Oedipus and Theseus must be living in a world in which there are no democracies whatsoever. So Oedipus has asked whether Athens was governed by a system which, as the answer reveals, could not have been invented yet. Sophocles has not just committed an anachronism, as Euripides had done in the *Suppliant Women*; he has deliberately made Oedipus ask an impossible question.

Sophocles is clearly going to a lot of trouble, and even running the risk of ridicule, to contradict Euripides' account of Athens in the heroic age. When Euripides' Theban Herald assumes that Athens is ruled by a king, this is a perfectly natural thing for him to do, and in fact Euripides expects us to realize this. The effectiveness of Theseus' proud answer is greatly increased by our awareness that the Athenian system is an extraordinary exception, that Athenian democracy is unique. The rather awkward parallel passage in the *Oedipus at Colonus* shows that Sophocles was very much aware of the democratic myth, and perhaps even of Euripides' version of that myth. Theseus must, therefore, be presented very clearly and deliberately as a king. This does not mean, however, that Sophocles is distancing his hero from the democratic city of the fifth century. Theseus is, rather, the mouthpiece of the city's higher ideals; the city is represented through him.

In their myths, the Athenians boasted that their country had always been a place of sanctuary for the oppressed. The Theseion was especially famous as an asylum for people in distress, which was only natural, since the hero himself had come to represent all that Athens stood for. The official funeral orations for the war dead celebrated the moral courage of the Athenians in protecting the children of Heracles and in recovering the bodies of the Seven against Thebes, and both of these myths had, of course, been dramatized by Euripides. Such myths stood in stark contrast with the real attitudes of the Athenians and the strict citizenship law of Pericles, which had been passed in 451/0 B.C. Nevertheless, poets still wrote plays about refugees who had been welcomed to their city by the Athenians of the heroic age. If we exclude the *Suppliant Women* of Aeschylus (where Argos is, however, an equivalent of Athens[3]), the first such play that survives, although it is

rather a special case, is the *Eumenides* of Aeschylus. It tells of the temporary sheltering of Orestes, and the permanent reception of an unusual band
of suppliants, the Furies, who become resident aliens in Athens at the end
of the play. Orestes himself is not a suppliant, and he is quite adamant on
this point.[4] He is therefore subject to the ordinary laws of the land and must
stand trial before the Areopagus for his alleged offences.

Oedipus, on the other hand, is a perfectly legitimate suppliant (ἱκέτην,
44), and as such he refuses to move from the grove of the Eumenides. The
Coloniate, who arrives on the scene, knows only that Oedipus is an odd-
looking man and that he has committed sacrilege, but even so he will not
disturb him in any way without appealing to the city. This does not, of
course, mean that Athens is careless about offences against religion. In fact,
it has a reputation for placing great importance on piety, and Creon appeals to this concern of the Athenians when he tries to persuade them to
expel Oedipus. Similarly, in Euripides' *Medea*, the Chorus after celebrating the holy nature of Athens, wonder how the Athenians will ever welcome a murderess like Medea into their country. And yet, in each case, the
suppliant is welcomed by the Athenian people or by Aegeus. The refugees
are not subject to the ordinary laws of the land; they do not even have to
prove that they are innocent; in fact, all these plays condemn the very idea
of an inquiry into their innocence. They are welcomed simply because they
are in trouble and need help.

In its structure, the *Oedipus at Colonus* is close to the normal suppliant play, where the suppliants ask for sanctuary and are granted their request after an initial refusal; where a villain comes and tries to snatch them
away, and the local ruler comes to their rescue, even if he has to fight a
battle against the oppressors of the refugees. It can, therefore, be compared
with other plays of this type by Aeschylus and Euripides. In its themes it is
strikingly similar to the *Eumenides*, since we have once again a polluted
murderer in Oedipus, the ominous presence of the Eumenides, and even
the Areopagus lurking in the background. It almost reads as an answer to
Aeschylus, because it contradicts much of what he says there, and later we
shall have to explore the relationship between the two plays. If we turn first
to the two suppliant plays of Euripides, we shall see that the themes explored by Aeschylus in the *Eumenides* go through a gradual but continuous development, and that the *Oedipus at Colonus* emerges as the natural
culmination of this literary evolution. The action in Euripides' *Children of
Heracles* is similar to that of the *Eumenides*.[5] In the *Eumenides* Orestes
leaves Athens, but his enemies, the Furies, become "resident aliens"
(μέτοικοι, 1011 and 1018) and remain as chthonic powers that protect the
city; in the *Children of Heracles*, the Heraclids leave Athens, but their
enemy, Eurystheus, (for no immediately apparent reason) becomes a "resi-

dent alien" (μέτοικος, 1033), remains in the land as a hero, and protects the city. In Euripides' *Suppliant Women* the suppliants themselves repay Athens for her generosity,[6] but they do not reward her by donating the remains of a hero.[7] Instead, they bury in the earth the sacrificial knife that was used when they swore eternal friendship with the Athenians (1205–1209). The knife, which will be buried by the place where the Seven against Thebes were cremated,[8] will have precisely the same effect as the bodies of the heroes themselves would have.[9] This concession is, however, extracted from the Argives at the last moment, and only by the intervention of Athena as a dea ex machina. In the *Oedipus at Colonus*, things work out more smoothly. Theseus plays the same role for Oedipus as Athena had done for the Furies or Demophon for Eurystheus, since he gives him a permanent home and sanctuary in Athens. Athens is rewarded directly for its welcoming of Oedipus, since Oedipus himself will protect the land,[10] but there is a slight twist to this reward. The people of Colonus have actually rejected Oedipus; it is their king, Theseus, who welcomes him. The people have failed their country (258–262); their king upholds the true ideals of Athens.

A Local Assembly of the People

The title of the play is polemical. Sophocles is asserting that Oedipus is at Colonus, that this is where he came to at the end of his life and was buried. This is by no means something that everybody would have accepted. There were also versions of the Oedipus myth that stated he was buried at Thebes, at Eteonos, or in Athens itself.[11] Sophocles would naturally have Oedipus buried in Attica rather than in Boeotia, but why does he choose Colonus rather than Athens? Is it simply a matter of local patriotism? Does Sophocles wish to honor his own deme? Colonus does seem to dominate the play,[12] and the place is obviously very important for Sophocles. He was enrolled in the deme of Colonus, the place-name appears in the title of the play, and we also find that the word for "place" (χῶρος) occurs no less than ten times in the play (and seven of these occurrences appear in the Prologue).[13] On every occasion it refers to the sacred grove on the hill of Colonus, or what Oedipus calls "the place," for it is the only relevant place as far as he and this play are concerned. The first stasimon is an ode to Colonus alone and nowhere else, as Knox remarks: "This is Attica, not Athens; the city is not mentioned."[14] Knox goes on, however, to argue that the various allusions of the song really represent the greatness of the city. It would indeed be possible to extend their application to Athens, as Knox has done,[15] but it is vitally important to note that Sophocles himself does not do this. The ode thus maintains the contrast between the city of Athens and the country of

Attica that has been developed earlier. Right from the start of the play, Sophocles has continuously drawn a sharp distinction between the city,[16] Athens, and the "place" (χῶρος, 15 and 24), Colonus. This does not mean, however, that Attica is disunited in any way; what we have is a division of power between the local deme and the central government, between the popular assembly and the king of Athens.

The "place" is described as "holy" twice (χῶρος δ' ὅδ' ἱρός, 16, and χῶρος μὲν ἱερός, 54), and as a place that it is improper to walk on (37), a place that is untouchable and that no one may live in (39). It is an area dedicated to chthonic powers, and it is an entrance (a "bronze threshold," 57) to the Underworld. It is holy to the Eumenides (42), and they are called the special protectors of this deme (δημούχαις θεαῖς, 458). The city, on the other hand, is the source of political power, and it is seen as exercising this power almost in opposition to the deme. In the first words that she speaks (14–18), Antigone draws a contrast between the city with all its fortifications and this holy place which needs no such protection, which has been left, quite literally, intact (ἄθικτος, 39). The Coloniate likewise contrasts the locals ("those who are named after this god" 65) with the king, who lives up in the city (κατ' ἄστυ, 67). At 78–80 he goes to some trouble to point out that he will refer the matter of Oedipus' staying at the grove in Colonus not, as we might expect, to the authorities in the city, but rather to his fellow demesmen at Colonus ("the demesmen right here, not those in the city," 78). The Coloniate says he is afraid to expel Oedipus from the holy grove without the permission of the state (πόλεως δίχα, 47–48), but for him the state is the assembly of the demesmen. They have the power to decide this matter by themselves (κρινοῦσι, 79).

The local government is fully democratic, but when Oedipus asked whether power lay in the hands of the people, the Coloniate answered that the real government of the place lay with the king in the city (τοῦ κατ' ἄστυ βασιλέως, 67). This admission gives more point to his distinction between the city and the demesmen. Later the Chorus will tell us that Theseus possesses the city as an inherited possession (πατρῷον ἄστυ, 297), and there is a slight touch of resentment in their insistence that he is the king of the *city*. The word *polis* would have been suitably ambiguous, since it means both city and state, but the word *astu*, which they insist on using, means the city alone, the city as opposed to and resented by the country folk of Colonus. Later, when Theseus comes along, he will make it quite clear to them that he is king of the entire state, that Colonus is completely subject to his will. He makes no attempt to find out what, if anything, the demesmen have decided about the matter; he immediately offers to help Oedipus on behalf of the entire state (556–562). Oedipus, however, refuses to go to Athens with Theseus and insists on staying at Colonus (643–644). He has been rejected by the people and defended by the king, but he will benefit the entire land, not just the center of royal power in the city.

If Oedipus refuses to go to Athens, there is, however, a sense in which Athens comes to Oedipus, or rather to Colonus. This place has assumed all the chthonic power of Athens. Sophocles makes this quite clear by having Oedipus die there, and even more so by locating the home of the Eumenides in the grove at Colonus. Oedipus is in a very similar situation to that of Orestes in the *Eumenides* of Aeschylus; both of them came to Attica after wandering all over Greece. In Orestes' case, however, the Erinyes were reconciled to him and to the country that received him only after he had undergone a trial for murder. In Sophocles' play, the Eumenides are already Attic goddesses. Their power to benefit the land and guarantee its fertility (Aeschylus, *Eumenides* 912–1020) has already taken effect and is described in the first Stasimon (*Oedipus at Colonus*, 668–719). Their chthonic power does not radiate from their cave under the Areopagus, but is centered on Colonus itself. Unlike Orestes, Oedipus does not have to face a trial, and rather than being chased by relentless Furies to Athens, he actually seeks them out himself. He knows within himself that he has already been reconciled to them. The model of the Eumenides is, however, always in the background, and if in Aeschylus' play there is at first open hostility and in the end an uneasy alliance between the Eumenides of the Areopagus and the goddess of the Acropolis, some of this conflict survives in the contrast drawn between Colonus and Athens, the holy place and the *astu*.

The notion that Oedipus is someone who should, perhaps, be expelled from Attica, comes up only twice in the play. It is raised by the Coloniate elders and by Creon. Each of them has some claim to the authority on which such a pronouncement could be based. The elders, by living at Colonus, have a special knowledge of the region and its divine powers (62–63). Only a local could have access to this sort of information (τῇ ξυνουσίᾳ, 63), and the Chorus notice immediately that Oedipus is not native to these parts (οὐδ' ἔγχωρος, 124–125). The Coloniates are called after the hero buried there (65), and they belong to the region just as much as Colonus himself does. As equal and indistinguishable demesmen (δημόται, 78), who insist on referring to themselves only as Coloniates,[17] they constitute the government of Colonus (ἔφοροι χώρας, 145). They have the right to decide (κρινοῦσι, 79) whether they should receive Oedipus or not. Their discussion (λέσχη, 167) is not, therefore, merely the idle chatter that Hesiod warns the prudent farmer to avoid (*Works and Days*, 493). It is the serious and authoritative discussion that takes place in a political assembly of the people.[18] They insist that the correct procedure of a democratic assembly should be adhered to. If Oedipus has a message for them, he must deliver it publicly in the proper way (ἵνα πᾶσι νόμος, 168). He must leave behind his special position in the sacred grove and speak as any other citizen would.[19]

Antigone realizes what they are getting at; they want her and Oedipus to act in an egalitarian manner, just like other citizens (ἀστοῖς ἴσα χρὴ μελετᾶν, 171). Oedipus must share in the political equality of the Coloniates. At first sight, this might seem to be perfectly fair, but the problem with Oedipus is that he cannot act as a citizen of Athens, or of any other country for that matter. He is without any citizenship (ἀπόπτολις, 208), too wretched to be able to stand up to anyone, even in a fair debate. As a suppliant, he has given up his claim to be treated as an equal, and gained instead the right to be protected as a harmless inferior.[20] Deep down, the Chorus know this, and although they ask him to speak in the normal (νόμος, 168) democratic manner, their first instinctive reaction is to look upon him as someone who is completely abnormal (ἄνομον, 142). As soon as they discover who he is, they return to the deep-seated fear he aroused at first by his terrible appearance.[21] They are afraid that his abnormal actions[22] will bring some curse upon them and their country.[23] Using the same words as they had used in guaranteeing him asylum,[24] they go back on their promise.

The favor they had promised Oedipus, that of asylum, was one that Oedipus had no right to expect, as Antigone acknowledges (49). This does not mean, of course, that the Chorus had the right to withdraw this favor (χάριν, 232) once they had granted it. Later, when things turn better for him, Oedipus will praise the Athenians as the only men who still practice piety, decency, and honesty.[25] At this point, however, the Chorus have broken all these rules of Athenian behavior, as Oedipus complains immediately afterwards (260–262). The only defense they offer for their cynical action is that Oedipus had deceived them by not telling them his name. They were entitled, therefore, to punish him (τίνειν, 230) by denying him the favor they had promised him and by using deceit against him in turn (230–233). They tacitly admit that when they granted him the right to speak among them as an equal,[26] this was simply a ploy to get him away from his place of sanctuary. By the end of the Parodos, they admit that he is equal only to Antigone, and that in wretchedness alone (254–255). It was, therefore, quite unfair of them to demand that he should participate in a debate as their equal.

It is disappointing to see the Coloniates act in this way since their local deme is the closest thing in this play to the normal machinery of Athenian democracy. There is, however, only too clear a parallel for such behavior in Thucydides' *Histories*. In the Melian Dialogue, the Athenians offer the representatives of Melos what seems to be a fair chance to discuss their future in an open debate. In fact, this fairness (ἐπιείκεια) is a complete sham, because behind the delegates of the Athenians lies their military might (τὰ τοῦ πολέμου). The Melians have as little chance of prevailing in the dialogue as Oedipus has in the play.[27] The Athenians may have started the war with a name for decency (τὸ ἐπιεικές, 1: 76, 4),[28] but in his last speech Pericles told them that their empire was a tyranny, and that they would have to maintain their tyranny through fear of what might happen to them if they were to relax their hold over their allies. How far they could go when moved by such fear comes out in a speech of Cleon some years later. Cleon condemned decency and pity as being unsuitable qualities in men who would rule an empire such as theirs (3: 40, 2). Cleon made this statement in the debate over the revolt of Mytilene. On that occasion the Athenians relented and did not follow his advice, but later again, in the case of Melos, they carried out these cynical precepts to the end. In the play of Sophocles, the Chorus suppress the demands of kindness (χάρις, 230–232) and pity (οἶκτος, 255) as if they had been taught in the school of Cleon. So if the Chorus are Athenian democrats, they also share the faults of Athenian democracy toward the end of the fifth century.

There is, however, an important difference between the mythical world of the play and the political world of the fifth century as Thucydides portrays it. When the Athenians decided that they would ignore the pleas of the Melians, there was no higher power to which their victims could appeal. The Athenians made it quite clear that there was little point in appealing to the distant gods, who were more likely to be on the side of the powerful, if anything. In Sophocles' play, on the other hand, things are not quite so bleak. The Chorus do respect the local goddesses. The problem is that their relation to the local goddesses is literally one of blind fear; they do not even dare to look at the goddesses (129–130). In depicting them in this way, Sophocles is probably presenting as true a picture of the average Athenian as we might derive from the sophistic politicians that Thucydides portrayed in the Melian Dialogue. If, in the dramatic structure of the *Histories*, the Sicilian defeat appears as a punishment for imperial *hybris*, Thucydides also acknowledges that some of the blame for the extent of that defeat must go to the religious scruples of Nicias. The attitude of the Chorus is not, therefore, a nostalgic re-creation of Athenian piety before the war, since even Thucydides realizes that some people like this could still be found after almost two decades of war. The arguments used by the Chorus may sometimes seem to test the limits of piety, but their fear of the gods is genuine. Oedipus plays on this fear by making the Chorus as terrified (ταρβεῖν, 292) of expelling him as they are of letting him stay (τρέμοντες, 256). Oedipus can invoke religious scruples, and they will have a real effect on the Chorus.

This genuine respect for religion is not the only way in which Sophocles' Athenians differ from the corrupted sophists of Thucydides. There is another factor in the play ensuring that its ending will not be tragic. In this play the higher principles of Athens are not just an ideal from which the city has unfortunately deviated. They are still present in the person of Theseus, who embodies these principles.[29] The Chorus are thus released from the dilemma that Oedipus had put them in, by being able, and in fact obliged, to refer the matter to this higher authority (295). This is not to suggest that Theseus "is" Pericles, or that he represents "Athens before the plague." After all, the Funeral Oration of Pericles is very idealistic, and it hardly describes "Athens before the plague" either. The speeches of Pericles and Theseus put forward a set of ideals that the city is no longer even trying to live up to. The Athenians have rejected these standards, they have cast decency aside. They may have hoped that by ruling their empire harshly, they would strengthen their control over the other Greeks, but in fact a more moderate administration might have saved the empire by making it more acceptable to the Allies. Similarly, the Chorus may hope to evade the wrath of the chthonic powers of Attica by acting in a formalistic and punctilious manner toward Oedipus, but in rejecting a suppliant they are in fact committing an even greater offence against the goddesses.

Nevertheless, the fear of the Chorus is authentic. Realizing that the matter is more complicated than they thought, they decide to refer it to the king (294–295). For the time being, they will put aside their fear of Oedipus and his awful deeds, if he will make the proper prayers to the Eumenides (490–492) and cleanse himself of this sacrilege at least. As demesmen of Colonus, their automatic reaction was to reject Oedipus as an intruder, but Theseus imposes on them their higher duty as Athenian citizens to come to the aid of refugees. Oedipus had promised them that if they, the members of this deme, accepted him, the entire state would benefit. Theseus commands them to put Athens above Colonus. Later, when Creon will come to drag Oedipus away, the Chorus will regard this as an attack on the entire state (842 and 879). When they shout for help, "O, all you people, come quickly,"[30] they echo the cry of the Herald who proclaimed the synoecism of Attica, "O, all you people, come here."[31] Their thinking is no longer narrow-minded and chauvinist; Theseus has changed them into high-minded patriotic Athenians.

Creon and the Areopagus

When Creon tries to bring Oedipus with him to Thebes, he claims to be acting on behalf of justice (742) and piety (760), but if the religious fear of the Chorus is genuine and disappears once Oedipus agrees to perform the necessary rituals, the same cannot be said for Creon's scruples. Since he is in the presence of Athenians, he can hardly tell the truth, which is that he wants Thebes to benefit from the tomb of Oedipus and not Athens, especially since this benefit would probably accrue during a war between these two countries. Oedipus, on the other hand, has no scruples about revealing Creon's intention to benefit Thebes at the expense of Athens (785–786), and he does not hesitate to side with Athens against what had once been his country. As soon as his aims are thus exposed, Creon drops his mask, and the play turns, for this second Episode, into a normal suppliant play, with a villain forcibly dragging refugees away from their sanctuary.

When Theseus arrives, Creon suddenly has to justify his behavior. He does not want to make this a dispute between Athens and Thebes for the possession of a hero's tomb. Instead he focuses on two points alone, that this is simply a family matter and that Oedipus is ritually impure. Both of these issues recall the status of Orestes in Aeschylus' *Eumenides*. Creon is trying to convince Theseus that Oedipus is not a holy suppliant but rather a criminal like Orestes. It is in this context that Creon brings up the Areopagus (947), which until now has not been mentioned in the play, in spite of the major role that the Eumenides have in it. Sophocles is clearly recalling the part that the Eumenides play in the trial of Orestes and the office given to them by Athena in Aeschylus' play. The goddess had appointed them to be the guardian spirits of the Areopagus in all subsequent trials. Creon must be referring to these goddesses when he says that the Areopagus is "chthonic" (χθόνιον, 948).[32] Every time it is used in the play, this adjective refers to those powers of the earth and the Underworld that are so important to the plot of the tragedy. In describing the Areopagus as "chthonic," Sophocles is acknowledging that it is an institution endowed with the power of the Underworld, and the reason it has this force, the reason that people respect and fear its decisions, is that the Eumenides have lent it their authority.

Creon is appealing to the prestige of the Areopagus on three different levels. First, he is appealing to it as the sanctuary of the Eumenides, or at least to the fear of these guardians that he expects Theseus and the Athenians to share. This accounts for the emphasis placed by all characters on the family throughout this episode, and it explains Creon's demand that Athens should not interfere with his "blood-relatives" (942–943). He is deliberately setting things up so that Oedipus will not appear simply as a suppliant to whom the Athenians might grant sanctuary or not, depending on how generous they happened to be feeling. Instead, he is twisting Oedipus' situation so that he must appear as the accused in a type of trial that will come under the jurisdiction of the Areopagus, one involving kindred blood. In effect, Creon is appealing to the religious power of the Eumenides, and he is asking them to punish Oedipus through their secular arm, the

Areopagus. Although such scruples may have genuinely troubled the Chorus earlier, we know that an appeal on this religious level will no longer have any effect. Oedipus by now has clearly been accepted by the Eumenides at Colonus. Creon himself will discover this shortly afterward, when Oedipus invokes against him the very goddesses that Creon had hoped to find on his side (1010–1013).

Second, Creon is also appealing to the political power of the Areopagus as the censor of morals at Athens. By the end of the fifth century this power was long gone. The Areopagus could only exercise it under rare circumstances, and only when it had been asked to do so by the Assembly. Creon cannot, therefore, go above the heads of the people and appeal to the Areopagus. Once again, he has made a clever legalistic argument, but he proves to be out of touch with the spirit of Athens on this moral issue, just as he had been on the religious one.

Third and last, he appeals to the old role of he Areopagus in the Athenian constitution. According to him, the Areopagus is the true governing body of Athens, not Theseus, and he describes this body as one that plans well (εὔβουλον, 947).[33] It is the presence of this *boule* (a word that means both council and counsel, and Creon is playing on these two meanings) that makes Athenians free. Slaves, Aristotle tells us, are without *boule* (the deliberative power in a human soul),[34] and this is why they are not free. Likewise, without the *boule* (the deliberative power in a political body) of the Areopagus, Creon warns us, Athens would be a servile state (πόλιν . . . δούλην, 917). Creon's aim in this speech is to appeal to an authority which, he hopes (ᾧ πίστιν ἴσχων, 950), will be superior to that of Theseus. Theseus responds rather testily by saying that whatever body Creon can place his hopes in (ἀλλ' ἔσθ' ὅτῳ σὺ πιστός, 1031) is little short of traitorous. This puts an end to Creon's vigorous attempts to draw the Areopagus into the picture.[35]

Creon is not, however, entirely unsuccessful in his appeal to the Areopagus, because if Theseus ignores Creon's suggestion that the matter should actually be referred to the Areopagus, he does take over its functions himself. Oedipus is in effect put on trial in this play, and the trial is conducted as if it were taking place on the Areopagus. Creon and Oedipus deliver formal speeches in the presence of Theseus, with the accuser speaking first and the accused last, as was the procedure in Athenian trials.

There were two unworked rocks on the Areopagus called the Rock of Outrageous Violence ("Ὕβρις), from which the accused spoke, and the Rock of Shamelessness, or Unforgivingness ('Αναιδεία), from which the prosecutor made his accusations.[36] At Colonus Oedipus also speaks from a platform of bare rock (192).[37] He is sitting on this rock when the Chorus consider expelling him, and later when Creon accuses him of patricide and incest. Apart from Creon, nobody else ever says that Oedipus is guilty of outrageous violence, but throughout the play, it is made clear that his accusers are guilty of shamelessness and unforgivingness (ἀναιδεία) in condemning him. When the Chorus command that Oedipus should leave, Antigone begs them to show some shame (αἰδώς, 247). Later they ask Oedipus about his experiences, but he says that the things he suffered were shameless (ἀναιδῆ, 516), so that it would, therefore, be wrong and shameless for the Chorus to ask him about them. His great accuser is, of course, Creon, and when Creon later accuses him, Oedipus calls him shameless (ὦ λῆμ' ἀναιδές, 960). At 863, when Creon has threatened he will drag Oedipus off to Thebes, he calls Creon's speech a "shameless statement" (φθέγμ' ἀναιδές). Creon is using his rights as a prosecutor ruthlessly and excessively. He has mercilessly exposed the disasters of Oedipus' life (962–964), and he seems to forget that he is bringing shame on himself and his family too: "who do you think you are disgracing—an old man like me or yourself?" (961); "Are you not ashamed (ἐπαισχύνεσθαι), you wretch, forcing me to speak of marrying my own mother, who happens to be a blood-relative of yours?" (978–979). Creon's behavior is condemned so often that we almost forget that unforgivingness was assumed to be a natural spirit of revenge, which might be found in any prosecutor, but Creon goes far beyond what is permitted in a prosecutor. He becomes guilty of outrageous violence himself, as the Chorus tell him, and as he himself cynically admits (883). He has gone so far that he is no longer a prosecutor; he has become a criminal himself. In fact, the only person explicitly accused of outrageous violence in the play is not Oedipus, the original outlaw, but his prosecutor, the self-righteous Creon. He is condemned for this by the Chorus (ὕβρις, 883), by Oedipus (καθυβρίζειν, 960), and by Theseus himself (ὕβριν, 1029).

The Areopagus was right beside the sanctuary of the Holy Goddesses (the *Semnai*), and the grave of Oedipus was also there.[38] Sophocles, however, transfers all its sacred power to Colonus, where the grove plays the same role for Oedipus as the Areopagus would have done in the legends of the city. The grove at Colonus is both the place of trial and the burial ground of Oedipus. Oedipus can thus answer Creon's charges by invoking against him the Eumenides of Colonus (τάσδε τὰς θεάς, 1010), whom Creon has insulted by laying hands on their suppliant. The Eumenides are only out to get normal criminals, like Orestes. They cannot harm an exceptional man like Oedipus who is soon to become a hero, because he is beyond pollution and cannot therefore be condemned by them. He is, on the contrary, so free from pollution that he alone is fit to enter their grove as an equal.

The Rules of Supplication

How can a mere suppliant like Oedipus be a peer of the Holy Goddesses? How can a mere suppliant also be a savior? We might almost think that the gods have cheated Creon and the Thebans, that they have deliberately hidden Oedipus' true nature from them. As a result of these divine tricks, the Thebans fail to treat Oedipus with the respect he deserves as a future hero, and thus they lose him to the Athenians. The play almost seems to be a version of the story of the Frog Prince. Theseus welcomes a beggar, and suddenly it turns out that this beggar is especially favored by the gods and will become a hero on his death. Some scholars do, in fact, accept a version of this view and argue that the gods, having treated Oedipus as a beggar for so long, take pity on him in the end and compensate him by making him a hero.[39] This is not to praise Sophocles very highly; it reduces the level of his technique in the *Oedipus at Colonus* to that of a poor playwright who is forced to end an awkward play by suddenly introducing a deus ex machina. To find out what Oedipus really is, to see how both sides of his nature can be compatible, we must first see what Oedipus is not, we must look at the mistaken interpretation of his character. This erroneous view is the one that is presented by Creon.

Creon treats Oedipus as if he were impure (ἄναγνος), and actually calls him that in his presence (945). It is quite obvious that Creon sincerely believes that Oedipus is impure, because he is afraid to allow him to be buried inside Theban territory. He will bury him on the border instead (785). He doesn't fully believe that Oedipus really will become a hero; he is worried that Thebes might be polluted by the presence even of the body of a man who had killed his own father and slept with his mother. Creon decides to play it safe, and he is by no means unreasonable in feeling this way. The Sicyonians, for example, were afraid to bury their liberator, Aratus, within the city walls. They only agreed to do so after Apollo's oracle at Delphi officially declared him to be a hero and gave them permission to bury him inside the city.[40] When they heard this, they changed his funeral into a public celebration. Creon's scruples are, therefore, quite justifiable, but it is not until the very end of the play that we realize how greatly he has underestimated Oedipus. Sophocles deliberately makes the end of Oedipus unclear; we know only that it is wondrous (θαυμαστός, 1665) and awesome (δεινός, 1,651). Before Oedipus disappears, his daughters wash him and dress him in white (1601–1603), which was the traditional color for a shroud.[41] Normally, this preparation of the body would take place after death. By inverting the usual procedure, Sophocles is showing his audience that Oedipus' passing away cannot really be interpreted as a death.

The white robes of Oedipus should perhaps be viewed not as a shroud but as festive garments, such as the Sicyonians wore to celebrate the heroization of Aratus.

Creon is quite right to question whether Oedipus is of heroic stature, but he is still wrong in thinking that Oedipus is impure. Even if we look upon Oedipus as merely an ordinary suppliant, he must be pure, because all suppliants are by definition holy and pure.[42] In Euripides' *Children of Heracles*, Eurystheus in a rather convoluted phrase says that if he is murdered, he will be "not pure for his killer" (οὐχ ἁγνός . . . τῷ κτανόντι κατθανών, 1011). The important point is not whether Eurystheus is a good and pure person in and of himself, but that however bad and polluted he may be, anyone who kills him will incur even greater pollution.[43] The suppliant is automatically considered to be pure, and he will bring pollution upon anyone who attacks him. Conversely, the grove of the Eumenides, though holy (ἱερός, 16 and 54) and untouchable itself (ἄθικτος, 39), will bring pollution upon anyone who trespasses there. If we look at the other suppliant plays, we shall find that the place where the suppliants seek sanctuary is always pure and holy.[44]

The sanctuary is pure and untouchable, but it is not polluted by the suppliant, since he is too weak to violate it. Similarly, it would be a very serious violation for any normal man to enter the women's quarters of another man's house, but a suppliant may do this with impunity.[45] As Parker has remarked of certain criminals,[46] it seems that suppliants in losing their honor also lose their ability to pollute. They are pure almost by default. The gods vent their anger on ordinary men, but a suppliant is too weak and humble for them to notice him. He is put in the same category as small children[47] or as animals, which, as Herodotus points out,[48] act as they please even in temples.

The suppliant is beneath the notice of the gods, but he is not beneath that of his fellow men. In fact, they have a special obligation to look after these especially weak members of human society, or rather outcasts from human society. Theseus is fully aware that he is dealing with such an outcast, and as soon as he comes onto the stage, he describes Oedipus in terms that are deliberately disgusting. He speaks of the bloody destroyed eyes of Oedipus (552), but if he realizes the hideous condition of Oedipus, he mentions it only to show that he himself will not be alienated by it. The Chorus had been horrified by Oedipus' frightful appearance (150–154); Theseus on the other hand not only accepts Oedipus as he is, but promises to do anything, short of some really frightful deed, to oblige Oedipus (560). The Chorus had told Oedipus that Theseus would come as soon as he discovered who the suppliant was. This he did not learn from the Coloniate (303–305), so his motivation in coming to see the unknown suppliant is divorced from any notion of possible benefit to himself or his city. Theseus is moved by pity alone (σ' οἰκτίσας, 556). He is completely above the worries about accepting a polluted man that had troubled the Chorus, and he is equally above the quarrel between Thebes and Athens for the possession of Oedipus' corpse.[49] He accepts Oedipus simply and solely because he is a stranger in distress (562–568).

This willingness to help an unfortunate is the sort of Athenian spirit that Oedipus had hoped to meet; his hopes are not fulfilled until Theseus enters. Oedipus had presented himself to the Coloniates as a suppliant, presuming that this would be enough to win him their support. He deliberately concealed the benefits he could bring to Athens; he wanted these benefits to be a reward rather than a bribe. He wanted, therefore, to appeal to them simply as a suppliant; and both he and Antigone made traditional appeals of supplication to the Coloniates.[50] Oedipus was eventually forced to reveal to the Chorus what he could do for Athens (287–291), since this was the only way he could change their hostile attitude (292–295). The negative reaction of the Chorus belied the good reputation that Athens had acquired (259–262); Theseus will reaffirm it.

Oedipus in fact makes a double supplication to the community, both directly by appealing to the Chorus and indirectly by supplicating at a public sanctuary.[51] Theseus acknowledges that Oedipus made a legally correct supplication both to the citizens and to himself (πόλεως . . . προστροπὴν ἐμοῦ τε, 558), but unfortunately for himself, Oedipus made a mess of things and provided the Chorus with a way of escaping their obligations. The Chorus induced him to leave the grove of the Eumenides, and Oedipus, using a technical term found in cases of supplication, declared "you have raised me up" (ἀνεστήσατε, 276). Normally, this technical term denotes the action of a person who accepts a suppliant. When, for example, Achilles accepts Priam's supplication at the end of the *Iliad*, Homer says "he raised the old man up by his hand" (γέροντα δὲ χειρὸς ἀνίστη, 24: 515). The supplication of Oedipus, however, is not quite as clear a case. An essential feature of Priam's supplication is that he and Achilles touch each other; Homer stresses this physical contact again and again.[52] This contact is essential if a supplication is to have effect,[53] but in the case of Oedipus, such contact is unthinkable. Even after Theseus has welcomed Oedipus and rescued him and his daughters from Creon, Oedipus still does not dare to touch his savior (1130–1138), and he never established any physical contact with the Coloniates. Oedipus has only made a verbal supplication to the Chorus, which is not binding, though he has made the necessary physical contact with the holy grove. When he moves away from the grove, however, this contact is broken, and his supplication has lost all its validity. The Chorus have not acknowledged his verbal supplication as binding and they

have not performed the ritual act of raising him from his suppliant position (though Oedipus mistakenly believes that they have); they have merely
tricked him into leaving his place of sanctuary, and such trickery is quite
within the rules of supplication.⁵⁴ Once he has voluntarily left their grove,
he has lost his claim on the Coloniates. Theseus is therefore under no religious obligation to take care of him, and this makes the *Oedipus at Colonus*
very different from the other suppliant plays. He refuses, however, to take
advantage of the ignoble loophole the Chorus have created and considers
himself and his city bound in honor to help Oedipus.

A Higher Authority

Sophocles deliberately makes Theseus' defense of Oedipus completely gra-
tuitous. In fact, it is not clear whether Theseus looks upon Oedipus as a
guest-friend (ξένος) or as a suppliant (ἱκέτης). These two social roles are
in some ways surprisingly similar,⁵⁵ but it is rare for someone to play both
of these roles at once.⁵⁶ When Theseus realizes who the suppliant is, he
welcomes Oedipus and speaks of him as his personal guest-friend (ξένος)
and the guest-friend of the Coloniates.⁵⁷ This word (ξένος) can mean simply "foreigner," but at 632 Theseus reveals that Oedipus is more than just
a stranger, he is a particularly close type of guest-friend. He is, in fact, a
"war-friend" (δορύξενος) and as such he is always welcome to share
Theseus' home (632–633). At the same time, Theseus also acknowledges
that Oedipus is a "suppliant of the gods" (ἱκέτης δαιμόνων, 634). In effect, Theseus is treating Oedipus as someone who deserves the sympathy
owed to a suppliant and the respect and guarantee of aid owed to a guest-
friend. Oedipus himself uses a peculiar expression to describe his condition; he describes himself as a "guest-friend in distress" (τὸν κακούμενον
ξένον, 261). Ellendt is right in saying that we should understand this as a
paraphrase for "suppliant,"⁵⁸ but it is a very important expression, because
it reveals that Oedipus is both a guest-friend (ξένος) and a suppliant
(ἱκέτης). Under normal circumstances, a guest-friend is equal to his host,
and their relationship is based on mutual advantage; a suppliant, on the other
hand, acknowledges that he is inferior to his host, and that he can only beg
for protection without offering anything in return.⁵⁹ Oedipus' circumstances
are, however, far from normal.

The play celebrates Athens as a sanctuary for refugees, but Athens'
justice is to be rewarded. If Oedipus has, however, the power to reward
Athens, then he is something more than an ordinary suppliant, for an ordinary suppliant is, almost by definition, incapable of repaying his benefactor. In normal cases of supplication, the person who offers shelter to the
outcasts is called their savior (σωτήρ).⁶⁰ Oedipus himself begs for "salva-

tion" (σωτηρία) when he asks the Chorus to protect him from Creon (725). Oedipus, however, is not only a suppliant in need of a savior; he is also a savior himself to the land that welcomes him. This is very unusual, but not unique. There is one previous suppliant play where something very similar happens, and this is Euripides' *Children of Heracles*. In that play, as we have seen already, Athens is indeed rewarded for protecting the Heraclids, but she is rewarded not by the suppliants themselves but by their persecutor, Eurystheus. It is Eurystheus who provides a precedent for Oedipus as a hero who will reward Athens simply by being buried in her territory, and also for Oedipus' unusual role as savior. At the end of Euripides' play, Eurystheus makes the following declaration:

> καὶ σοὶ μὲν εὔνους καὶ πόλει σωτήριος
> μέτοικος ἀεὶ κείσομαι κατὰ χθονός.[61]

> A friend to you and a savior to your city
> I will lie as a resident-alien forever under the earth.

In the *Oedipus at Colonus* the old suppliant is repeatedly called the savior of Athens (460, 463, and 487). The most interesting case is at line 487, since in that line the full ambiguity of Oedipus' position is expressed in the oxymoron, "a savior suppliant" (ἱκέτην σωτήριον). Ellendt was so shocked by this phrase that he gave the word for savior (σωτήριον) a new meaning, "saved," which occurs nowhere else in Greek literature.[62] Other scholars have ruined this line by changing the word from "savior" (σωτήριον) to "saviors" (σωτηρίους), so that it would refer to the Eumenides rather than Oedipus.[63] The paradoxical expression, however, describes Oedipus' position exactly. He is a helpless suppliant and a guest-friend and a savior.

Creon cannot be blamed for not recognizing that Oedipus was destined to become a hero on his death; his real failure is that he did not realize that Oedipus was extraordinary. The everyday rules cannot apply to Oedipus. He either deserves respect as a savior and a hero, or sympathy as a helpless suppliant; Creon gives him neither. He is either favored by the gods and above pollution, or so wretched as to be below it; Creon casts him aside as impure. Theseus assumes that Oedipus is exceptionally unfortunate, and offers to help him in every way; his generosity is rewarded because he discovers in the end that Oedipus is also exceptionally blessed.

Theseus' real reason for receiving Oedipus is that he himself knows what it is like to be an outsider (562ff.), and he realizes that this misfortune could strike any man (566–568). Theseus has determined to treat as guests men who are merely suppliants. He does not act as if he were living in the well-organised world of the Homeric princes, where everything could

be arranged by exchanges of gifts. He realizes that there are also the unwelcome and unavoidable gifts of the gods. He bases his behavior not on
the reciprocity of gifts between men, not on the favors he may one day
demand from Oedipus in return for his present kindness, but on what
Archilochus calls the rhythm that governs mankind, on the balancing out
of fortune and misfortune that the gods oversee (fr. 128, *IEG*). This balance sheet is drawn up not by the warrior nobleman, who calculates what
he has received from and what he owes to his "guest-friends," but by the
gods, who determine what each man will be given.

The Homeric hero defended his honor by harming his enemies and
helping his friends, and he did so with the violence of those who are governed by their passions. The sense of honor that moves Theseus is quite
different. It is because he is truly noble (γενναῖος) that he is not motivated
by any passion or sentimentality in agreeing to oblige Oedipus (1636). The
same nobility prevents him from feeling any of the vindictive anger that
Creon's outrageous behavior might reasonably have aroused (904). Oedipus blesses Theseus for his nobility (γενναίου) which, he sees, is the true
cause of Theseus' concern for Oedipus and his daughters (1042). It was,
once again, his nobility (γενναῖον) that led him to receive Oedipus in the
first place, as Oedipus himself realizes (569). By using the word "nobility" (τὸ γενναῖον) again and again, Sophocles draws attention to the unusual light in which he views this ideal. It is much closer to the endurance
that kept Odysseus alive than to the virtues of the normal Homeric heroes.
It is a quiet virtue based on the bearing of one's own misfortunes, and on
the realization that others have suffered similar ills, or worse. For Oedipus, "nobility" is that inner component which, along with his awful experiences and the passing of time, has taught him to be content with his lot
(8). Even the Coloniate can recognize at a glance (ὡς ἰδόντι, 76) that Oedipus, in spite of his awful appearance, is "noble" (γενναῖος, 76), just as
Odysseus conserves his nobility under his beggarly disguise. Sophocles
makes a direct link between his conception of what is noble and Odysseus'
great virtue of endurance at 1640f., when he has Oedipus make, in rather
difficult Greek, the following request of his daughters: "Enduring what is
noble in your hearts, you must leave this place" (τλάσας χρὴ τὸ γενναῖον
φρενί / χωρεῖν τόπων ἐκ τῶνδε). Ellendt gives an extremely good interpretation of the peculiar phrase, "enduring what is noble in your hearts,"
when he paraphrases it as "enduring what is noble, for by enduring it the
nobility of one's character is revealed."[64]

This new ideal of nobility is personified by Theseus, and it is an ideal
to which Sophocles would like his country to return. It lies not in success
or victory, but rather in enduring misfortune, or, if you happen to be lucky
yourself, in coming to the aid of those who are less so. Euripides' *Suppli-*

ant Women and Sophocles' *Oedipus at Colonus* are obviously quite different plays, but the images they present of human existence and how we should react to life are surprisingly similar. They both proclaim that success is largely a matter of luck, and that true greatness lies in admitting this and regarding both prosperity and misfortune as burdens that must be borne in common. Euripides believed that this nobility was something the Athenian people possessed, and that their king could be fully confident that they would act upon it; Sophocles believed it was something to which they had to be recalled, a virtue that had to be inculcated in them once again, even against their will. Whether such nobility is an ideal the Athenians uphold or one they have betrayed, this distinguishing mark of the Athenian character is always embodied in the person of Theseus, its proud or disappointed hero.

Notes

1. Thucydides 8: 97, 2.
2. Ehrenberg shows that there is a fundamental disagreement between the rationalist and sceptical new Athens of Pericles and the old polis that Sophocles loved, which held onto traditional religion and its "unwritten laws" (Ehrenberg 1954, 153–154 and 157–159). It is not clear whether the Sophocles, mentioned as one of the *probouloi* of 413 B.C. by Aristotle (*Rhetoric*, 3: 1419 a 26), is our poet or a politician who happened to have the same name.
3. Vidal-Naquet 1986, 180.
4. He repeatedly asserts that he is οὐ προστρόπαιος, *Eumenides* 237 and 445.
5. Vidal-Naquet 1986, 190.
6. This element does appear in Euripides' *Medea*. Medea promises to cure Aegeus of his childlessness (717–718) if he will grant sanctuary to her, but this personal favor is quite different from a permanent benefit to the entire people of Athens.
7. The sons of the suppliant women, the famous Seven against Thebes, were supposedly buried at Eleusis, but according to Euripides they are brought to Argos for burial (*Suppliant Women* 1210). A sanctuary is set up, however, to commemorate their cremation (*Suppliant Women* 1211–1213).
8. The Seven against Thebes are cremated near Eleusis, but they are not buried there (see previous note). The only thing that is buried is the knife, which acts as a sort of surrogate for the bodies of the seven heroes.
9. The knife will terrify the Argives (*Suppliant Women* 1208) and give them a "sorry return" (κακὸν νόστον, *Suppliant Women* 1209) if they dare to attack Athens, just as the corpse of Eurystheus will be hostile to the Dorians (*Children of Heracles* 1034) and give them a "sorry return" if they are so ungrateful as to attack Athens (κακὸν νόστον, *Children of Heracles* 1042). In Sophocles' play, the body of Oedipus will have a similar effect, though Oedipus expresses it in rather different terms (*Oedipus at Colonus* 616–623).

10. In the other suppliant plays, the connection between the generosity of Athens and its reward is indirect. Athena defends Orestes, but the Furies bless the land; Demophon welcomes the children of Heracles, but Eurystheus guards the land; Theseus fights for the Argive women, but the sacrificial knife protects Attica. The *Oedipus at Colonus* is the only one of these plays in which the same person is defended by Athens and protects Athens; this makes Oedipus a very peculiar figure.

11. Thebes: Homer, *Iliad* 23: 679–680. The sanctuary of Demeter at Eteonos: scholium to line 91 of *Oedipus at Colonus*. The Areopagus: Pausanias 1: 28, 7. Colonus: *Oedipus at Colonus, passim*; Aelius Aristides, 3 (*To Plato: In Defence of the Four*) 188. See Frazer 1898, 366–367 and Kearns 1989, 50 and 208–209.

12. Kirkwood 1986, 150.

13. "In the present play its explicit importance is limited to its opening and its close, but once established it will no doubt stick in the mind of the audience, with the help of the stage picture" (Winnington-Ingram 1980, 249, note 7).

14. Knox 1964, 154.

15. Ibid., 154–155. Note the precision of the *Dramatis Personae*, which describes the Chorus as a Χορὸς Ἀττικῶν γερόντων.

16. In line 15 Sophocles uses the ambiguous term πόλις, which can of course mean city or state, but πύργοι in the previous line makes it quite clear that he is referring to the city, the ἄστυ.

17. The Coloniate emphasizes that they are all called after the local hero, that they all use their demotic name. They adhere strictly to the wishes of Cleisthenes that citizens should abandon the gentile name in favor of the more egalitarian demotic name.

18. "Reisig correctly observes that it should be understood not as any type of everyday discussion, but as one to which a report is made so that a decision may be reached. Thus λέσχη in tragedy has the same meaning as ἀγορά (assembly) or συνέδριον (council)" (Ellendt 1872, 412, *sub voc.* λέσχη). Jebb discusses the word λέσχη in a note to *Antigone* 158ff., in which he refers the reader to *Oedipus at Colonus* 167. "Here λέσχη is not the meeting, but the discussion which is to take place there" (Jebb 1891, 39–40). For my argument, the important point is not whether the word refers to the meeting or the discussion that takes place during it, but that it does have a political meaning.

19. The expression ἀβάτων ἀποβάς ("step away from this place where no one should step," 167) alludes by contrast to the βῆμα ("step" or "platform") from which any citizen could address the Athenian Assembly.

20. The suppliant's "behaviour indicates that he has temporarily opted out of the 'contest system' of social relationships that characterises normal behaviour between non-φίλοι." (Gould 1973, 94.) Supplication is "a plea for the protection of an acknowledged and magnanimous superior (and thus an acceptance of harmless inferiority) . . . ." (Gould 1973, 100).

21. When they meet him, they say he is "frightening to look at, frightening to listen to" (141); when they discover he is Oedipus, they are frightened once again: "fearing what may come from the gods" (256).

22. "You are going too far; yes, you are going too far!" (περᾷς γὰρ περᾷς, 155–156); "further trouble" (πέρα χρέος, 235). The adverb πέρα has the connotation of "excessive," or "going beyond the norm."

23. "You will not bring down further curses, not if I can help it" (154); "lest you bring further trouble on my city" (236).

24. "Nobody will ever drag you away from this abode" (ἐκ τῶνδ' ἑδράνων, 176); "Get back away from this abode" (τῶνδ' ἑδράνων ἐκτόπιος, 233). The word ἕδρανα (abode) misleadingly suggests that this is a place where Oedipus may stay in complete security.

25. "Piety" (1125), "decency," and "not telling lies" (1127).

26. Themistocles, when he supplicated King Admetus of Molossia, pointed out that it was dishonorable for a host to pretend that a suppliant was his equal, and to use this as grounds for punishing him. He should only act this way towards someone who really was his equal: "It is honorable to take vengeance only on people of your own rank and provided they are equal to you" (Thucydides, 1: 136, 4).

27. Kirkwood 1986, 101–102.

28. Ibid., 101.

29. Reinhardt 1979, 208.

30. ἰὼ πᾶς λεώς . . . μόλετε σὺν τάχει (884–885).

31. δεῦρ' ἴτε πάντες λεῷ (Plutarch, *Life of Theseus*, 25, 1).

32. Ellendt suggests that the word "chthonic" may in this case mean that the institution has its roots fixed deep in the national soil (Ellendt 1872, *sub voc.* χθόνιος), and Jebb takes it to mean simply "local" (ἐγχώριον), but he admits that the only other such use of the word is found at *Ajax* 202 in the expression, χθονίων . . . Ἐρεχθειδᾶν, "the chthonic descendants of Erechtheus" (Jebb 1889, 153, note to line 948). This is not a good parallel, because in saying that the Athenians are descended from Erechtheus, Sophocles is not merely saying that they are native to Attica, but that they are actually descended from the very soil of Attica. In the *Oedipus at Colonus*, it would be very confusing to use the word "chthonic" in this sense of "local," since it literally means "of the earth" everywhere else in the play.

33. Sophocles, as Jebb notes, is playing on the name of the Areopagus (ἡ ἐξ Ἀρείου πάγου βουλή) when he uses the word εὔβουλον (Jebb 1889, 153, note to line 947). He is also playing on the two senses of βουλή, council and counsel.

34. "For a slave does not have the faculty of deliberation (τὸ βουλευτικόν)" (Aristotle, *Politics*, 1: 1260 a12).

35. We can trace from this a development that occurs in the treatment of suppliants in tragedy. In the *Eumenides*, written shortly after Ephialtes had reduced the power of the Areopagus, the declaration by this court that Orestes is free of guilt is the major theme of the play. Roughly a generation later, in the *Suppliant Women* of Euripides, Theseus presumes to pass judgement on the actions of Adrastus, but is rebuked for it. By the end of the century, the thought of doing so is expressed only by the villain of the piece, Creon.

36. Pausanias 1: 28, 5. Orestes recalls the two βάθρα of the Areopagus at *Iphigeneia at Aulis*, 961–963.

37. Musgrave's emendation, αὐτοπέτρου βήματος ("a platform of bare rock"), would be very convenient for my interpretation, but even the manuscript reading, ἀντιπέτρου βήματος ("a rocky platform"), will not change the meaning of the expression greatly, and λᾶου (a "stone" or "boulder," 196) suggests that the stone is not worked. Presumably this stone is no different from the one just within the boundaries of the grove, which was specifically described as ἀξέστου πέτρου ("unworked rock," 19) by Antigone.

38. Pausanias 1: 28, 6–7

39. Linforth rejects these views and claims that there is no real case of compensation by the gods in Greek mythology (Linforth 1951, 102).

40. Plutarch, *Life of Aratus*, 53: 2–4. See discussion of this passage in Parker 1983, 42–43.

41. Garland 1985, 24.

42. ἱκέται δ' ἱεροί τε καὶ ἀγνοί (Pausanias, 7: 25, 1). See discussion of this passage in Gould 1973, 100.

43. See Genesis 4: 18 where Cain is hardly the purest of men (indeed he has just been cursed), but Yahweh still promises that whoever kills Cain will suffer a sevenfold vengeance.

44. In Aeschylus' *Suppliant Women*, the Danaids sit ἐν ἀγνῷ (223). Andromache, in Euripides' play, takes refuge at the ἀγνὸν τέμενος or ἀγνὸν βωμόν of Thetis (*Andromache* 253 and 427). Megara, in the *Madness of Heracles*, seeks sanctuary at the ἀγνοῖς ἑστίας . . . βάθροις (715), and Aethra, in Euripides' *Suppliant Women*, stays at the ἀγναῖς ἐσχάραις of the Eleusinian goddess (33).

45. Odysseus' supplication of Arete is a good example of this. It is discussed by Gould, who mentions parallels from other Mediterranean societies (Gould 1973, 98).

46. "It looks as if, in the case of the traitor and temple-robber, the law of the gods ensuring the right of burial ceased to apply. One might even conclude that, with their honor, they lost the power to pollute" (Parker 1983, 46).

47. Children do not pollute the city if they are buried inside it: "The . . . Greek communities . . . presumably felt that no great contagion could proceed from such insignificant bones" (Parker 1983, 41).

48. Herodotus says that only Greeks and Egyptians object to copulating in temples. All other nations find nothing wrong with this, and argue that if it were displeasing to the gods, then animals would not do it (Herodotus 2: 64).

49. "The Theseus of Sophocles is not the ideal patriot that he always is in Euripides. . . . He himself stands outside the opposing positions" (Reinhardt 1979, 213). "If Theseus, the model-sovereign of the model-city, distinguishes—though Oedipus does not—the city of Thebes from its rulers, this is, in short, more in keeping with the logic of his character than with that of the tragedy as a whole" (Vidal-Naquet 1986, 186).

50. Ἱκετεύομεν (241): Antigone. Ἱκνοῦμαι (175) and ἱκέτην (284): Oedipus.

51. Gould suggests that in the Bronze Age, the suppliant would have had recourse to the hearth in the palace, which would have served both as the personal altar of the king, and the common altar of his people. Thus, supplication at

an altar is always an appeal to the community as a whole (Gould 1973, 94, note 100).

52. "With his own hands he grasped the knees of Achilles and kissed his hands" (24: 478). "I endured reaching my hand to the face of the man who killed so many of my children" (24: 506). "He took the old man by the hand" (24: 507). "He raised the old man by the hand" (24: 515).

53. Gould 1973, 77, 81 and 84–85. Only "complete" supplication with physical contact is valid. In the *Medea* and *Hippolytus* physical contact with the hand is described as βιάζεσθαι (*Medea* 339 and *Hippolytus* 325), and it makes the supplication of Medea and the Nurse binding on Creon and Phaedra respectively. See Gould 1973, 85–87 for an analysis of these two passages.

54. Gould 1973, 82–83.

55. Ibid., 79.

56. "Odysseus seems to oscillate between the role of ξένος and that of ἱκέτης. . . . But Odysseus' is a peculiar, even a unique, case" (Gould 1973, 93, note 94a).

57. Ellendt lists these cases where ξένος is used in the special sense of "guest" ("someone who is joined to us by a certain bond of obligation") rather than "stranger": it is used by the Chorus of Oedipus at 1637; of Theseus by Oedipus at 1119 and 1206; and of the Coloniates by Oedipus at 822 and 844 (Ellendt 1872, 479, *sub voc.* ξένος).

58. "Understand it as suppliant" (Ellendt 1872, 479, *sub voc.* ξένος).

59. Gould 1973, 88–89, 92 note 94a, and 94.

60. Danaus declares to his daughters that the Argives are "saviors (σωτῆρες) without a doubt" (Aeschylus, *Suppliant Women* 982). The Corinthian women use the same term when they ask Medea where she will be able to find refuge: "What friendship abroad or home or land will you find as a savior (σωτῆρα) from your troubles?" (Euripides, *Medea* 359–361). Similarly, Iole uses this term when she tells the sons of Heracles to remain grateful to Athens: "Always consider them to be your saviors (σωτῆρας) and your friends" (Euripides, *Children of Heracles* 312).

61. Euripides, *Children of Heracles* 1032–1033.

62. "But it clearly means *safe* at OC 487: δέχεσθαι τὸν ἱκέτην σωτήριον. Bothe and Reisig, however, think it is used actively, but this view does not pay proper attention to the fact that Oedipus had said he was bringing safety to the land of Attica at line 460; for it would be out of place to mention that benefit in a prayer appealing to the gods" (Ellendt 1872, 712, *sub.voc.* σωτήριος). Campbell follows him in his note to line 487 (Campbell 1879, 180).

63. Pearson 1964 and Dawe 1979 follow Bake in emending to σωτηρίους. Jebb 1889, Dain and Mazon 1960, *LSJ*, and Kamerbeek 1984 all retain and justify the manuscript reading in their note to this line.

64. "*ferentes quod generosum est*, in quo ferendo generosa indoles conspicitur" (Ellendt 1872, 142, *sub.voc.* σωτήριος).

7

Theseus Enters History

Thucydides

At around the same time as the *Oedipus at Colonus* was produced, Thucydides wrote the first extant version of the story that Theseus had united the Athenians into one state. Herodotus had mentioned Theseus in a passing reference to his abduction of Helen. There we learn that the Deceleans were quite annoyed with him for irresponsibly dragging them into a war against the Spartans. In effect, the Deceleans betrayed Theseus by revealing Helen's whereabouts to the Dioscuri, but "even the Athenians themselves admit" that this was a good thing to do[1] and that the Deceleans were acting out of concern for the country as a whole.[2] Thucydides will suggest a similar resentment against the king's power on the part of the demesmen of Attica, and we have already seen an element of this attitude in Sophocles' play. Thucydides presents Theseus as a forerunner of Pericles, and his ambiguous attitude to the mythical king reflects his uncertain views about Athenian foreign policy. The mythical unification of Attica is directly compared with the unpopular plan of Pericles for defending the state. Pericles ordered the Athenians to come together into the city and ensure its survival, but to abandon the countryside and allow the Spartans to plunder it with impunity. In Thucydides' work, Pericles becomes, in effect, a second and more radical synoecist. His policy continues that of Themistocles, who had argued that the Athenians should rely on their naval defenses[3] and had persuaded them to refortify the city and build the Long Walls after the Persian Wars.[4] Both these policies had been the making of Athens, and Thucydides seems to approve of Themistocles and Pericles. Nevertheless, he is well aware of the hardship that Pericles' decision caused the Athenians, and he seems to wonder whether the path of glory was really the best one for Athens in the long run. He is also the only writer to wonder whether even the synoecism of Theseus might not have been gained at too high a price, since later writers are unanimous in proclaiming it as a great and extraordinary achievement.

Modern scholars are not sure when the synoecism of Attica occurred, though it obviously took place at some time in the prehistoric period.[5] The Greeks themselves had no doubts; they were certain that Attica had been united during the reign of Theseus a generation before the Trojan War, and the *Marmor Parium* gives 1259/8 B.C. as the exact date.[6] For the Athenians, the important thing was that the population formed one homogeneous body, and that this unity had existed since mythical times.[7] There were two separate traditions about the synoecism of Attica. One told that the Athenians had no urban civilization whatsoever, the other that they had already been organized into twelve cities by Cecrops. The first version stresses that the Athenians had been scattered throughout the land.[8] They had lived in villages, and devoted themselves to working in the fields.[9] This version makes Theseus a sort of civilizing hero; until he comes along, the Athenians are like Arcadian aborigines. His real achievement is not just that he united Attica, but that he introduced them to civilized life in the first place. Thucydides, however, belongs to the second tradition. According to this version of the myth, there were already cities in Attica and Theseus united them into one big state. Most of the sources state that there were eleven or twelve cities, and Philochorus even gives a list of them.[10] Thucydides obviously has this version of the myth in mind when he says that the Athenians used to live "in cities,"[11] and that these cities had their own councils and magistrates (2: 15, 2).[12] Like the other representatives of this version, Thucydides stresses that Theseus united the Athenians into *one* polis,[13] the polis *as it now is*,[14] and he contrasts this new political arrangement with the previous division into several cities.

Thucydides believes that this development was a very difficult one for the Athenians, and that regional loyalty had always been of particular importance to them.[15] Even as late as the first years of the Peloponnesian War, the country districts that the inhabitants of Attica come from are, for them, their real native land;[16] they come to Athens as to a foreign country.[17] When they are forced to abandon the countryside, the reluctance they feel is not something new that suddenly hits them in 431 B.C. They have had this attachment to their region since the time of the early kings before Theseus; they felt this way after the synoecism; and they maintain this strong regional loyalty in Thucydides' own day.[18] Thucydides tells us that the temples in their local regions are "ancestral," a word which implies that they are not only very ancient but also especially sacred.[19] Cleisthenes himself, when he reorganized the tribes and demes, did not dare to interfere with the ancestral religious customs of the Attic regions.[20] Thucydides also remarks that the strong feeling of regionalism in Attica springs from their attachment to the "old-fashioned constitution," and according to Aristotle the return to the "ancestral constitution" under Theramenes was quite popular.[21] A similar spirit of conservative regionalism can be found in Aristophanes' comedies, and also in the *Oedipus at Colonus*.

Thucydides believes that the spirit of regionalism against which Theseus has to fight is a very old mode of thought. This can be seen not only in Thucydides' analysis of such local patriotism in Attica, but also in the similarity between the behavior of Athenian country people and that of the prehistoric Greeks in Thucydides' work. Like the primitive Greeks, the early inhabitants of Athens kept to themselves and refused to come together.[22] In fact, they were even more reluctant to move to Athens than entire Greek peoples were to move to a new country.[23] In the normal course of events, Attica would have been invaded by others, but it was saved from invasion by the poverty of its soil (1: 2, 5). The reluctance of Attica's inhabitants to unite did, however, keep their country weak, and it even subjected Attica to several internal wars (2: 15, 1). They were standing in the way of Athenian greatness, but as in Aristophanes, it is not absolutely clear that the shrewdness of these country folk may not in the long run be wiser than all the fine schemes of the great men in the city.

In deference to such regional sentiment, Theseus must allow the country people "to manage their own affairs as they had done previously." Thucydides uses the very same expression when he is describing the early Greek peoples; they also "manage their own affairs."[24] The inhabitants of Attica thus enjoyed a measure of autonomy that was normally possessed only by separate states. In fact, Thucydides refers to life before the unification of Attica as "autonomous living."[25] Among the Greeks, "autonomy" was a technical term denoting the condition of a semi-independent state that was in the sphere of influence of a greater power. An important passage for determining the meaning of autonomy in Greek thought also provides a close historical parallel for Theseus' synoecism. This is the passage in the first book of Herodotus' *Histories* where he describes the unification of Media under Deioces. The Medes used to be "autonomous" and they lived in villages, just like the Athenians before Theseus.[26] Deioces sets himself up as king, and forces them to build a capital city, Ecbatana, and to pay more attention to it than to the villages they came from.[27] The unifications of Attica and Media, and the language used to describe them are too close for a reader to feel entirely comfortable about the progress that Athens has made by becoming united. Theseus is beginning to look suspiciously like an oriental despot, and there is a further element in the rivalry between his centralized government and local autonomy that strengthens this comparison. Autonomy was often connected with "ancestral customs," since tradition was about the only higher power that the weaker state in such an arrangement could appeal to, if it was wronged by the more powerful state.[28] We have seen that the autonomous inhabitants of Attica were indeed very much attached to such "ancestral customs," to their ancestral temples, and to their ancestral constitution. These are things that all Greeks greatly admired, and autonomy itself is not a notion with negative connotations. It may be true that the Chorus of Sophocles' *Antigone* uses this word in a negative way to describe the heroine's behavior, but she is the great defender of ancestral customs, and she stands up for them against a despot.[29] Sophocles does not necessarily wish us to agree with the Chorus that her autonomy is a negative characteristic. It would, of course, be a gross exaggeration to say that Thucydides portrays Theseus as a power-hungry oriental despot whose sole desire is to deprive people of their autonomy, or as a bullying tyrant who delights in trampling upon ancestral customs. Nevertheless, it is extremely significant that Thucydides does not present Theseus as a champion of enlightenment and progress doing battle against the forces of darkness and backwardness. He appears as a very ambitious and farsighted ruler, but Thucydides seems to question whether these ambitions and visions are really for the best. If Theseus started the unification of Attica, Pericles brought it to its awful logical conclusion, by sacrificing the Attic countryside to his ambitions; and if Theseus set Athens on the road to glory, Pericles showed her just where that road might lead her.

The last speech of Pericles recorded by Thucydides (2: 63, 2–3) exposes the brutal nature of Athenian ambition. He admits that their empire is unjust, he even admits that it is a tyranny, but, he tells them, it is too late to turn back now; they must pursue the course they have taken to the end. The love of Athenian power that he had inspired in the Funeral Oration now turns out to be the sinister "lust for tyranny" that had inspired Deioces.[30] Pericles denounces those who might have some misgivings about the path on which Athens has marched. According to him, they are idle, they are cowardly, and they would be incapable of surviving, even if they were to be given the opportunity of minding their own business (significantly, the phrase he uses is "living autonomously").[31] The enemy, for Pericles, is the spirit of regional loyalty that would confine its horizons to Attica alone, that would gladly forgo the doubtful glory of controlling an empire. He has no real answer to the misgivings of the quiet country people of Attica; all he can say to them is that it is too late, and that the justice of their complaints is therefore irrelevant.[32]

Pericles is, of course, quite right, in the sense that Athens has been pursuing its aggressive path to glory for a very long time. As far as

Thucydides is concerned, Pericles is following in the footsteps of Themistocles and of Theseus. The synoecism represents the major turning point in Athenian history, and this event is so far back in the past, that it is a little late to think of turning back now. The greatness of Athens would have been impossible without the synoecism of Attica by Theseus.[33] From that time on, Attica remained free from internal strife (1: 2, 5), her stability attracted immigrants of the best type, and this influx made her even greater still (1: 2, 6). Thucydides considers this achievement of Theseus' as a definite sign that he was indeed a "brilliant" leader, and thus he puts Theseus in the same league with Themistocles, who founded the Athenian navy and set Athens on the road to supremacy, and Pericles, who completed the work of Themistocles.[34]

In spite of this, Thucydides does not accept the normal Athenian legend of a great progressive march from unification to democracy to the empire, a movement that started with Theseus and whose every stage was attributed to him through ever bolder flights of anachronism. On the contrary, he sees this process as one that it was indeed too late to change, but not too late to question. He seems to fluctuate between the optimistic belief of his country's leaders that Athens could have pulled anything off, even the Sicilian expedition, and the suspicion that the entire imperial adventure was madness. These very legitimate doubts were felt by country people in the fifth century, as Aristophanes shows us so often, and Thucydides believes that the people of Attica have quietly entertained these doubts throughout the whole of Athenian history. This history starts with Theseus, and he is the epitome of Athenian glory, though by the end of the fifth century, it was time to wonder whether this glory was not all vanity.

Hellanicus

Thucydides mentioned Theseus in his great work which encompassed the entire Greek world, but he obviously could not pay a great deal of attention to him. The work of another fifth-century historian is quite different in its emphasis, and it marks a turning point in the treatment of the Athenian hero. This work is the *Atthis* of Hellanicus, a somewhat older contemporary of Thucydides.[35] Hellanicus, although he was actually from Lesbos, was the first historian to write a history devoted entirely to Attica. As part of this history, he had to give an account of the entire career of Theseus. He is, therefore, the first historian to have written a complete biography of the hero. Seven fragments survive from this portion of his *Atthis*. Unlike the Atthidographers who came after him, Hellanicus makes no attempt to rationalize the more outlandish stories about Theseus,[36] or to whitewash the hero's character.[37] His Theseus is closer to the wild man found in legends before the fifth century than he is to the civic hero presented in Athenian tragedy. If Hellanicus alters any details in the myth, it is only to reconcile these events with the accepted chronology of the heroic age. Otherwise, he is quite content to follow the old myths about Theseus. He portrays him as an Athenian version of Heracles, with all the faults of that hero, just as the Athenian Treasury at Delphi had done a century earlier.

In the Cretan adventure,[38] Minos appears as a real fiend.[39] He comes to Athens in person and chooses the victims himself (in the normal version they cast lots among themselves). None of the young men are allowed to bring a weapon, so their chances of surviving against the Minotaur are negligible.

Hellanicus tells us that Theseus founded the Isthmian Games for Poseidon because he wanted to imitate the Olympic Games that Heracles had inaugurated for his father, Zeus.[40] Theseus is, therefore, deliberately setting out to be a second Heracles, and Hellanicus does not seem to find it at all embarrassing that Athens should have a derivative hero.[41] Hellanicus also reduces the importance of Theseus' battle with the Amazons by the Euxine Sea. He concludes that since Theseus belonged to a later generation, he cannot have been Heracles' partner in this war.[42] Theseus must, therefore, have gone on a purely private expedition (ἰδιόστολον), in which he took "the Amazon" (Antiope) as a captive.[43] The Amazons waited for the Crimean Bosporus to freeze, crossed over, invaded Attica, and fought there for four months before they were defeated.[44]

If, in the work of Hellanicus, Theseus seems to be no more than a latter-day imitator of Heracles, he is also presented as quite an unsavory character. Rather than covering up Theseus' abduction of Helen, Hellanicus makes it, if anything, even worse. In the interests of accurate chronology, he says that Theseus was fifty years old at the time,[45] and he adds that Helen was only seven![46] The only reason Theseus commits this peculiar crime is that he and his friend Peirithous had agreed that they both would marry daughters of Zeus, and Helen has the misfortune to fulfill this requirement. He leaves her at Aphidna with his mother Aethra, and then the pair of them go off to Hades to abduct Persephone. Meanwhile, the Dioscuri, enraged at their inability to find their sister, lay Attica to waste and take Aethra as a captive.[47] Theseus is a highly irresponsible character, who has brought destruction on his country for the sake of a silly agreement with his equally disreputable friend.

Hellanicus has, therefore, written about four of the five adventures that appeared in the old stories told about Theseus up till the middle of the sixth century. Only the story of his battle against the Centaurs is missing, and that could easily have been described in a lost portion of his *Atthis*. His characterization of Theseus is no different from the one that appears in those earlier tales. The historical tradition of Theseus, founded by Hellanicus, starts off at much the same level as the mythical tradition had several centuries earlier. The development his character goes through in the *Atthides* is in some ways similar to the changes it underwent in the poetic tradition. The Theseus of Philochorus is definitely a more civilized and moral person, just as the Theseus of Euripides' *Suppliant Women* is better than the character who appears in Homer or Hesiod, but the motivation behind these developments in the two traditions is completely different. With the exception of Cleidemus, who invents all kinds of new details and tries to write an adventure story in which Theseus appears as a contemporary (fourth-century) soldier-statesman,[48] the historians are trying to rationalize the unnatural elements out of the story, to reconcile it with other traditions, and to whitewash the Athenian hero. They are also responsible for many of the stories that attribute various innovations in political and religious life to Theseus. They are not interested in Theseus as a complex personality or an ambiguous role model, such as we found him to be in the literary works of the fifth century. He is for them no more than a convenient name to which they can attach various achievements. They often display considerable ingenuity in doing so, but their aim is not, after all, to create a good story or pass on messages about life.[49]

With the advent of the Atthidographers Theseus leaves the poets and becomes the property of historians and politicians. The extent of this change may be judged by noting the sources of Plutarch's biography. Plutarch is, of course, a historian himself, but even so it is remarkable that he depends almost entirely on the Atthidographers for information about the career of a man who is, after all, a mythical figure, and that he rarely takes material from the poets.[50] The one sphere in which Theseus remained a figure who could arouse some interest and controversy was that of the political debates over the development of the Athenian constitution. In these arguments, Theseus was declared by the various factions to have been the inventor of their political program. These stories told about Theseus are far from being exercises of the mythopoeic imagination, since whatever interest they possess derives not from their characterization or plot, which are always rather flat, but rather from the intensity of the political debate in which their creators were engaged.

The fourth century marks the end of the age of the city-state. These little republics had seen the rise of hero cult, and when they started to decline, their myths and heroes went down with them. The mythical heroes no longer had the hold over the popular imagination that they once had enjoyed in the heyday of the polis. Perhaps the historians of Attica were vaguely aware of this decline, and this may in part have been why they decided to preserve these traditional stories for posterity. With their work, the evolution of Theseus as an Athenian hero comes to an end. He had started out as a hero in primitive tales of adventure, and then he developed into a model of everything that Athens stood for, and now he had finally become a subject of antiquarian interest and academic investigation.

But let us end with an image of Theseus in his heyday, and in that of his city-state itself. We should think of him as he was described in the stories that the Athenians heard from their parents and their poets. Euphranor's nostalgic painting captures the paradox of this image that had meant so much to the Athenians during their century of greatness. There one saw Theseus, an ancient hero-king, standing by democracy and the people as their patron and benefactor, a friendly royal spirit protecting their democratic constitution.

Notes

1. The Deceleans performed a deed, which was beneficial for all time, as even the Athenians themselves admit." (Herodotus 9: 73, 1).

2. "The Deceleans, or according to other people Decelus himself, were angry at the arrogance of Theseus and feared for the entire land of the Athenians . . ." (Herodotus 9: 73, 2).

3. Herodotus, 7: 141–144 and Plutarch, *Life of Themistocles*, 10.

4. Thucydides, 1: 89–90.

5. Estimates range from the thirteenth century (Padgug 1972) to the tenth century (Diamant 1982) to the eighth century (Moggi 1976).

6. *FGrH*, 239 (*Marmor Parium*) fr. A20.

7. The myth of autochthony also promoted this idea of Athenian unity.

8. Σποράδην, Isocrates 10 (*Helen*) 35. Dispersos . . . separatim, Valerius Maximus, 5: 3, 3.

9. They lived in villages or "demes": Isocrates 10 (*Helen*) 35; Cicero, *Laws*, 2: 5; Diodorus, 4: 61, 8; Valerius Maximus, 5: 3, 3. They live a rural life: Cicero, *Laws*, 2: 5; Valerius Maximus, 5: 3, 3.

10. Theophrastus, *Characters*, 16, 6 and the *Marmor Parium*, (*FGrH* 239 fr. A20) state that there were twelve cities. Charax says that there were eleven (*FGrH* 103 fr. 43), and Philochorus just lists eleven names (*FGrH* 328 fr. 94), though one has probably dropped out of the manuscript. Perhaps Charax did not include Athens itself.

11. κατὰ πόλεις, Thucydides, 2: 15, 1. Moggi points out that this phrase alone suggests that Thucydides was aware of the version of the myth that told of a previous synoecism into twelve cities by Cecrops (Moggi 1976, 3).

12. Plutarch must be basing his account of the synoecism on this version too, because he refers to the *prytaneia* (city halls), councils, and magistrates of the previous system (*Life of Theseus*, 24, 4).

13. "He forced them to use this one polis" (Thucydides, 2: 15, 2). The one new city is contrasted with the other previous cities: τῶν ἄλλων (Thucydides, 2: 15, 1). Later versions emphasize that the newly united Athens consists of one single polis, as distinct from the several preexisting ones: "into one (polis)" (Theophrastus, *Characters*, 26, 6); "into one polis" (*FGrH* 328 Philochoros fr. 94); "into one city . . . and into one people of one polis" (Plutarch, *Life of Theseus*, 24, 1); "Having created one council chamber and city hall, common to everyone" (Plutarch, *Life of Theseus*, 24, 3).

14. "What is now the city" (Thucydides, 2: 15, 2); "the present city" (*FGrH* 328 Philochoros fr. 94).

15. "From very early times this [regional loyalty] had been a characteristic of the Athenians above all other peoples " (Thucydides 2: 15, 1).

16. "Each one felt that he was in fact leaving his own state" (Thucydides 2: 16, 2).

17. Thucydides refers to the move Pericles forces upon them as an ἀνάστασις (2: 14, 2) or a μετάστασις (2: 16, 1). These words are normally used of mass deportations and migrations from a people's native land.

18. "From very early times" (2: 15, 1); "after they were synoecised" (2: 16, 1); "and up until this war" (2: 16, 1).

19. "Leaving behind what had been their ancestral temples throughout the ages" (Thucydides, 2: 16, 2).

20. Aristotle, *Constitution of the Athenians*, 21, 6.

21. Their temples mean so much to them because they have been theirs "since the times of the old-fashioned constitution" (Thucydides 2: 16, 2). The Athenians are delighted when Theramenes restores the "ancestral constitution" (Aristotle, *Constitution of the Athenians*, 35, 2–3).

22. 1: 2, 2 and 2: 15, 1–2.

23. Of the early Greeks, Thucydides says: "At first there were migrations, and people easily left their own land" (1: 2, 1). When he speaks of the early inhabitants of Attica, he says by contrast: "They did not easily make migrations" (2: 16, 1).

24. The people of Attica: Νεμομένους τὰ αὑτῶν ἑκάστους (Thucydides, 2: 15, 2). The early peoples of Greece: Νεμόμενοι τὰ αὑτῶν ἕκαστοι (Thucydides, 1: 2, 2).

25. αὐτονόμος οἴκησις (Thucydides, 2: 16, 1).

26. "They were all autonomous" (Herodotus, 1: 96, 1). "The Medes used to live in villages" (Herodotus, 1: 96, 2).

27. "He forced them to build one city" (Herodotus, 1: 98, 3). Compare the description of the synoecism of Attica: "He forced them to use this one city" (Thucydides, 2: 15, 2).

28. Ostwald 1982, 9.

29. αὐτόνομος ζῶσα (Sophocles, *Antigone* 821) literally means "living autonomously," but the Chorus mean something like "living by your own rules," or "being too headstrong." Ehrenberg argues that Antigone's defense of tradition against Creon (Ehrenberg 1954, 31–34 and 54–61) is an implicit attack on the

autocratic style and irreligious scepticism of Pericles (Ehrenberg 1954, 94–96 and 153–154).

30. "But you must in fact contemplate every day the power of this city and become her lovers (ἐραστάς)" (Thucydides, 2: 43, 1); "Since your [control over the empire] is a tyrannical power (τυραννίδα), and although it may seem unjust to have acquired it, it would be dangerous to abandon it" (Thucydides, 2: 63, 2). Compare Deioces who "fell in love with tyrannical power" (ἐρασθεὶς τυραννίδος, Herodotus, 1: 96, 2).

31. "If they were to live autonomously (αὐτονόμοι οἰκήσειαν) by themselves" (Thucydides, 2: 63, 3). Compare the "autonomous living" (αὐτονόμῳ οἰκήσει) of the early people of Attica (Thucydides, 2: 16, 1).

32. "You can no longer get out of it" (Thucydides 2: 63, 2). The casual way in which he says "although it may seem unjust to have acquired it" (Thucydides, 2: 63, 2) suggests that he considers this a rather tiresome question.

33. "It became great because everyone contributed to it" (Thucydides, 2: 15, 2). The same view is found in the other writers who mention the synoecism: Xenophon, *The Art of Hunting*, 1, 10 (where he refers to the synoecism by the expression "having made his country much greater"); Isocrates 10 (*Helen*) 35; Pseudo-Demosthenes, 59 (*Against Neaira*) 75; Diodorus 4: 61, 8; Valerius Maximus 5: 3, 3.

34. Thucydides applies the adjective ξυνετός to Theseus (2: 15, 2) and to Themistocles (1: 74, 1 and 1: 138, 2); at 2: 34, 6 he says that Pericles is μὴ ἀξυνετός. The only other people he calls ξυνετοί are Archidamus (1: 79, 2), though it is not a Spartan virtue (1: 138, 2), and the oligarchs of 411 B.C. (8: 68, 4). Cleon, on the other hand, condemns this virtue (3: 37, 3), but Thucydides believes that such contempt for intelligence is just the sort of thing you would expect to find once a country starts going to the dogs (3: 82, 4; 3: 82, 5; and 3: 83, 3).

35. He is cited by Thucydides at 1: 96. He was born around the beginning of the fifth century, and died either in 412 B.C. or shortly after 406 B.C.

36. Plutarch declares explicitly that this is *his* aim: "Let us then purify the mythic element and make it submit to rationalization and assume the appearance of history" (Plutarch, *Life of Theseus*, 1). See Ampolo and Manfredini 1988, xi–xvii.

37. Cleidemus, for example, gets rid of the Minotaur altogether, and Demon claims that the Minotaur was really a general of Minos' army who happened to be called Taurus.

38. *FGrH*, 323a (Hellanicus) fr. 14.

39. Cleidemus clears his good name by putting Theseus' expedition to Crete under the reign of Minos' successor, Deucalion.

40. κατὰ ζῆλον Ἡρακλέους, *FGrH*, 323a (Hellanicus) fr. 15. In his commentary to this fragment, Jacoby suggests that the Athenian prohedria at the Corinthian Games gave rise to this story.

41. Philochorus, who tries to idealize Theseus and explain away any unattractive features in the legend, did not like the idea that the Athenian hero should merely follow the Doric one, so he made Theseus a partner, not an imitator, of Heracles (Pearson 1942, 115).

42. Pearson 1942, 19 and 115.

43. *FGrH*, 323a (Hellanicus) fr. 16a.

44. Ibid., fr. 17.

45. Ibid., fr. 18.

46. Ibid., fr. 19.

47. Ibid., fr. 20.

48. Pearson 1942, 65–66 and 151–152.

49. See Kirk's definition of myth (Kirk 1974, 28–29).

50. Pearson 1942, 17. Plutarch himself declares his contempt for poetic myths in the introduction to his biography of Theseus, and at various points in the narrative, which are briefly discussed by Ampolo and Manfredini (Ampolo and Manfredini 1988, xi and xiv).

Bibliography

Abbreviations

EG   *Epigrammata Graeca*. Edited by D. L. Page. Oxford: Clarendon Press, 1975.

EGF   *Epicorum Graecorum Fragmenta*. Edited by Malcolm Davies. Göttingen: Vandenhoek & Ruprecht, 1988.

FGrH   *Die Fragmente der Griechischen Historiker*. Edited by Felix Jacoby. Leiden: E. J. Brill, 1957–1969.

IEG   *Iambi et Elegi Graeci ante Alexandrum Cantati*. Edited by M. L. West. Oxford: Clarendon Press, 1972.

LSJ   *A Greek-English Lexicon*. Edited by Henry George Liddell, Robert Scott, and Sir Henry Stuart Jones. Oxford: Clarendon Press, 1968.

PLF   *Poetarum Lesbiorum Fragmenta*. Edited by Edgar Lobel and Denys Page. Oxford: Clarendon Press, 1955.

PMG   *Poetae Melici Graeci*. Edited by D. L. Page. Oxford: Clarendon Press, 1962.

RE   *Real-Encyclopaedie der classischen Altertumswissenschaft*. Edited by August Friedrich von Pauly, Georg Wissowa, and Wilhelm Kroll. Stuttgart: J. B. Metzler, 1893–1980.

TGF   *Tragicorum Graecorum Fragmenta*. Edited by Augustus Nauck, revised by Bruno Snell. Hildesheim: Georg Olms, 1964.

TrGF   *Tragicorum Graecorum Fragmenta*.

Volume 1: *Didascaliae Tragicae. Catalogi Tragicorum et Tragoediarum. Testimonia et Fragmenta Tragicorum Minorum*. Edited by Bruno Snell. Göttingen: Vandenhoeck and Ruprecht, 1986.

Volume 2: *Fragmenta Adespota*. Edited by Bruno Snell and Richard Kannicht. Göttingen: Vandenhoeck and Ruprecht, 1981.

Volume 3: *Aeschylus*. Edited by Stefan Radt. Göttingen: Vandenhoeck and Ruprecht, 1985.

Volume 4: *Sophocles*. Edited by Stefan Radt. Göttingen: Vandenhoeck and Ruprecht. 1977.

Secondary Works

Adkins, A. W. H. 1960. *Merit and Responsiblity*. Oxford: Oxford University Press.

Ameis, K. F., and C. Hentze. 1879. *Anhang zu Homers Odyssee*. Leipzig: Teubner.

Ampolo, Carmine, and Mario Manfredini. 1988. *Plutarco. Le Vite di Teseo e di Romolo*. Milan: Arnoldo Mondadori Editore.

Andrewes, A. 1974. *The Greek Tyrants*. London: Hutchinson University Library.

Austin, M. M., and Pierre Vidal-Naquet. 1980. *Economic and Social History of Ancient Greece*. Berkeley, Los Angeles, and London: University of California Press.

Avery, Harry C. "'My Tongue Swore, But My Mind Is Unsworn.'" *TAPA* 99 (1968): 19–35.

Barrett, W. S. 1964. *Euripides, Hippolytus*. Oxford: Clarendon Press.

Barron, John P. 1972. "New Light on Old Walls: The Murals of the Theseion." *JHS* 92 (1972): 20–45.

———. 1980. "Bacchylides, Theseus and a Woolly Cloak." *BICS* 17 (1980) : 1–8.

Barthes, Roland. 1970. *Mythologies*. Paris: Editions du Seuil.

Bérard, Claude. 1974. *Anodoi, essai sur l'imaginaire des passages chtoniens*. Institut Suisse de Rome.

———. 1982. "Récupérer la mort du prince: héroïsation et formation de la cité." In *La mort, les morts dans les sociétés anciennes*, edited by G. Gnoli and Jean-Pierre Vernant, 89–105. Cambridge: Cambridge University Press, and Paris: Maison des Sciences de l'Homme.

———. 1983. "L'héroïsation et la formation de la cité: un conflit ideologique." In *Architecture et société de l'archaïsme grec à la fin de la république romaine*, 43–59. Paris: Centre National de la Recherche Scientifique, and Rome: École Française de Rome.

Bernabé, Albertus. 1987. *Poetarum Epicorum Fragmenta*. Leipzig: B. G. Teubner.

Berns, Gisela. 1973. "Nomos and Physis. (An Interpretation of Euripides' Hippolytos.)" *Hermes* 101 (1973): 165–187.

Blomqvist, Jerker. 1982. "Human and Divine Action in Euripides' Hippolytus." *Hermes* 110 (1982): 398–414.

Boardman, John. 1964. *The Greeks Overseas*. Harmondsworth: Penguin Books.

———. 1967. *Pre-Classical. From Crete to Archaic Greece*. Harmondsworth: Penguin Books.

———. 1972. "Herakles, Peisistratus, and His Sons," *Révue archéologique* (1972): 57–72.

———. 1975. "Herakles, Peisistratus, and Eleusis." *JHS* 95 (1975): 1–12.

———. 1978a. "Exekias." *AJA* 82 (1978): 11–25.

———. 1978b. *Greek Sculpture, the Archaic Period: A Handbook*. New York and Toronto: Oxford University Press.

———. 1982. "Herakles, Theseus and Amazons." In *The Eye of Greece*, edited by Donna Kurtz and Brian Sparkes, 1–28. Cambridge: Cambridge University Press.

———. 1984. "Image and Politics in Sixth Century Athens." In *Symposium Amsterdam*, edited by H. A. G. Brijder, 239–247. Amsterdam: Allard Pierson Museum.

———. 1989. "Herakles, Peisistratus, and the Unconvinced." *JHS* 109 (1989): 158–159.

Bolling, George Melville. 1925. *The External Evidence for Interpolation in Homer*. Oxford: Clarendon Press.

Bond, Godfrey W. 1981. *Euripides Heracles*. Oxford: Clarendon Press.

Bothmer, Dietrich von. 1957. *Amazons in Greek Art*. Oxford: Clarendon Press.

Bowra, C. M. 1964. *Pindar*. Oxford: Clarendon Press.

Brelich, Angelo. 1956. "Theseus e i suoi avversari." *Studi e materiali di storia delle religioni* 27 (1956): 136–141.

Bremmer, Jan. 1986. "What Is a Greek Myth?" In *Interpretations of Greek Mythology*, edited by Jan Bremmer, 1–9. Totowa, New Jersey: Barnes and Noble.

Brommer, Frank. 1978. *Hephaistos. Der Schmiedegott in der antiken Kunst.* Mainz am Rhein: Verlag Philipp von Zabern.

———. 1982. *Theseus*. Darmstadt: Wissenschaftliche Buchgesellschaft.

Burian, Peter. 1985. "Logos and Pathos." In *Directions in Euripidean Criticism*, edited by Peter Burian, 129–155. Durham, North Carolina: Duke University Press.

Burkert, Walter. 1985. *Greek Religion*. Translated by John Raffan. Cambridge, Massachusetts: Harvard University Press.

Bury, J. B., and Russell Meiggs. 1975. *A History of Greece*. London: Macmillan.

Calame, Claude. 1990. *Thésée et l'imaginaire athénien.* Lausanne: Éditions Payot.

Campbell, Lewis. 1879. *Sophocles. Volume I. Oedipus Tyrannus. Oedipus Coloneus. Antigone*. Oxford: Clarendon Press.

Carter, L. B. 1986. *The Quiet Athenian*. Oxford: Clarendon Press.

Catling, H. W. 1982. "Archaeology in Greece, 1981–82." *A.R.* (1981–1982): 3–62.

Christensen, Kerry A. 1984. "The Theseion: A Slave Refuge at Athens." *American Journal of Ancient History* 9 (1984): 23–32.

Clairmont, Christoph W. 1983. *Patrios Nomos. Public Burial in Athens during the Fifth and Fourth Centuries B.C. British Archaeological Reports (International Series)*. 161 (1983).

Coldstream, J. N. 1976. "Hero-Cults in the Age of Homer." *JHS* 96 (1976): 8–17.

Conacher, D. J. 1967. *Euripidean Drama: Myth, Theme and Structure*. Toronto: University of Toronto Press.

Connor, W. R. 1970. "Theseus in Classical Athens." In *The Quest for Theseus*, edited by Anne G. Warde, 143–174. London: Pall Mall Press.

———. 1987. "Tribes, Festivals and Processions: Civic Ceremonial and Political Manipulation in Archaic Greece." *JHS* 107 (1987): 40–50.

Dain, Alphonse, and Paul Mazon. 1960. *Sophocle, III. Philoctète, Oedipe à Colone.* Paris: Les Belles Lettres.

Davie, John N. 1982. "Theseus the King in Fifth-century Athens." *G&R* 29 (1982): 25–34.

Davies, Malcolm. 1989. *The Epic Cycle.* Bristol: Bristol Classical Press.

Davison, J. A. 1958. "Notes on the Panathenaea." *JHS* 78 (1958): 23–42.

Dawe, R. D. 1979. *Sophocles. Tragoediae, II: Trachiniae. Antigone. Philoctetes. Oedipus Coloneus.* Leipzig: Teubner.

Détienne, Marcel. 1967. *Les maîtres de vérité dans la Grèce archaïque.* Paris: François Maspero.

————. 1977. *Dionysos mis à mort.* Paris: Gallimard.

———— and Jean-Pierre Vernant. 1974. *Les ruses de l'intelligence—la métis des grecs.* Paris: Flammarion.

Deubner, Ludwig. 1932. *Attische Feste.* Berlin: Verlag Heinrich Keller.

Diamant, Steven. 1982. "Theseus and the Unification of Attica." *Hesperia* Supp. 19 (1982): 38–47.

Dodds, E. R. 1951. *The Greeks and the Irrational.* Berkeley, Los Angeles, and London: University of California Press.

Dontas, George S. 1983. "The True Aglaurion." *Hesperia* 52 (1983): 48–63.

Dugas, Ch. 1943. "L'évolution de la légende de Thésée." *REG* (1943): 1–24.

Dugas, Ch., and R. Flacelière. 1958. *Thésée: Images et récits.* Paris: Editions E. de Boccard.

Dumézil, Georges. 1979. *Mariages indo-européens.* Paris: Payot.

Edmonds, John Maxwell. 1957. *The Fragments of Attic Comedy.* Leiden: E. J. Brill.

Ehrenberg, Victor. 1954. *Sophocles and Pericles.* Oxford: Basil Blackwell.

Ellendt, Friedrich. 1872. *Lexicon Sophocleum.* Berlin: Borntraeger.

Ferguson, William Scott. "The Attic Orgeones." *Harvard Theological Review* 37 (1944): 61–140.

Figueira, Thomas J. 1984. "The Ten Archontes of 579/8 at Athens." *Hesperia* 53 (1984): 447–473.

Finley, John H., Jr. 1968. "Pindar's Beginning." In *The Poetic Tradition*, edited by Don Cameron Allen and Henry T. Rowell, 3–26. Baltimore: Johns Hopkins University Press.

Finley, M. I. 1973. *Democracy Ancient and Modern.* New Brunswick, New Jersey: Rutgers University Press.

————. 1986. *The Use and Abuse of History.* London: The Hogarth Press.

Foley, Helene P. 1985. *Ritual Irony: Poetry and Sacrifice in Euripides.* Ithaca and London: Cornell University Press.

Frazer, J. G. 1898. *Pausanias's Description of Greece.* Volume II. *Commentary on Book I.* London: Macmillan.

Friis Johansen, K. 1945. *Thésée et la danse à Délos.* Copenhagen: Munksgaard.

Fuks, Alexander. 1953. *The Ancestral Constitution.* London: Routledge and Kegan Paul.

Gamble, R. B. 1970. "Euripides' 'Suppliant Women': Decision and Ambivalence." *Hermes* 98 (1970): 385–405.

Garland, Robert. 1985. *The Greek Way of Death.* Ithaca: Cornell University Press.

Gennep, Arnold van. 1909. *Les rites de passage.* Paris: Editions Nourry.

Gernet, Louis. 1982a. *Anthropologie de la Grèce antique.* Paris: Flammarion.

———. 1982b. *Droit et institutions en Grèce antique.* Paris: Flammarion.

Goossens, Roger. 1962. *Euripide et Athènes.* Brussels: Académie Royale de Belgique.

Gould, John. 1973. "Hiketeia." *JHS* 93 (1973): 74–103.

Grube, G. M. A. 1941. *The Drama of Euripides.* London: Methuen.

Harrison, Evelyn B. 1977. "The Sculptures of Alkamenes for the Hephaisteion. Part I, The Cult Statues." *AJA* 81 (1977): 137–178.

Herter, Hans. 1936. "Theseus der Jonier." *Rheinisches Museum* 85 (1936) 177–239.

———. 1939. "Theseus der Athener." *Rheinisches Museum* 88 (1939): 244–326.

———. 1973. "Theseus." In Pauly, *RE* , Supp. Volume 13.

Hoffelner, Klaus. 1988. "Die Metopen des Athener-Schatzhauses. Ein neuer Rekonstruktionsversuch." *MDAI (A)* 103 (1988): 77–117.

Huxley, George. 1969. *Greek Epic Poetry.* Cambridge, Massachusetts: Harvard University Press.

———. 1973. "The Date of Pherecydes of Athens." *GRBS* 14 (1973): 137–143.

Jacoby, Felix. 1945. "Some Athenian Epigrams from the Persian Wars." *Hesperia* 14 (1945): 157–211.

———. 1947a. "Some remarks on Ion of Chios." *Classical Quarterly.* 41 (1947): 1–17.

———. 1947b. "The First Athenian Prose Writer." *Mnemosyne* 13 (1947): 13–64.

———. 1949. *Atthis.* Oxford: Clarendon Press.

Jeanmaire, Henri. 1939. *Couroi et Courètes. Essai sur l'éducation spartiate et les rites d'adolescence dans l'antiquité hellénique.* Lille: Bibliothèque de l'Université.

Jebb, R. C. 1889. *Sophocles: The Oedipus Coloneus.* Cambridge: Cambridge University Press.

———. 1891. *Sophocles: The Antigone.* Cambridge: Cambridge University Press.

Jones, A. H. M. 1986. *Athenian Democracy.* Baltimore: Johns Hopkins University Press.

Kamerbeek, J. C. 1984. *The Plays of Sophocles. Commentaries. Part VII. The Oedipus Coloneus.* Leiden: E. J. Brill.

Kearns, Emily. 1989. *The Heroes of Attica.* London: Institute of Classical Studies.

Keuls, Eva. 1984. "Patriotic Propaganda and Counter-cultural Protest in Athens as Evidenced by Vase Painting." In *Symposium Amsterdam*, edited by H. A. G. Brijder, 256–259. Amsterdam: Allard Pierson Museum.

Kirk, G. S. 1974. *The Nature of the Greek Myths.* Harmondsworth: Penguin.

———. 1985. *The Iliad: A Commentary. Volume I: Books 1–4.* Cambridge: Cambridge University Press.

Kirk, G. S., and J. E. Raven. 1971. *The Presocratic Philosophers.* Cambridge: Cambridge University Press.

Kirkwood, G. M. 1958. *A Study of Sophoclean Drama*. Ithaca, New York: Cornell University Press.

———. 1986. "From Melos to Colonus: Τίνας Χώρους 'Αφίγμεθ' . . . ;" *TAPhA* 116 (1986): 99–118.

Knox, Bernard M. W. 1964. *The Heroic Temper*. Berkeley, Los Angeles, and London: University of California Press.

Kovacs, David. 1980. "Shame, Pleasure, and Honor in Phaedra's Great Speech (Euripides, *Hippolytus* 375–387)." *American Journal of Philology* 101 (1980): 287–303.

Kroll, John H., and Nancy W. Waggoner. 1984. "Dating the Earliest Coins of Athens, Corinth and Aegina." *AJA* 88 (1984): 325–340.

Kron, Uta. 1976. *Die zehn attischen Phylenheroen*. Berlin: Deutsches Archäologisches Institut.

Kullmann, Wolfgang. 1960. *Die Quellen der Ilias (Troischer Sagenkreis)*. *Hermes Einzelschriften*. Volume 14. Wiesbaden: Frank Steiner Verlag.

Leaf, Walter. 1900. *The Iliad*. London and New York: Macmillan.

Lesky, Albin. 1966. *A History of Greek Literature*. Translated by James Willis and Cornelis de Heer. New York: Crowell.

Lévêque, Pierre, and Pierre Vidal-Naquet. 1964. *Clisthène l'Athénien*. Paris: Macula.

Lévi-Strauss, Claude. 1958. *Anthropologie structurale*. Paris: Librairie Plon.

Linforth, Ivan M. 1951. "Religion and Drama in 'Oedipus at Colonus'." *U. Cal. Publ. in Class. Phil.* 14 (1951): 75–191.

Loraux, Nicole. 1981a. "Cité Grecque." In *Dictionnaire des mythologies*, edited by Yves Bonnefoy, Volume 1, 203–209. Paris: Flammarion.

———. 1981b. *Les enfants d'Athéna*. Paris: François Maspero.

———. 1986. *The Invention of Athens*. Translated by Alan Sheridan. Cambridge, Massachusetts, and London: Harvard University Press.

Luschnig, C. A. E. 1980. "Men and Gods in Euripides' Hippolytus." *Ramus* 9 (1980): 89–100.

MacKendrick, Paul. 1981. *The Greek Stones Speak*. New York: St. Martin's Press.

March, Jennifer R. 1987. *The Creative Poet*. London: Institute of Classical Studies.

Mazon, Paul. 1992. *Hésiode. Théogonie—Les travaux et les jours—Le bouclier*. Paris: Les Belles Lettres.

Meiggs, Russell, and Davis Lewis. 1969. *A Selection of Greek Historical Inscriptions to the End of the Fifth Century B.C.* Oxford: Clarendon Press.

Meinecke, Augustus. 1839. *Fragmenta Poetarum Comoediae Antiquae*. Berlin: G. Reiner.

Merkelbach, R. 1973. "Der Theseus des Bakchylides (Gedicht für ein attisches Ephebenfest)." *ZPE* 12 (1973): 59–62.

Mylonas, George E. 1951. "The Cult of the Dead in Mycenaean Times." In *Studies Presented to David Moore Robinson*, edited by George E. Mylonas and Doris Raymond, Volume 1, 64–105. Saint Louis: Washington University Press.

Moggi, Mauro. 1976. *I sinecismi interstatali Greci*, Volume 1. Pisa: Edizioni Marlin.

Moore, Mary B. 1986. "Athena and Herakles on Exekias' Calyx-crater." *AJA* 90 (1986): 35–39.

Mossé, Claude. 1979. "Comment s'élaborer un mythe politique: Solon, "père fondateur" de la démocratie athénienne." *AnnESC* 34 (1979): 425–437.

Neils, Jenifer. 1987. *The Youthful Deeds of Theseus*. Rima: Giorgio Bretschneider Editore.

Nilsson, Martin P. 1932. *The Mycenean Origins of Greek Mythology*. Berkeley, Los Angeles, and London: University of California Press.

————. 1941. *Geschichte der griechischen Religion*. Munich: C. H. Beck'sche.

————. 1951. *Cults, Myths, Oracles, and Politics in Ancient Greece*. Lund: C. W. K. Gleerup.

————. 1953. "Political Propaganda in Sixth Century Athens." In *Studies Presented to David Moore Robinson*, edited by George E. Mylonas and Doris Raymond, Volume 2, 743–748. Saint Louis: Washington University Press.

————. 1964. *A History of Greek Religion*. New York: Norton.

Nock, Arthur Darby. 1944. "The Cult of Heroes." *Harvard Theological Review*. 37 (1944): 141–174.

Orban, Marcel. 1981. "«*Hippolyte*»: Palinodie ou Revanche?" *Les études classiques* 49 (1981): 3–17.

Ostwald, Martin. 1982. *Autonomia: Its Genesis and Early History*. Scholar's Press.

Padgug, Robert A. "Eleusis and the Union of Attica." *GRBS* 13 (1972): 135–150.

Parke, H. W. 1977. *Festivals of the Athenians*. Ithaca, New York: Cornell University Press.

Parker, Robert. 1983. *Miasma*. Oxford: Clarendon Press.

Pearson, Lionel. 1942. *The Local Historians of Attica*. Lancaster, Pennsylvania: Lancaster Press.

————. 1964. *Sophoclis Fabulae*. Oxford: Clarendon Press.

Pélékidis, Chrysis. 1962. *Histoire de l'éphébie attique*. Paris: Éditions Broccard.

Podlecki, Anthony J. 1971. "Cimon, Skyros, and Theseus' Bones." *JHS* 91 (1971): 141–143.

————. 1975. "Theseus and Themistocles." *Rivista storica dell' Antichità*. 5 (1975): 1–24.

————. 1986. "Polis and Monarch in Early Attic Tragedy." In *Greek Tragedy and Political Theory*, edited by Peter J. Euben, 76–100. Berkeley, Los Angeles, London: University of California Press.

Polignac, François de. 1984. *La naissance de la cité grecque*. Paris: Éditions la Découverte.

Price, Theodora Hadzisteliou. 1973. "Hero-Cult and Homer." *Historia* 22 (1973): 129–144.

Pritchett, W. Kendrick. 1985. *The Greek States at War. Part IV*. Berkeley, Los Angeles, and London: University of California Press.

Reckford, Kenneth J. "Phaethon, Hippolytus, and Aphrodite." *TAPA* 103 (1972): 405–432.

Reinhardt, Karl. 1979. *Sophocles*. Translated by Hazel Harvey and David Harvey. New York: Barnes and Noble.

Rhodes, P. J. 1981. *A Commentary on the Aristotelian Athenaion Politeia*. Oxford: Clarendon Press.

Russo, Carlo Ferdinando. 1965. *Hesiodi Scutum*. Florence: La Nuova Italia.

Schefold, Karl. 1946. "Kleisthenes." *Museum Helveticum* 3 (1946): 59–93.

———. 1966. *Myth and Legend in Early Greek Art*. Translated by Audrey Hicks. New York: Harry N. Abrams.

———. 1992. *Gods and Heroes in Late Archaic Greek Art*. Translated by Alan Griffiths. Cambridge: Cambridge University Press.

Schefold, Karl, and Jung, Franz. 1988. *Die Urkönige, Perseus, Bellerophon, Herakles und Theseus in der klassischen und hellenistischen Kunst*. Munich: Hirmer Verlag.

Schmitt, Arbogast. 1977. "Zur Charakterdarstellung des Hippolytos im 'Hippolytos' von Euripides." *Würzburger Jahrbücher für die Altertumswissenschaft*. N.F. 3 (1977): 17–42.

Sealey, Raphael. 1976. *A History of the Greek City States 700–338 B.C.* Berkeley, Los Angeles, and London: University of California Press.

Segal, Charles. 1979. "The Myth of Bacchylides 17: Heroic Quest and Heroic Identity." *Eranos* 77 (1979): 23–37.

Seltman, C. T. 1974. *Athens. Its History and Coinage Before the Persian Invasion*. Chicago: Ares Publishers.

Shapiro, H. A. 1988. "The Marathonian Bull on the Athenian Acropolis." *AJA* 92 (1988): 373–382.

———. 1989. *Art and Cult under the Tyrants in Athens*. Mainz am Rhein: Verlag Philipp von Zabern.

Shaw, Michael H. 1982. "The ἦθος of Theseus in 'The Suppliant Women.'" *Hermes* 110 (1982): 3–19.

Simon, Erika. 1976. *Die griechischen Vasen*. Munich: Hirmer Verlag.

———. 1983. *Festivals of Attica: an archaeological commentary*. Madison, Wisconsin: University of Wisconsin Press.

Skutsch, Otto. 1987. "Helen: Her Name and Nature." *JHS* 107 (1987): 188–193.

Snodgrass, Anthony. 1980. *Archaic Greece. The Age of Experiment*. Berkeley, Los Angeles, and London: University of California Press.

———. 1982. "Les origines du culte des héros dans la Grèce antique." In *La mort, les morts dans les sociétés anciennes*, edited by G. Gnoli and Jean-Pierre Vernant, 107–119. Cambridge: Cambridge University Press, and Paris: Maison des Sciences de l'Homme.

Sourvinou-Inwood, Christiane. 1979. *Theseus as Son and Stepson*. London: Institute of Classical Studies.

Stanford, W. B. 1959. *Homer. Odyssey. Books I to XII*. London: Macmillan.

Taylor, Michael W. 1981. *The Tyrant Slayers. The Heroic Image in Fifth Century B.C. Athenian Art and Politics*. New York: Arno Press.

Thompson, Homer A. 1966. "Activity in the Athenian Agora 1960–1965." *Hesperia* 35 (1966): 37–54.

Thompson, Homer A., and R. E. Wycherley. 1972. *The Agora of Athens (The Athenian Agora Vol. XIV)*. Princeton: American School of Classical Studies at Athens.

Tod, Marcus N. 1985. *Greek Historical Inscriptions: From the Sixth Century B.C. to the Death of Alexander the Great in 323 B.C.* Chicago: Ares.

Toepffer, Johannes. 1889. *Attische Genealogie*. Berlin: Weidmann.

———. 1897. *Beiträge zur griechischen Altertumswissenschaft*. Berlin: Weidmann.

Tyrrell, Wm. Blake. 1984. *Amazons. A Study in Athenian Mythmaking*. Baltimore: Johns Hopkins University Press.

Vanderpool, Eugene. 1974. "The 'Agora' of Pausanias I, 17, 1–2." *Hesperia* 43 (1974): 308–310.

Van der Valk, M. 1964. *Researches on the Text and Scholia of the Iliad*. Leiden: E. J. Brill.

Vernant, Jean-Pierre. 1962. *Les origines de la pensée grecque*. Paris: Presses Universitaires de France.

———. 1968. *Problèmes de la guerre en Grèce ancienne*. Paris and the Hague: Martin & Co.

———. 1974. *Mythe et société en Grèce ancienne*. Paris: François Maspero.

———. 1985. *Mythe et pensée chez les Grecs*. Paris: Editions la Découverte.

Vidal-Naquet, Pierre. 1981. *Le chasseur noir*. Paris: François Maspero.

———. 1986. "Oedipe à Athènes." In *Mythe et tragédie en Grèce ancienne*, edited by Jean-Pierre Vernant and Pierre Vidal-Naquet, 149–173. Paris: Editions la Découverte.

Vlastos, G. 1964. "Isonomia politike." In *Isonomia. Studien zur Gleichheitvorstellung im griechischen Denken*, edited by Jurgen Mau and Ernst Günther Schmidt, 1–35. Berlin: Akademie-Verlag.

Vox, Onofrio. 1983. "Teseo odissiaco." *QUCC* 44 (1983): 91–97.

———. 1984a. "Prima del trionfo: i ditirambi 17 e 18 de Bacchilide." *A.C.* 53 (1984): 200–209.

———. 1984b. "Bacchilide e Timocreonte contro Temistocle." *Prometheus* 10 (1984): 117–120.

Webster, T. B. L. 1967. *The Tragedies of Euripides*. London: Methuen.

West, M. L. 1966. *Hesiod: Theogony*. Oxford: Clarendon Press.

———. 1978. *Hesiod: Works and Days*. Oxford: Clarendon Press.

———. 1985. *The Hesiodic Catalogue of Women*. Oxford: Clarendon Press.

Whitley, James. 1988. "Early States and Hero Cults: a Re-Appraisal." *JHS* 108 (1988): 173–182.

Wilamowitz-Möllendorff, Ulrich von. 1937. *Kleine Schriften*. Berlin: Weidmann.

Will, Edouard. 1972. *Le Monde grec et l'Orient*. Paris: Presses Universitaires de France.

Winnington-Ingram, R. P. 1960. "Hippolytus: A Study in Causation." In *Euripide. Entretiens sur l'Antiquité classique. Tome VI*. Geneva: Fondation Hardt.

Index